P



# HappyHour GUIDEBOOK

2013 EDITION

**Portland Happy Hour Guidebook**

*Seventh Edition*



ISBN: 978-0-9791201-5-2

Self-published with all content including research, reviews, illustrations, maps, and design by Cindy Anderson

Cover photos: Seres, Mama Mia, and Bazi Bierbrasserie by Cindy Anderson; Mint/820 by Steve Woods; Thirst by Leslie Palmer; and Gilt Club by Jamie Dunn. Author photo by Cassy Cole. Editing (partial copy) by Mary Beth Saddoris (writebrainediting@gmail.com). Locally printed in the U.S. by Choose Local Printing (www.chooselocalprinting.com); Bill Yancey (503) 680-3128; Portland, Oregon

Due to the fluid nature of the ever-changing Portland Happy Hour scene, Half-Full Enterprises cannot accept responsibility for any complications that may arise from using the information in this book. Every effort has been made to maintain accuracy, but things change, and Half-Full Enterprises cannot guarantee that the information in this book is or will be accurate. The opinions expressed in this book are just that, opinions of the author. The author did not receive any endorsement earnings (or bribes!) from any bar/restaurant/tavern in the writing of this book. Finally, you are responsible for your own actions, before, during and after using the information provided in this book. Drink responsibly! Half-Full Enterprises is not liable for any irresponsible actions on your part, including but not limited to drunk dialing, hooking up with an ex-boyfriend or girlfriend, hurting yourself or hurting someone else.

***Coupons** are provided as a courtesy. Menus may change or restaurants may close, and neither the author nor the publisher makes any warranty or representation about the validity or enforceability of the coupons. Originals only. May not be good on holidays. Please use coupons wisely — and nicely.*

**Half-Full Enterprises**
10350 N. Vancouver Way, Suite 173; Portland, OR 97217
www.happyhourguidebook.com
pdxinfo@happyhourguidebook.com

# Dedication

This past year has delivered me some whopper blows, and some wonderful angels.

To my best-ever, full-of-sweetness Mom, who I thank for... everything and more. And it's so cute you would read my books cover-to-cover.

To my amazingly, ever-optimistic Uncle Phil, for reminding me that the sun's coming out any minute now!

And to my unbelievably wonderful, dear friend, Dawnie, who I thank for her infectious attitude of never holding back happiness.

## website info

www.
happy hour guide book
.com

news & changes

parties

facebook

twitter

contact information

best-of lists

ideas

newsletter

# Contents

# Keep smilin'!

☐ Step out of your comfort zone and discover a new place you've never tried before. Explore!

☐ Revisit a long-time, classic favorite.

☐ Hit at least three Happy Hours a month :-)

☐ Visit a friend in a different side of town. Try a couple places in a new neighborhood.

☐ Play tourist right here in Portland – and go to Happy Hour near your chosen site.

☐ Invite a new friend to meet out at Happy Hour.

☐ Invite an old friend, or maybe two or three!

☐ Ask a networking contact to meet for a drink. Happy Hour can be much more fun than coffee.

☐ Make a monthly date night with your special someone. Or maybe make that weekly...

☐ Pick up "drinkercising" as a hobby – plan some exercise or walking along with that Happy Hour!

☐ Follow **"Portland Happy Hour Guidebook"** facebook page for all kinds of fun ideas!

# Map Information

Plus some scattered places "Out & About"
—and—
Beaverton, Lake Oswego, Tigard, Vancouver

- ● Black dots mark restaurant location
- ★ Stars indicate places that go until 7:00pm
- O White dots indicate limited Happy Hour info

# Rating System

As fun as this so-called *job* is, I take it very seriously. I am in a unique positon of having personally analyzed literally hundreds of Happy Hours, and have devised a formula to rate Happy Hours in comparison to others:

## Food

Exclusively focused on food served at Happy Hour only. Considers taste, discounts, healthy alternatives, and uniqueness (i.e. not the usual bar menu).

**3** – Delicious food, lots of options and discounted well.

**2** – Pretty good food food and/or discount.

**1** – Negligible discounts, few selections, or possibly bad taste. It will be explained in that section.

## Drinks

Not all about being the cheapest, but need discounts!

**3** – Good deals, variety, and quality drinks.
**2** – Pretty good, but need more variety or discounts.
**1** – Eh. Not that impressed. Not trying or expensive.

## Atmosphere

Looks matter! As a rule, this book covers the nicer places in town. Good vibes? Stunning decor? What?

**3** – Upscale and unique decor and/or gorgeous views.
**2** – Nice enough, but not quite stunning.
**1** – More of a bar than a restaurant. Low on style and decor. Women may be uncomfortable when alone.

## "Magic Points"

An arbitrary point is often added to the overall score to make up for not using half-points. Sometimes a place is better than the sum of three parts! Overall score is shown in large type.

# Stars & High Scores

## Stars

**Perfect Tens** – You'll see a big star to call it out.

**Personal favorites** – Three stars and "Favorite!"

**Bonus Stars** – Sometimes an overall score doesn't quite do the place justice. This especially happens in places that do not offer drink specials. Here and there, I just *had* to assign a star!

Remember to check our website every once in a while for changes and closures.

**www.happyhourguidebook.com**

And please let us know if you see information that needs changing.

# Notes & Disclaimers

**Accuracy of information:** Things change! Graciously accept this fluidity and adjust your attitude accordingly. As of this writing, the information herein is current. Every effort has been made to present information accurately. Check the website for updates.

**Crowd scene:** An element that can greatly vary. I elected not to try to qualify the type of person typically visiting a certain place, but rather encourage you to reserve judgement as well and be accepting and tolerant—and even friendly—to your fellow bar patrons. Also, please be aware that the more popular places get crowded. Be flexible, prompt, and patient. I hope this book will encourage you to get out there and explore! Every place in this book is worth checking out.

**Service:** I didn't comment on this aspect as "one bad apple doesn't spoil the whole bunch." Be aware that sometimes it's service via bartender only, and you'll have to order at the bar. If things are taking a while, be proactive, yet polite.

**Tipping:** Servers may have to make just as many trips for you as a regular diner. Please consider the effort—not the totally low bill—and be extra-generous for good service!

**Rating and Judging:** All judging is based on Happy Hour only. You may find you have different opinions of places. I called 'em as I saw 'em and in comparison to others. Take your own notes for future reference throughout the book. Record your adventures within and it can be a fun walk down Memory Lane!

**Do not drink and drive (but of course).**

**Happy Hours are often relegated to bar area only.** Mostly, I've commented on the restaurant atmosphere overall, including outdoor seating (which may not always be available to the Happy Hour crowd). Ask before you are seated to confirm available service.

# Factoids & Tipsys

- Be sure to become a **facebook fan!** Get clued in to Happy Hour action and chime in with your opinions and experiences too. Win contests and get deals!

Portland Happy Hour Guidebook

- Lots of places go all night ('til close) on Sunday or on another weeknight. Look for the ★s in this book to most easily find **extended hours.**

- Check out the website's **MAPS** tab. View these maps on your iPhone! Refer to the restaurant's rating page in book for full information, ratings & exact hours.

- Be aware of the Happy Hour **end-time** and pad your order by at least 10 minutes. Confirm with your waiter if you made it on time.

- Incorporate another **activity** such as a movie, concert, the Chinese Gardens, or a long walk into your night out.

- Not all places can accommodate larger **groups.** Call first. It's fun to organize a get-together!

- Sign up for the **email** list at your favorite restaurants. You'll be in the know about special events and offers. And maybe get a coupon here and there too.

- Live in gratitude—most cities do not have Happy Hours. I know—shocking! And we have the best.

- Things change! Please **report changes** you find to: pdxinfo@happyhourguidebook.com. Also, sign up for the monthly newsletter to be in-the-know.

- Check in with the **website** to keep up with changes!

**www.happyhourguidebook.com**

# Playing Favorites

I love this group of restaurants on the cover! And I love that they represent a wide array of Happy Hour possibilities from cocktailing, to fine dining, to pursuing the best in beer. When looking for ideas, it gives you a great little group to start with, and here's why:

## Bazi Bierbrasserie

(SE Hawthorne & 32nd)

It's all the rave among beer geeks, and a nice place to go for everyone. It's a Belgian-style beer bar with 17 craft beers on draft, plus bottles and full bar. Unique brasserie-style food menu. Sharp owner, talented bartenders. Be sure to try their famous beer cocktails!

## Gilt Club

(NW Broadway & Everett)

In a nutshell, a most lush and gorgeous space! I was an immediate fan, mostly for the drinks and swanky vibe in the place, but later for the food as well. Not only do they make some of the city's finest crafted cocktails, they also have delicious food at dinner. And now they've expanded their Happy Hour menu!

## Mama Mia Trattoria

(SW 2nd Ave. & Washington)

Mama mia! Recently, when I peeked at their Happy Hour menu online, my eyes almost popped out of my head! They've always had a lot of options at Happy Hour, but now it's a crazy-huge menu, and all kinds of options at the low price points of $2.00, $3.00 and $4.00! And they've added drink specials! New owners have taken the food up a level too. Beautiful private party room available, and surprise! Incredible cheese-burgers! And of course, great Italian food as well.

# Playing Favorites

## Mint/820
(NE Russell near Mississippi)

My very first Happy Hour when I moved to Portland – I was very impressed! They set a high bar, and started me on the path... Incredible cocktails, great patio, and very cool lounge. Plus a nice restaurant next door, the Mint part of 820 (Latin-American-inspired Northwest menu). Also, FYI, the owner Lucy Brennan, wrote a bartending guide, "Hip Sips." Beautifully designed, but requires skills, so I'll just sip here. Often.

## Seres
(NW Lovejoy & 11th Ave.)

Sigh. I just love Seres. It just tastes so good, and it's so good for you too! They focus on using top-quality, mostly organic ingredients. Sustainably-caught, naturally-raised, no hormones, etc. I only know it tastes extraordinary! Essentially, you will find traditional Chinese food like fried rice or Kung Pao chicken, but notice a lighter, more pure quality than many typical places. The restaurant itself is very serene, and I love stepping inside into immediate-relaxation mode. Plus, parking isn't too bad in this neighborhood.

## Thirst Bistro
(On the Waterfront near RiverPlace Marina)

We are so lucky to have two rivers right in Portland – and so lucky to have Thirst to enjoy overlooking the Willamette! I love this Riverplace Esplanade area, and I love Thirst! I've actually had some of the best meals I've had in Portland here, and probably the best value too. Pacific NW inspired cuisine – and wine tasting bar. They also have a couple of incredible event spaces. Cozy lounge areas with fireplaces, floor-to-ceiling windows, and a wonderful sunny piazza patio! Love it!

# ★10

- ☐ 23 Hoyt
- ☐ Allium
- ☐ Amalfi's
- ☐ Aquariva
- ☐ Aura
- ☐ Aviary
- ☐ Banya
- ☐ Bartini
- ☐ Blue Agave
- ☐ Bluehour
- ☐ Box Social
- ☐ Brasserie Montmarte
- ☐ Bugatti's
- ☐ Café Castagna
- ☐ Café Nell
- ☐ Central
- ☐ Cha
- ☐ Charlie's Bistro
- ☐ Chart House
- ☐ Ciao Vito
- ☐ Claim Jumper
- ☐ Clarklewis
- ☐ Cocotte
- ☐ Clyde Common
- ☐ Decarli
- ☐ Departure
- ☐ Dr. Sushi
- ☐ Driftwood Room
- ☐ Equinox
- ☐ Farm Café
- ☐ Gilt Club
- ☐ Giorgio's
- ☐ Gustav's
- ☐ Hall Street Grill
- ☐ Hayden's
- ☐ Bugatti's
- ☐ Hazel Room
- ☐ Hokusei
- ☐ Hudson's
- ☐ Jantzen Beach
- ☐ Jimmy Mak's
- ☐ Jo-Bar
- ☐ Karam
- ☐ La Calaca
- ☐ Lapellah
- ☐ Lincoln
- ☐ Mama Mia
- ☐ Manzana's
- ☐ Market
- ☐ McCormick & Schmick's
- ☐ McGrath's
- ☐ Meriwether's
- ☐ Metrovino
- ☐ Mextiza
- ☐ Mint/820
- ☐ Ned Ludd
- ☐ Nel Centro
- ☐ Newport Seafood
- ☐ Oba
- ☐ The Original
- ☐ Paadee
- ☐ Pambiche
- ☐ Papa Haydn
- ☐ Parish
- ☐ PF Chang's
- ☐ Pope House
- ☐ Portland City Grill
- ☐ Press Club
- ☐ Red Star
- ☐ Ringside Fish House
- ☐ Riverview
- ☐ Ruth's Chris
- ☐ Salty's
- ☐ Saucebox
- ☐ Seres
- ☐ Serratto
- ☐ Shiraz
- ☐ Silk
- ☐ Sinju
- ☐ Soi9
- ☐ Split
- ☐ Stanford's
- ☐ Tapalaya
- ☐ Terrace Kitchen
- ☐ Thai Orchard
- ☐ Thirst
- ☐ Three Degrees
- ☐ Tommy O's
- ☐ Touché
- ☐ Trader Vic's
- ☐ Trebol
- ☐ Tucci
- ☐ Uptown Billiards
- ☐ Urban Farmer
- ☐ Voicebox
- ☐ Wassabi
- ☐ Wild Abandon

# "Best-of" Listings

## OUTDOOR PATIOS & DECKS

**River Decks**

Beaches
Island Café
Jantzen Beach Bar
McMenamin's
on the Columbia
Newport Seafood Grill
Riverview
Salty's
The Deck
Thirst
Three Degrees
Who Song & Larry's

**Sky High Views**

Departure
Noble Rot
Windows

**Views from Inside**

Chart House
Portland City Grill

**Pleasant Patios**

Amalfi's
Casa Naranja
del Inti
Farm Café
Firehouse
Fish Sauce
Grant House
Jamison
Meriweather's (dinner)
Mextiza
Moloko
Nel Centro
Ned Ludd
Papa Haydn Sellwood
Radio Room
Stickmen Brewery
Tin Shed
Yakuza

**Delightful Decks**

Bernie's
Caldera
Mint/820
Nightlight
Touché
Wild Abandon

More exceptional patios or decks, but no Happy Hours: Channel's Edge, DiPrimi Italian, Prost, Roadside Attraction, Veritable Quandry

# "Best-of" Listings

## AMERICAN FOODS

**Best Pizzas**

Cafe Castagna
Firehouse
Lucca
Nel Centro
Nostrana
Oven & Shaker
Pazzo
Porcelli's
Serratto
Shiraz
Sunshine Tavern
Touché

**Steakbites**

23 Hoyt
El Gaucho
Morton's
Ringside
Clyde's Prime Rib
Portland City Grill
Ruth's Chris
Urban Farmer

**Southern**

Irving St. Kitchen
Pope House
Tapalaya

**Best Burgers**

23 Hoyt
Cafe Castagna
El Gaucho
Grant House
Jake's Famous
Jake's Grill
Joe's Burgers
Little Bird
McCormick & Schmick's
Metrovino
Mint/820 (lambburger)
Morton's
Ringside (all)
Ruth's Chris
Salty's
Saucebox
Serratto
Star Bar

Not my list, but I often hear about:
Bar Bar
Gruner
Jo-Bar
Moonshine Kitchen
Pause
Slow Bar
Tiger Bar

# "Best-of" Listings

## INTERNATIONAL FOODS

**Asian/Thai/ Vietnamese**

Bamboo Sushi
Bambuza
Banya
Departure
Dr. Sushi & BBQ
Dragonwell
E-San
Fish Sauce
Ginger Pop
Hokusei
Kin
Lela's Bistro
Masu
Mee-Sen
Paadee
Ping
PF Changs
Samurai Blue
Saucebox
Seres
Shigezo
Silk
Sinju
Soho
Soi9
Yama Sushi

**French**

Brasserie Montmarte
Chez Machin
Cocotte
Little Bird
Petite Provence
St. Jack

**German**

Gruner
Gustav's (all)
Prost*
Spints
Widmer Gasthaus

**Indian**

East India Company
Vindalho

**Alpine/Northern**
Broder
Slide Inn

# "Best-of" Listings

## INTERNATIONAL FOODS

### Italian

Amalfi's
Carpaccio
Ciao Vito
Giorgio's
Mama Mia
Serratto
Touché
Tucci
Via Delizia

### Middle-Eastern

Berbati's
Cypress
Habibi
Hoda's
Karam
Shiraz
TarBoush

### South of the Border

Blue Agave
Casa del Matador
Cha
Isabel
La Calaca Comelona
Las Primas
Mextiza
Mi Mero Mole
Oba
Pambiche
Trebol

### European-Style Pubs

Alberta St. Pub
County Cork
Highland Stillhouse
Horsebrass Pub*
Kell's
Leaky Roof
Moon & Sixpence*
Paddy's
Rose & Thistle Pub
Thirsty Lion

### International Flavors

Bluehour
Cruz Room
Living Room Theaters
Metrovino
Muu-muu's
Nel Centro
North 45
Salvador Molly's

* No Happy Hour

# "Best-of" Listings

## LOUNGING AND LINGERING

**Cocktails**

Bartini
Beaker & Flask*
Box Social
Central
Clyde Common
Gilt Club
Jo-Bar
Kask*
Mint/820
Observatory
Olive or Twist*
Rum Club
Teardrop Lounge
Vault
Vintage Lounge

**Bookish Good Looks**

Bread & Ink Café
Dig a Pony
Irving St. Kitchen
Palace of Industry
Press Club
Tugboat Brewery
Secret Society

* No Happy Hour

**Retro/Mod**

Crush
Jinx
Mellow Mushroom
Moloko
The Original
Pour

**Retro/Old School**

Clyde's Prime Rib
Doug Fir
Driftwood Room
Jake's
Gold Dust Meridian
Hubers
Jimmy Mak's
Ringside Steakhouse
Ron Tom's
Savoy Tavern & Bistro
Trader Vic's
Wilf's

**Speakeasy Style**

Beech St. Parlor
Camellia Lounge
Central
Circa 33
Hazel Room
Hobo's
Interurban
Sapphire Hotel
Secret Society
Sidecar 11

**You know how there's always so many restaurants you want to try, but then you forget which ones they are?**

Here's some lists to help remind you!
May be especially helpful when hosting visitors.

Take notes on these pages (there's lots of white space) and peruse when deciding:

# Where should we go to eat?!

**Best Breakfasts**
Arleta Library Café
Autentica
Broder
Country Cat
Helser's
Mother's
Petite Provence
Sanborn's
Screen Door
Simpatica
Tasty & Sons
Zell's

Breakfast is huge in this town –
Get the **"Breakfast in Bridgetown"** book!
By Paul Greald
There's an app too.

**Casual & Award-Winning**
(Including best pizzas and burgers)

Apizza Scholls
Biwa
Boke Bowl
Dove Vivi
Firehouse
Foster Burger
Ken's Artisan Pizza
Little Big Burger
Oven & Shaker
Podnah's Pit
Pok Pok
Tanuki
Via Tribunali

**Best Gluten-Free**
Corbett Fish House
Mac & Cheesery
Mama Mia Trattoria
Mi Mero Mole
Natural Selection
Northwest Public House
Portobello Vegan Trattoria
Seasons and Regions
Slide Inn
Thirst Bistro

Overall, restaurants are becoming more and more responsive to this situation.

In general, these foods have lots of options: Asian, Indian, Mediterranean, Mexican, Peruvian
ENJOY!

**www.glutenfreeportland.org**

**Best Sandwiches**
Big Ass Sandwiches
Bunk
Grain & Gristle
Kenny & Zuke's
Lardo
Laurelhurst Market
Meat Cheese Bread
Olympic Provisions
Petisco
Streetcar Bistro

**Coolest new concept: Ocean Complex**
Bridging the gap between food carts and brick & mortar restaurants, with places by some Portland's best chefs! At NE Glisan & 24th:

24th & Meatballs
Basa Basa
Slowburger
Uno Mas
Pie Spot

**Special Showpieces**
Benson Hotel
Chart House
Departure
Food Carts
Gracie's/Driftwood Room
Hale Pele
Portland City Grill
Salty's
Tony Starlights
Trader Vic's
Urban Famer
Voodoo Donuts

**Foodie Focused**

Beast
DOC
Genoa
Gruner
June
Le Pigeon
Luce
Ned Ludd
Nostrana
Paley's Place
Tabla

**More Recent City Bests**

Aviary
Bamboo Sushi NW
Bollywood Theater
Boxer Sushi
Cocotte
Imperial
Kin
Little Bird
Market
Mextiza
Noisette
Ox
Paadee
Riffle
Roe
Smallwares
St. Jack
Vie
Wafu
Woodsman Tavern
Xico

**Established City Bests**

23 Hoyt
a Cena
Acadia
Accanto
Andina
Bamboo Sushi
Bluehour
Castagna
Clarklewis
El Gaucho
Farm Cafe
Gilt Club
Giorgio's
Higgins
Jake's
Karam
Lincoln
Mama Mia Trattoria
Masu
Meriwether's
Metrovino
Navarre
Nel Centro
Noble Rot
Nostrana
Oba
Park Kitchen
Patanegra
Ringside
Saucebox
Seres
Serratto
Three Doors Down
Thirst
Toro Bravo
Wildwood
Yakuza

## Happy Hour All Night

Enjoy at: **Gotham Tavern** (NE map)

The Gotham Tavern

**Get Happy Hour prices on food 'til close.**

## ★ FREE Small Plate ★

Enjoy at: **Hazel Room** (Hawthorne map)

The Hazel Room tea lounge

**Buy one delicious Happy Hour item, get a second one free!**

## ★ $15.00 off! ★

Enjoy at:

**Jantzen Beach Bar & Grill**

(Waterfront map)

Jantzen Beach BAR & GRILL

**Take $15 off your dinner bill.**

## Gotham Tavern

2240 North Interstate Avenue
Portland, OR 97227
(503) 517-9911
www.gothamtavern.com

*Good for whole table, but limited to one single tab/payment. Not good with any other offer. Expires 12/30/13.*

## The Hazel Room

3279 SE Hawthorne Blvd.
Portland, OR 97214
(503) 756-7125
www.thehazelroom.com

*Buy any Happy Hour menu item and get one of equal or lesser value free! Valid only during Happy Hour. Not good with any other offer or take-out. Maximum two free menu items per table. Beverage purchase required. Expires 12/30/13.*

## Jantzen Beach Bar & Grill

909 N Hayden Island Dr.
Portland, OR 97217
(503) 978-4554
www.redliontheriver.com

*For lunch or dinner checks totalling $50 or more (amount prior to discount) . Expires 12/30/13. Can not be combined with any other discounts or offers, including Happy Hour. One coupon per table.*

## ★ FREE Sandwich ★

Enjoy at: **Las Primas** (North/NE map)

LAS PRIMAS
PERUVIAN KITCHEN

**Buy any regular sandwich, get a Happy Hour sandwich free!**

## ★ 1/2 Price Entree ★

Enjoy at: **Macadam's** (Out & About Map)

Macadam's
Bar & Grill

**Buy one entree, get 2nd half-price!**

# Las Primas

3971 N Williams Ave.
Portland, OR 97227
(503) 206-5790
www.lasprimaskitchen.com

*Buy any regular sandwich and get a Happy Hour sandwich free. Valid anytime (lunch, happy hour or dinner). Not good with any other offer or take-out. Maximum one coupon per table. Expires 12/30/13.*

# Macadam's Bar & Grill

5833 SW Macadam Avenue
Portland, OR 97239
(503) 246-MACS
www.macadamsbarandgrill.com

*Buy any dinner entree and get a second one of equal or lesser value half-price. Requires purchase of two beverages. Expires 12/30/13. Cannot be combined with any other offer or dinner specials. One coupon per table.*

## Burgers & Bubbles $14

Enjoy at: **Metrovino** (Pearl map)

METROVINO

**Enjoy our world-class cheeseburger with a glass of bubbles!**

## Happy Hour All Night

Enjoy at: **Mint | 820** (NE map)

*mint* 820

**Get Happy Hour prices on food 'til close.**

# Metrovino

139 NW 11th Avenue
Portland, OR 97209
(503) 517-7778
www.metrovinopdx.com

PORTLAND Happy Hour GUIDEBOOK Recommended!

*Good for whole table. Not good with any other offer. Expires 12/30/13. Subject to availability.*

# Mint/820

816 N Russell St
Portland, OR 97227
(503) 284-5518
www.mintand820.com

PORTLAND Happy Hour GUIDEBOOK Recommended!

*Good for whole table. Not good with any other offer. Expires 12/30/13.*

## ★ $10 off Lunch Entree! ★

Enjoy at: **Salty's** (Waterfront map)

Salty's COLUMBIA RIVER SEAFOOD GRILL

**Buy two lunch entrees, save $10!**

## ★ $10 off Dinner Entree! ★

Enjoy at: **Salty's** (Waterfront map)

Salty's COLUMBIA RIVER SEAFOOD GRILL

**Buy two dinner entrees, save $10!**

## Book a Private Event at Salty's!

Enjoy at: **Salty's** (Waterfront map)

Salty's COLUMBIA RIVER SEAFOOD GRILL

**FREE round of appetizers and a champagne toast for your group!**

## Salty's on the Columbia

3839 NE Marine Drive
Portland, OR 97211
(503) 288-4444
www.saltys.com/portland

*Buy any two lunch entrees and get $10.00 taken off your total bill. Requires purchase of two beverages. Expires 12/30/13. Cannot be combined with any other offer, Happy Hour, or specials. One coupon per table.*

---

## Salty's on the Columbia

3839 NE Marine Drive
Portland, OR 97211
(503) 288-4444
www.saltys.com/portland

*Buy any two dinner entrees and get $10.00 taken off your total bill. Requires purchase of two beverages. Expires 12/30/13. Cannot be combined with any other offer, Happy Hour, or specials. One coupon per table.*

---

## Salty's on the Columbia

3839 NE Marine Drive
Portland, OR 97211
(503) 288-4444
www.saltys.com/portland

*Free round of appetizers & a champagne toast for your group! Must book through our catering dept. and meet minimum party size. Expires 12/30/13. Not good with any other offer.*

## FREE Happy Hour Pool

Enjoy at: **Uptown Billiards Club**
(Nob Hill map)

## ★ 2-for-1 Rate ★

Enjoy at: **Voicebox Karaoke**
(Nob Hill map)

**Buy one individual rate hour – get one free.**

## Uptown Billiards Club

120 NW 23rd Avenue
Portland OR 97210
(503) 226-6909
www.uptownbilliards.com

*Coupon good for one hour of free pool on one table. Minimum $10.00 food purchase required. Not redeemable for cash. Expires 12/30/13.*

## Voicebox Karaoke

2112 NW Hoyt
Portland, OR 97209
(503) 303-8220
www.voiceboxpdx.com

*Good for one guest at the $4 or $7 per hour or $10 tuesday rate. Maximum value $10. No cash value. Limited to two coupons per suite, per party. Subject to suite availability. Reservations recommended. Party size minimums may apply. Expires 12/30/13.*

# A few of my favorite things...

**To help you find even more HAPPY-ness in life, check out all these fun and brilliant businesses!**

## Brewcycle

It's a party—on a bar bike! Pedal away and experience your favorite breweries in a whole new way.

It's a blast!

BREWCYCLE
PORTLAND

www.brewcycleportland.com
971.400.5950

## Northwest Food & Wine Festival

Portland's legendary food and wine festival with the best of Northwest wines, spirits and beers – and food! Enjoy the highest quality cuisines from the area's well-known chefs and restaurants. This is the best one – don't miss it!

And... November 16th, 2013!

*The Northwest Food & Wine Festival*

**November 10, 2012**
DoubleTree by Hilton Lloyd Center | 4:00–8:00pm

www.nwwinefestival.com
971.400.5950

## Portland Food Adventures

If I could "force" you to go to one of these, I would!
I never knew dining could be THIS amazing.
Really – you MUST try it!

WOW!

www.portlandfoodadventures.com
Six food experiences for the price of one!

## Lardo

A superb sandwich shop with beer garden too!
Seasonal ingredients and a rotating menu of
playful, delicious sandwiches. Craveable!

Exceptional!

www.lardopdx.com
503.234.7786

## Ride On

A brilliant concept that not everyone knows about,
but may one day need to use. Call Ride On when you
shouldn't drive, and they'll drive your car for only $15!

Brilliant!

www.rideonportland.org
(503) 235-7433 (ride)

#### Beervana!

# Beervana Map

(Near Downtown)

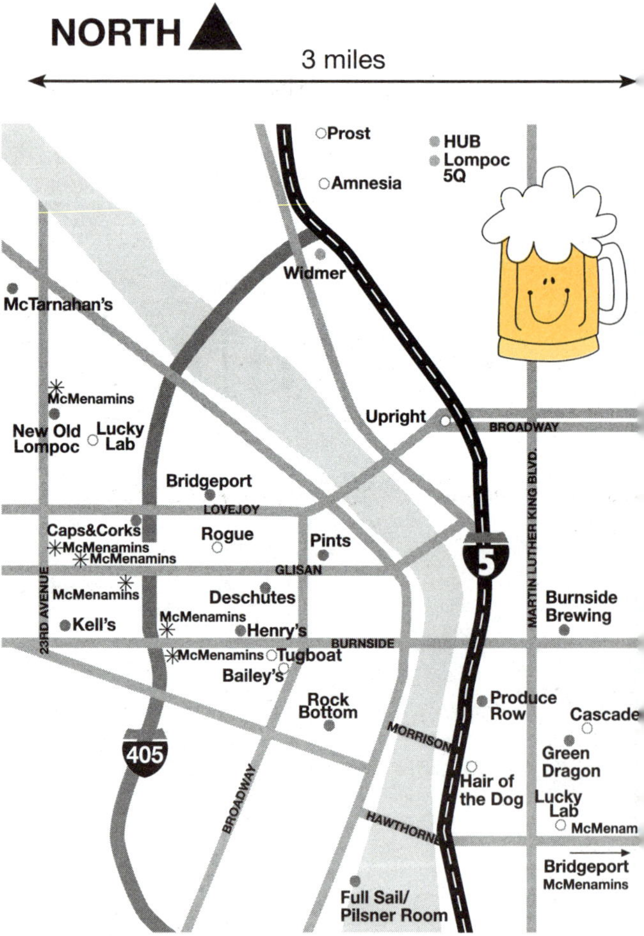

## Alameda Brewhouse

**Fremont Map** 4765 NE Fremont; (503) 460-9025
www.alamedabrewhouse.com

**Hoppy Hourss** 3:00–6:00pm Mon-Fri; 9:00pm–close Daily

**Food Deals** $4.00–$5.00 Half-off a dozen or so well-portioned appetizers: ravioli, cajun calamari, hummus, quesadillas, pizza, nachos, spinach dip, wings.

**Drink Specials** $3.00 house ales; $3.95 wines

**Atmosphere** Interior leans more towards a nicer restaurant than a casual microbrewery with clean, contemporary lines, colors, and stylings. Outdoor seating on active sidewalk at Happy Hour.

## Amnesia Brewing

**North/NE Map** 832 N. Beech; (503) 281-7708

**Hoppy Hours** 4:00–6:00pm Tues-Fri; ★All Night Mon
Beer special: $3.50 pints
Food specials: None (but cheap grub, though limited)
*Brewpub in the eclectic Mississippi neighborhood; alluring front patio hang-out; beer afficionados love it.*

## B.J.'s Brewhouse www.bjsrestaurants.com

**Waterfront Map** 12105 N. Center; (503) 289-5566
7390 NE Cornell, Hillsboro; (503) 615-2300

**Hoppy Hours** 3:00–7:00pm Mon–Fri and 10:00–11:00pm Sun–Thur

**Food Deals** $2.00 off appetizers (17 items)
All the bar basics with 1/2 price personal pizzas too.

**Drink Specials** $1.00 off pints and wells

**Atmosphere** Warm and friendly pub with golden beer-colored walls, red brick, big ol' beer vats and a long bar. Big – 125 National locations.

## Breakside Brewery www.breaksidebeers.com

**Northeast (off map)** 820 NE Dekum; (503) 719-6475

**Hoppy Hours** 3:00–6:00pm Sun–Thur; 9:00–close Daily

**Food Deals** $2.00–$6.00 About a dozen basic beer bites: wings, hummus, pretzel, nachos, grilled cheese & soup, chips & salsa, burgers, sliders.

**Drink Specials** $3.50 drafts; $1.00 off wine

**Atmosphere** Great care went into the design, so it's a fresh and clean take on the standard brewery trends of cement floors, giant wood beams, and garage-style roll-up doors. Outdoor picnic tables.

## Bridgeport Brewpub

**Pearl Map** 1313 NW Marshall; (503) 241-3612
www.bridgeportbrewandalehouse.com

**Hoppy Hours** 3:00–5:00pm Food; 3:00–6:00pm Beer
10:00pm–close Fri–Sat (food and beer deals)

**Food Deals** $2.50–$6.00 Giant menu! Cheeseburgers, brats, BBQ chicken, mac & cheese, pizza, and more!

**Drink Specials** $3.00 Imperial pints

**Atmosphere** Slick, big-city-style brewery, bakery and coffee shop in renovated loft building; cavernous open area with the brick, iron and wood; outdoor seating.

**Bridgeport Ale House** (beer brewed at their brewpub)

**Southeast Map** 3632 SE Hawthorne; (503) 233-6540
www.bridgeportbrewandalehouse.com

**Hoppy Hours** 3:00–5:00pm Tues–Fri
10:00pm–close Fri–Sat

**Food Deals** $2.00–$7.00 15 items with all the Happy Hour basics covered including salads, dips, burgers, pizzas, mac & cheese, poutine, sandwiches.

**Drink Specials** $3.00 pints (20 oz. Imperial Pints)

**Atmosphere** A smaller, neighborhood off-shoot of downtown's Bridgeport Brewpub with open windows to the street, sidewalk seating, and big central bar.

## Burnside Brewing

**Central Eastside Map** 701 E Burnside; (503) 946-8151
www.burnsidebrewco.com

**Hoppy Hours** 3:00-6:00pm Daily

**Food Deals** Limited menu with some very obscure items that somehow match the place... pickle plate, brat burger, fried sardines, pickled pork slider, white bean spread, duck confit cohiba/cigar roll, crepes.

**Drink Specials** $3.00 drafts (20 oz. Imperial pints $3.00 all night on Wed); $5.00 house wines

**Atmosphere** Big, open room with cement floors (much like most breweries), with added character from massive wood beams overhead, black walnut tables and designerly L-shaped bar. Very cool, and *huuuge*, chalkboard framed sign. Patio.

## Cascade Brewing Barrel House

**Southeast Map** 939 SE Belmont; (503) 265-8603
www.cascadebrewingbarrelhouse.com

**Hoppy Hours** 4:00–6:00pm Daily $1.00 off drafts

Lots of barrels, 16 taps, and cheap grub at all times – and lots of it! Bright green walls and visible barrels, picnic table seating, and outdoor patio.

## Coalition Brewing

**Lloyd Center-ish** 2724 SE Ankeny; (503) 894-8080
www.coalitionbrewing.com

**Hoppy Hours** 3:00–6:00pm Tues-Sun

**Food Deals** $2.00–$4.00 Ultra-cheap beer go-withs!

**Drink Specials** $3.50 pints; $10.00 pitchers; $5.00 house wines

**Atmosphere** Cozy little neighborhood place with good beer (with local, hand-picked guest home brews) located in the old Noble Rot space. It's both a pub and 10-barrel brewery. Come thirsty!

## Columbia River Brewing

**Northeast (off map)** 1728 NE 40th; (503) 943-6157
www.columbiariverbrewpub.com

**Hoppy Hours** 3:00–6:00pm and 9:00pm–close Daily

**Food Deals** $5.00–5.99 Big menu of good eats: ravioli, nachos, grilled stuffed portobello, artichoke dip, pizza, steak chimichangas, wings, veggie plate.

**Drink Specials** $3.00 drafts; $1.00 off all wines; $5.00 daily cocktail

**Atmosphere** Nice, open brewpub with refinished wood floors and tables, separated bar area, views of the "Brew House" beer vats, but all a bit too brightly lit.

## Deschute's Brewery

**Pearl Map** 210 NW 11th Ave.; (503) 296-4906
www.deschutesbrewery.com

**Hoppy Hours** 4:00–6:00pm Mon–Fri

**Food Deals** $3.00–$4.50 Mini-meals like ribs, pizza, sloppy joes, mac & cheese, fries, Caesar salad, pretzels, French onion soup, salad, fries, or pizza.

**Drink Specials** $3.50 beer-of-the-day (half-liter)

**Atmosphere** A "don't miss" for beer lovin' visitors and locals. Huge, and always crowded, cavernous interior captures the spirit of the Pacific NW, complete with bear totem poles, exposed brick, and lots of wood.

## Fourth Street Brewing

**Gresham** 77 NE 4th Street; (503) 669-0569
www.4thstreetbrewing.com

**Hoppy Hours** 4:00–6:00pm and 9:00–11:00pm Daily
★ All day Sunday and starts at 2:00pm on Saturday

**Food Deals** $2.95–$4.95 Big bar menu with soup or salad, fries or chips or dips, cheese plate, giant pretzels, nachos, sliders, skewers

**Drink Specials** $3.00 drafts; $4.00 wines; $3.00 wells

**Atmosphere** Nice brewery with bar and brewing in back, and dining in front. Nine big-screen TVs and pool.

## Golden Valley

**Beaverton** 1520 NW Bethany Blvd.
(503) 972-1599; www.goldenvalleybrewery.com

**Hoppy Hours** 3:00–6:00pm Daily

**Food Deals** $2.95–$4.95 A bit of everything: pork or beef sliders, ribs, oysters shooters, mac & cheese, tacos, hummus, grilled veggie quesadilla, hummus, fries.

**Drink Specials** $2.00 Beaverton Blonde
$3.00 drafts; $4.00 house red

**Atmosphere** A brand-new beacon in Beaverton that calls out for an immediate detour from the road. Warm and woody with wood floors, tables and trim, big wood bar and bar stools, and exposed wood ceiling.

## Hair of the Dog Brewery

**Southeast/CES Map** 61 SE Yamhill; (503) 232-6585
www.hairofthedog.com

**Hoppy Hours** No official Happy Hour

Big tasting room for one of our founding microbrewies (1993), with full kitchen and big, garage-style pub.

## Hopworks Bike Bar

**North/NE Map** 3947 N. Williams; (503) 287-6258
www.hopworksbeer.com

**Hoppy Hours** 3:00–6:00pm and 9:00pm–close Daily

**Food Deals** $2.25-$5.75 A dozen or so tasty bar treats to complement award-winning beers, plus a couple of desserts: pizza, giant pretzels, outstanding chicken wings, big salads, hummus, and soups.

**Drink Specials** $.75 cents off drafts

**Atmosphere** Organic beer, sustainable food, and stationary bicycles that actually generate electricity back into the building's grid when pedaled. Family-friendly with great beer garden. Bike frames overhang the bar at this northside HUB (note: not the Williams HUB building), and there's 99 bottles of beer on the walls!

## Hopworks Urban Brewery

**Southeast Map** 2944 SE Powell Blvd; (503) 232-4677
www.hopworksbeer.com

**Hoppy Hours** 3:00–6:00pm & 9:00pm–close Daily (Fri & Sat 10:00pm–midnight)

**Food Deals** $2.25–$4.75 Similar but smaller version of menu at the other HUB (see Bike Bar listed previously).

**Drink Specials** Beer is 75 cents off

**Atmosphere** Eco-brewpub with organic beer, fresh local ingredients, and a sustainable building. Very cool bike "rack" over bar. Bike-, banquet-, baby- and beer-garden-friendly. Lots of natural woods and light inside.

## Laurelwood Brewpubs

www.laurelwoodbrewpub.com

5115 NE Sandy; (503) 282-0622

6716 SE Milwaukie Ave; (503) 894-8267

PDX Airport Concourse A (503) 493-9427 (No HH)

PDX Airport Concourse E (503) 281-6753 (No HH)

1401 SE Rasmussen; Battleground, WA (360) 723-0937

**Hoppy Hours** 3:00–6:00pm and 9:00–10:00pm Daily

**Food Deals** $3.00– 5.00 Lotsa bar eats: burgers (meat or veggie), Caesar, garlic fires, tacos, pork sliders, fish & chips, nachos, artichoke dip, and hummus.

**Drink Specials** $3.00 drafts

**Atmosphere** Since 2001, neighborhood-, family- and friend-focused. Casual, neighborhood hangouts. "Portland's Original Certified Organic Brewery."

## Kell's and Old Town Pizza

Now making their own beer on-site!
See information on p.173 and p.255.

# Lompoc Brewpubs

www.newoldlompoc.com

**Hedgehouse**
3412 SE Division; (503) 235-2215

Hoppy Hours 4:00–6:00pm and 10:00pm–close Daily
Beer special: $3.50 pints; $2.50 pints on Tuesdays
Food deals: $2.00–$5.00 Finally! Deals on food too! Seven snacks like Welsh rarebit, nachos, beer cheese dip.

Family- and dog-friendly. Fun, super-big patio area outside; cute & cozy converted craftsman interior.

**Lompoc Fifth Quadrant & Sidebar Tasting Room**
3901 N. Williams; (503) 288-3996
Hoppy Hours 4:00–6:00pm and 10:00pm–close Daily
Beer special: $3.50 pints ($2.50 pints all day Tuesday) $1.00 off cocktails; Plus $3.00 Bloody Mary Sunday
Food deals: Half-off select appetizers (burger, wings, nachos, salad, hummus, beer cheese dip, fries).

Fresh and colorful, loft-style brewpub; long wooden booths for socializing; outdoor covered patio open to restaurant. Sidebar bonus room!

**Oaks Bottom Pub**
1621 SE Bybee; (503) 459-4988

Hoppy Hours 3:00–6:00pm and 9:00pm–close Daily
Beer special: $3.50 Lompoc pints ($2.50 Mondays); $1.00 off wine and wells; $3.00 Bloody Mary Sunday
Food deals: $4.00–$5.00 Best totchos ever! Plus pita-za hummus platter, shrooms, sliders, wings, fries.

Small but popular neighborhood haunt with a café appeal and outside seating on back patio.

# McMenamin's Breweries

See general overview and listings on p.63-64.

## Lucky Labs www.luckylab.com

**Lucky Labrador Brew Pub**
915 SE Hawthorne; (503) 236-3555

**Lucky Labrador Beer Hall**
1945 NW Quimby; (503) 517-4352

**Lucky Labrador Public House**
7675 SW Capitol Hwy.; (503) 244-2537

**Lucky Labrador Tap Room**
1700 North Killingsworth; (503) 505-9511

Save a buck off beer on "Miser Mondays" at the Hawthorne and Killingsworth locations, and Tuesdays at Capitol Hwy or Quimby. Decent and well-priced food, but no special HH deals. Casual favorites in big, woody spaces. Big rooms, dog- and family-friendly.

## Mashtun Brewpub

**North/NE Map** 2204 NE Alberta; (503) 548-4491
www.themashtunbrewpub.com

**Hoppy Hours** 3:00–6:00pm Daily

**Food Deals** $2.50–$6.00 Tasty basics that go well with beer and pool. Generous servings of tots!

**Drink Specials** $3.00 house beers; $3.00 wells

**Atmosphere** Very casual and warehouse-y pub with big patio. Large and open garage-like space.

## Max's Fanno Creek

**Tigard** 12562 SW Main St; (503) 624-9400
www.maxsfannocreek.com

**Hoppy Hours** 3:00–6:00pm and 9:00pm–close Daily

**Food Deals** $2.00–$5.00 About a dozen bar eats like hummus, quesadillas, mushrooms, mac & cheese, nachos, Caesar, fish & chips, sliders, artichoke hearts.

**Drink Specials** $2.75 beer of the day (8 taps)

**Atmosphere** Very casual brewpub with central hand-painted pillar and few other quirky art pieces. Exterior looks almost like a convenience store.

## McTarnahan's www.macsbeer.com

**NW/Nob Hill** 2730 NW 31st Ave.; (503) 228-5269

**Hoppy Hours**
3:00–6:00pm Daily & 9:00pm–close Tues–Sat

**Food Deals** $3.00–$5.00 A dozen big bar bites like burgers (meat or SW bean/veggie), pork sliders, tacos, twice-baked potato, corndogs, stix, Caesar, fries, hummus, Scottish pie – and desserts too!

**Drink Specials** $3.50 drafts; $10.50 pitchers
$4.00 house wine or mimosas

**Atmosphere** A little bit of everything strewn throughout 3-4 rooms, with the patio being a highlight. Cozy and pubby back room, compared to the front bar with views of hi-def TVs and the giant, copper beer vats.

## Migration Brewing

**Lloyd Center-ish** 2828 NE Glisan Street; (503) 206-5221
www.migrationbrewing.com

**Hoppy Hours** 3:00–6:00pm Mon-Fri (and Blazer games)

**Beer special:** $3.50 pints; $1.00 off wine

**Food Deals:** $3.00-$5.00 Good eats grub

*Casual and low-key PDX-style microbrewery with large TV (movie nights) and outdoor picnic tables. Several of their own brews with 8 guest taps.*

## Pints

**Old Town Map** 412 NW 5th Ave.; (503) 564-2739
www.pintsbrewing.com

**Hoppy Hours** 3:00–6:00pm Mon–Sat

**Beer special:** $3.00 pints

**Food Deals:** $3.00 New HH menu: potato corn fritters, chicken tenders, fries, flatbread, sliders, hummus.

**Atmosphere** Coffehouse by day, urban taproom by night (find the cozy second back room with brick walls and working brewery). Locally roasted coffee *and* NW craft beers. What a perfect Portland concept!

## Raccoon Lodge

7424 SW Beaverton-Hillsdale Hwy.; (503) 296-0110
www.raclodge.com

**Hoppy Hours** 4:00–6:00pm / 9:00pm–close Mon–Fri
10:00am–2:00pm Sat–Sun (in the Den only)

**Food Deals:** $3.25–$4.95 Big bar menu with a bit of everything! Burgers, several varieties each of fries, rings, and sliders, nachos, satay, fish tacos, salads.

**Drink Specials** $3.50 three select microbrews 20 oz.

**Atmosphere** Home of Cascade Brewing Company (since 1998). Simple, clean, basic pub with pool and TV. Popular and enjoyable outdoor beer garden!

## Ram Brewery www.theram.com

11860 SE 82nd Ave; Happy Valley; (503) 659-1282
29800 SW Boones Ferry; Wilsonville (503) 570-0200
(19 locations throught the U.S.)

**Hoppy Hours** 3:00–6:00pm and 9:00pm–close Daily

**Food Deals** $2.99–$4.99 Three styles of sliders, three kinds of fries, calamari, potato skins, nachos, spinach dip, hummus, and armadillo eggs!

**Drink Specials** $3.25 drafts, wines, or wells

**Atmosphere** Big, bold, and woody befitting the Big Horn Brewing Company name and corporate style. Sports, family-friendly and outdoor eating area.

## Rock Bottom www.rockbottom.com

**Downtown East Map** 206 SW Morrison; (503) 796-2739
(34 locations throughout the U.S.)

**Hoppy Hours** 2:00–6:00pm Mon–Fri
9:00pm–close Sun–Thurs; 11:00pm–close Fri & Sat

**Food Deals** $1.95–$5.95 17 appetizer goodies!

**Drink Specials** $1.00 off pints, wine, cocktails (early)

**Atmosphere** Corporate-style open brewery; warm coppers mixed with wood under soaring lofted ceilings; bustling big bar area; sidewalk dining.

## Rogue Ales www.rogue.com

"Meeting Halls" are each different, and visiting each at least once should be on every beer lover's bucket list.

Portland

### Rogue Hall

1717 Southwest Park Ave; (503) 219-8000
**Hoppy Hours** 3:00–5:00pm Mon–Fri (food only)
**Food Deals:** $3.00–$5.00 bar food basics
Located in the heart of the PSU campus in the Vue Tower (formerly Paccini's). College bar casual with coffee too. Tiki Tuesdays (wear your aloha shirts).

### Rogue Ales Public House

1339 NW Flanders; (503) 222-5910
**Hoppy Hours** 3:00–5:00pm Mon–Fri (food only)
**Food Deals:** $3.00–$5.00 bar food basics
38 taps! A fun and rouge-ish interior with several bawdy bar rooms befitting the name and attitude. Often a much-welcomed retreat from all the Pearliness nearby. Fun outside seating in the summertime.

### Green Dragon

928 SE 9th Ave.; (503) 517-0606

Also home to Buckman Brewing (503) 241-3800
www.buckmanbrewery.com

**Hoppy Hours** 4:00–6:00pm Daily
**Food Deals** $3.00–$5.00 Fresh, tasty bar bites
**Drink Specials** No drink discounts, but 62 taps!!
**Atmosphere** Open, garage-style brewery with a utopian beer selection of 19 perfectly selected, rotating taps. Nice big beer garden! Next to the Q-hut.

**Visit them at PDX!** Concourse D (503) 282-2630

**Visit them on the Coast!**

**Brewer's on the Bay**
2320 OSU Drive; Newport, OR; (541) 867-3664

**Rogue Ales Public House**
748 SW Bay Blvd; Newport, OR; (541) 265-3188

## Salmon Creek Brewery

**Vancouver Map** 108 W Evergreen; (360) 993-1827
www.salmoncreekbrewpub.com

**Hoppy Hours** 3:00–6:00pm Tues–Sat

**Food Deals** $2.95–$7.95 Pub munchies made for beer: beer-battered onion rings, mushrooms, veggies, jalapeno and cheddar tots, fries, hummus, nachos.

**Drink Specials** $1.00 off almost all beer

**Atmosphere** A cozy little pub interior with hunter green walls, café curtains, tin ceilings, memorabilia and art, and twinking white lights everywhere. Charming, private patio with brick walls covered in ivy.

## Sasquatch Brewery

**Out and About Map** 6440 S.W. Capitol Highway
(503) 402-1999; www.sasquatchbrewery.com

**Hoppy Hours** 3:00–5:00pm and 9:00pm–close Daily

**Food Deals** $2.00–$6.00 Good beer go-withs like giant pretzel, herbed popcorn, cheese or meat plates, soup, greens, beet fritter, olives, fries or burger.

**Drink Specials** $3.50 beer of the Day; $4.00 wines

**Atmosphere** Casual brewery in converted craftsman house. Traditional dining room with wood floors and green walls. Summer fun on the new outdoor deck!

## Stickmen Brewery & Skewery

**Lake Oswego Map** 40 N State: Lake Oswego
(503) 344-4449; www.stickmenbeer.com

**Hoppy Hours** 3:00–6:00pm Mon–Fri

**Food Deals** $2.95–$5.95 Nice first-round Happy Hour menu for the new kids on the block: nori fries, tempura zucchini, Caesar, sliders, bento bowl, crawfish cakes, sausage roll, wings. Check skewers on regular menu.

**Drink Specials** $1.00 off wells

**Atmosphere** It's right on the lake! This is the former Oswego Lake House. They've really brightened up the place. Traditional, somewhat nautical decor.

# Tugboat Brewing Co.

**Downtown East Map** 711 SW Ankeny; (503) 226-2508
www.d2m.com/Tugwebsite

**Hoppy Hours** 4:00–7:00pm Mon–Fri
**Beer Special:** $1.00 off drafts

Downtown Portland's oldest microbrewery and the perfect rainy-day hideout. Completely cozy with lots of dark woods, loads of old books, and well-loved board games. A secret treasure for dark days and nights. Per their website: "nightly live jazz music, cool munchies, and nice beer for nice people."

# Widmer Gasthaus www.widmer.com

**North/NE Map** 929 N Russell; (503) 281-3333

**Hoppy Hours** 2:00–5:00pm Mon–Fri ('til 10pm Mon)
11:00am–close Sun

**Food Deals** $3.00–$8.00 ($2.00 off burgers Sun–Mon) Bar menu with lots of food to go with beer, but without the higher prices: BBQ pork sandwiches, pretzels, salads, hummus, fondue, soup, wings, burgers.

**Drink Specials** $1.00 off pints

**Atmosphere** One of Oregon's biggest and best. Nice looking space with bricks, wood pillars and trim, and beer-colored walls. Fun – and free – tours on Fridays and Saturdays (reservations are required).

# Volcanic Brewery!?

**Guest beers on tap?**
**Find it in a Tiki Hut?**
My very favorite Portland brewery! Lively brews by savage hop heads, Edward Querfeld and Steve Woods.

www.volcanicbrewery.com
www.facebook.com/
VolcanicBrewing

# Small Microbreweries

*No food served, but growler fills encouraged!*

## Captured by Porches

**Several locations** (off map); (971) 207-3742
www.capturedbyporches.com
Following in the food cart distribution plan, but with beer – and buses! Check website to find them. Genius!

## The Commons Brewery

**Southeast (off map)** 1810 SE 10th Ave; (503) 343-5501
www.commonsbrewery.com
Super simple and small, but living the dream! Eight house taps with occasional guests. Limited hours.

## Gigantic Brewing

**Southeast (off map)** 5224 SE 26th Ave; (503) 208-3416
www.giganticbrewing.com
Cool tap room with funny flair here and there. Garage style with outdoor picnic tables.

## Occidental Brewing Co.

**North (off map)** 6635 N. Baltimore; (503) 719-7102
www.occidentalbrewing.com
Simple tasting room in St. John's with a small bar area open the the brewing warehouse. Tiny beer museum!

## Upright Brewing

**North/NE** 240 N Broadway; (503) 735-5337
www.uprightbrewing.com
Bare-bones tasting room to enjoy samples, full beers, and occasional live music.

## Vertigo Brewing

**Hillsboro** 21420 NW Nicholas Ct; (503) 645-6644
www.vertigobrew.com
Big warehouse tasting room with barrel, picnic, and metal tables. Stand steady or sit and sip a spell.

*All about beer and food – and Happy Hour too!*

## Bazi Bierbrasserie

Top cover fave 2013!

**Southeast Map** 1522 SE 32nd Ave; (503) 234-8888
www.bazipdx.com

**Hoppy Hours** 3:00-7:00 pm Daily (plus 10:00pm–close)
★All day Sunday

**Food Deals** $3.00-$7.00 Wide-ranging menu of 10 items: grilled shrimp and kale, spinach salad, burgers, grilled cheese, salad, pork belly skewers, frites.

**Drink Specials** $1.00 off most beers; $1.00 off wine $3.50 wells; $5.00 cocktails (full bar including award-winning signature BEER cocktails!)

**Atmosphere** *The* place for Belgian beers on tap! They rotate 18 taps in all, and have another dozen or so bottles. Nice back bar area; lounge area with couches and tables up front. Roll-up garage door and lots of light. "A wine bar of beer."

## Caps & Corks

1000 NW 17th Ave; (503) 222-6435
www.capsandcorks.com

**Hoppy Hours** 3:00–6:11pm Daily (they cut ya slack :-)

**Food Deals** $3.00–$5.00 Wide array with the usual bar line-up, plus some fancy stuff like salad, dolmas and baked brie. More than 15 menu items, including a pretty good burger (and I don't think that often).

**Drink Specials** $3.50 select beer; $4.00 house wines $4.00 wells

**Atmosphere** Formerly the Emanon, now a popular stop on the super-fun BrewCycle tour. They have several coolers packed with hundreds of beers, plus a great wine shop. Extremely casual, especially for the Pearl.

## Concordia Ale House

**North/NE (off map)** 3276 NE Killingsworth
(503) 287-3929; www.concordia-ale.com

**Hoppy Hours** 3:00–6:00pm Mon–Fri; $2.00 Tuesdays (noon–mid Your choice of 26 bottles)

**Food Deals** $3.75 About 15 bar apps cover all the bases: nachos; plain, veggie or cheeseburgers; BBQ pork sandwich; cajun, garlic or chili cheese fries or tots; mac & cheese; quesadillas; or healthy salads.

**Drink Specials** Sadly, no drink deals.

**Atmosphere** A visit to Concordia's Great Wall of Taps is a feast for the eyes and a touch of paradise for the discriminating beer palette. Bar in back with 22 taps and over 150 bottles. Pool tables, keno et al., and TVs. Up front, family-friendly, neighborhood place.

## Henry's Tavern

**Pearl Map** 10 NW 12th Ave.; (503) 227-5320
www.henrystavern.com

**Hoppy Hours** 3:00–6:00pm Daily; 9:00pm–close Mon–Thur; 10:00pm–mid Fri–Sat; ★All day Sunday

**Food Deals** $3.95–$5.95 About 12 items: a couple salads, soup, mac & cheese, sushi roll, burger, killer Gorgonzola fries(!), prawns, hummus, dip, and more.

**Drink Specials** Sadly, no drink deals.

**Atmosphere** A popular, long-time Portland favorite. Warm, but very spacious ex-brewery; open two-story seating; huge center bar; loft-style bricks & iron; patio (not available for HH seating). More than 100 beers on tap with refrigerated bar top to keep them chilled!

## Highland Stillhouse

**Oregon City Map** 201 S. 2nd Street; (503) 723-6789
www.highlandstillhouse.com

**Hoppy Hours** 3:00–6:00pm Tues–Fri

**Food Deals** $4.00–$5.00 If you love haggis balls, you'll love the Highland Stillhouse! Or on the possibly less-interesting side, there's also wings, rings, shrimp cocktail, fried mushrooms, coconut prawns, mac & cheese, and sliders.

**Drink Specials** $1.00 off beer and wine (rotating beer specials with 18 choice taps)

**Atmosphere** Step inside and sample a whisky (there's more than 400 to try)! Stay and relax – the wall-to-wall Scottish decor transports you to a whole other time and country, and the upstairs is especially loaded with true tavern character. Outside patio.

## Hop & Vine www.thehopandvine.com

**North/NE Map** 1914 N Killingsworth; (503) 954-3322

**Hoppy Hours** 3:00–6:00pm Mon–Sat;
3:00pm–close Sunday★

**Food Deals** $2.00–$6.00 Limited Happy Hour menu: Olives, popcorn of the day, butter lettuce salad, cheeseburger, tomato soup with grilled cheese.

**Drink Specials** $1.00 off beer and wine

**Atmosphere** Everything to make a hoppy beer lover happy. And a large wall of wine makes it a bottle shop heaven too! Simple and mellow backyard picnic table seating, with hops and vines. Coffeehouse-like interior.

## Hophouse(s) www.oregonhophouse.com

**Hawthorne Map** 4111 SE Hawthorne; (503) 477-9619
**North/NE (off map)** 1517 NE Brazee; (971) 266-8392

**Hoppy Hours** 3:00–6:00pm and 9:00pm–close Daily
★All day Sunday

**Food Deals** $4.00 Good for beer drinkin' food, plus a little more: beer nuts, cheese curds, poutine, fries, crostini, chicken satay, deviled eggs, chicken sandwich, sliders, jalapeno corn fritters, and pulled pork.

**Drink Specials** $1.00 off select beer

**Atmosphere** The 15th Ave. location hosts 33 local taps and has outside seating. Hawthorne Hophouse, has "only" 24 taps. Not an overdose of personality to these places, but there *is* something very fun about them...

# More Pubs with a Big Beer Focus

**Dublin Pub**
6821 SW Beaverton-Hillside Hwy.; (503) 297-2889
www.dublinpubpdx.com
Happy Hours: 3:00–7:00pm Daily (5:00-7:00pm Sun)
Cheap grub and $3.00 microbrews or wells; $4 wines

59 beers on tap; over 50 more in bottles. Since 1983, a very popular Irish pub in Southwest PDX. Pool and frequent live music. Ultra-casual bar.

**Horsebrass Pub** www.horsebrass.com
4534 SE Belmont; (503) 232-2202
No Happy Hour Legendary English Pub style and has over 50 taps! "It's #7 of the 125 places to have a drink in the world before you die" ~ All About Beer Magazine

**Moon & Six-Pence**
2014 NE 42nd Ave; (503) 288-7802
No Happy Hour Super-casual and somewhat old, but that makes it seem more British, in a good way.

**Prost!** www.prostportland.com
4237 N. Mississippi; (503) 954-2684
No Happy Hour Highly popular place and worth going. Nice German pub w/over-sized beer mugs—and boots!

**Roscoe's** www.roscoespdx.com
8105 SE Stark; (503) 255-0049
Happy Hours: 2:00–6:00pm Daily; $1.00 wells
Big and well-chosen tap line-up, plus half-off bar menu

**Rose & Thistle Pub**
2314 NE Broadway; (503) 287-8582
Happy Hours: 3:00-7:00pm Sun-Thurs
$2.75 well, $3.50 20 oz micros
Haggis, scotch eggs, character, and a great patio!

**Saraveza** www.saraveza.com
1004 N Killingsworth; (503) 206-4252
200+ bottles and 10 rotating taps!
Happy Hours: 3:30-5:30pm Wed-Mon $1.50 1/2 pours
Very cool neighborhood pub! Fun, bottle-cap tables. Big menu focuses on pasties, pickling, house meats and Midwest treats.

# Bottle Shops & Taprooms

**1856**
1465 NE Prescott; (503) 915-0135; www.1856pdx.com
*NEW in 2012! Beer, wine, cider, vermouth, bitters, books. Tiny place with 350 beers and seven rotating taps.*

**Apex**
1216 SE Division; (503) 273-9227; www.apexbar.com
*Almost 50 taps with a wide variety of beer styles.*
*No food served, but next to a Mexican take-out. Giant patio, small bar. Very bike friendly, but no dogs.*

**Bailey's Tap Room**
213 SW Broadway; (503) 295-1004
www.baileystaproom.com
*20 Rotating Taps of Craft Ales and Lagers. Prime location downtown and cool place.*

**Beer Bunker**
7918 SE Stark St; (503) 254-8200
*Fun new bottle shop opened this year. Lots of old tin signs, office chairs, and hanging beer-can lights.*

**The BeerMongers**
1125 SE Division; (503) 234-6012
www.thebeermongers.com
*500+ beers and 8 rotating, mostly local taps.*

**Belmont Station**
4500 SE Stark; (503) 232-8538
www.belmont-station.com
*1,000 beers in the store; café next door to drink & dine.*

**Bottles**
5015 NE Fremont; (503) 287-7022
www.bottlesnw.com
Happy Hour: 4:00–6:00pm Daily; All Day Sunday
$3.50 drafts
*Cool and very casual neighborhood bottle shop with ribs, wings, sliders, eight rotating taps, and hundreds of bottles. Great outdoor beer garden!*

**Bridgetown Beerhouse**
915 N Shaver; (503) 477-8763
www.bridgetownbeerhouse.com
*Tiny, but conveniently located, northeast bottleshop.*

**By the Bottle**
104 W. Evergreen, Vancouver, WA (360) 696-0012
www.www.bottledbrews.com
*A store, taproom, a sight to see. Over 600 types of beer!*

**John's Marketplace**
3535 SW Multnomah Blvd; (503) 244-2617
www.johnsmarketplace.com
*The best in the West! They carry more than 800 different bottled beers and a big selection of kegs too. Great for winos as well – they carry over 400 different wines!*

**Plew's Brews**
8409 N. Lombard; (503) 283-2243
www.plewsbrews.com
Happy Hour 4:00–7:00pm Mon–Fri $3.00 pints

Funky and fun tasting room and possibly the best place in town to fill your growlers (only eight bucks)!

**Portland U-Brew & Pub**
6237 SE Milwaukie; (503) 943-2727
www.portlandubrewandpub.com
Happy Hour 3-6pm $.50-$1.00 off beer; $4.00 wines
$3.95-$6.95 Four sandwiches; four pizzas

*Make your own beer! Learn new important skills from friendly and knowledgeable staff. Relax – have a home brew! Brew on premises with everything you'll need. Fully stocked supply store for home brewing too. Fun!*

**Uptown Market**
6620 SW Scholls Ferry Rd; (503) 336-4783
www.uptownmarketpdx.com
*Specialty brew store with 700 bottles and 6 taps too. Homebrew and kegerator experts, consultants, and suppliers.*

# McMenamin's Hotels

**Crystal Hotel**
303 SW 12th Ave.; Downtown Portland; (503) 972-2670
Right across the street from the Crystal Ballroom.
Houses Al's Den for live music and the Zeus Café too.

**Edgefield**
2126 SW Halsey; Troutdale; (503) 669-8610
38-acre renovated "Poor Farm;" golf course, movie theater, beer garden, casual and fine-dining, wine bar, Jerry Garcia bar, Little Red Shed Pub, and Spa.

**Gearhart Hotel**
1157 N. Marion Ave; Gearhart (coast); (503) 717-8150
*New!* Eighteen guestrooms on a golf course with pub.

**The Grand Lodge**
3505 Pacific Ave.; Forest Grove; (503) 992-9533
Stately ex-Masonic lodge and nursing home near Wine Country; restaurants, bars, movies, soak tub.

**Hotel Oregon**
310 NE Evans Street; McMinnville; (503) 472-8427
Weekend get-away in wine country; rooftop bar (great for viewing UFOs), pub, back bar, Cellar Bar, billiards.

**Kennedy School**
5736 NE 33rd Ave.; Portland; (503) 249-3983
Detention Bar, Honors Bar, Boiler Room Bar, movies, soaking pool, beer garden, party rooms, restaurant.

**Old St. Francis School**
700 NW Bond; Bend; (541) 382-5174
Old 1936 Catholic schoolhouse transformed into a heavenly entertainment complex.

**White Eagle**
836 N. Russell; Portland (503) 335-8900
A small "rock 'n' roll hotel" with resident "spirits" (it's reportedly haunted), nightly bands, saloon, and outdoor, seasonal beer garden.

# McMenamin's Pubs

*Select favorites – see their website for all pubs.*

**Bagdad Theater/Greater Trumps**
3702 SE Hawthorne; (503) 236-9234
Arabian-Nights-inspired movie theater and secret pub.

**Blue Moon Tavern**
432 NW 21st Ave.; (503) 223-3184
Meandering bar with table-top fireplace in the round and pool tables; outdoor sidewalk seating.

**Chapel Pub**
430 N Killingsworth; (503) 286-0372
A sanctuary with lots of cozy rooms. Outdoor patio.

**Crystal Ballroom**
1332 W Burnside; (503) 225-0047
Awesome place to see concerts! The ballroom floor is spring-loaded so it bounces slightly, and there's '80s nights downstairs at Lola's (check calendar).

**McMenamins on the Columbia**
1801 SE Columbia River Dr.
Vancouver, WA; (360) 699-1521
Brews with views! See full review on page 86.

**McMenamins Tavern & Pool**
1716 NW 23rd Ave.; (503) 227-0929
Heated outdoor tables; big pool room.

**Mission Theater**
1624 NW Glisan; (503) 223-4527
$3.00 movies in old Swedish evangelical mission.

**Ram's Head**
2282 NW Hoyt; (503) 221-0098
Sophisticated manly-man haven.

**Ringler's Pub**
1332 W. Burnside; (503) 225-0627
Funky ex-auto garage.

**Zeus Café**
303 SWt 12th Ave.; (503) 384-2500
The latest and greatest in the brand-new Crystal Hotel.

# Waterfront

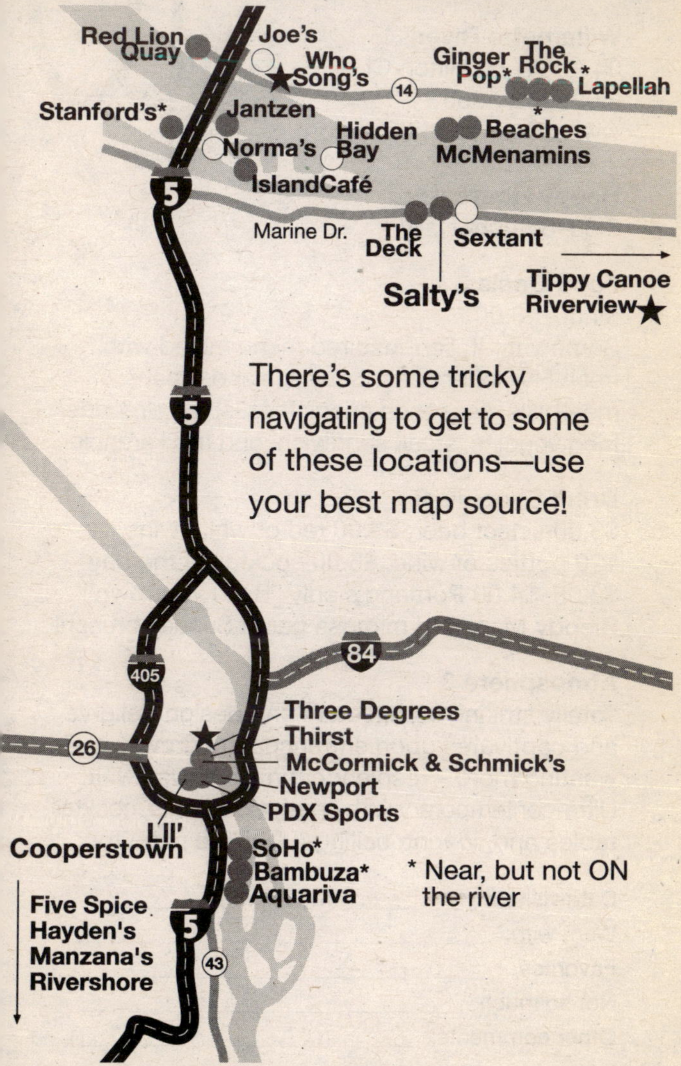


There's some tricky navigating to get to some of these locations—use your best map source!

# Aquariva

10

**Willamette River**
0470 SW Hamilton Ct
(503) 802-5850
www.aquarivaportland.com

**Happy Hours**
3:00–6:30pm Daily

**Food Deals 3**
$4.00–$8.00
Somewhat Italian-inspired menu mixed with fresh NW influences: Sauvie Island greens, meatballs, seasoned crispy fries, spicy almonds, fried veggies, steak sandwich, and fried arancini.

**Drink Specials 3**
$3.00 select beer; $5.00 red or white wine
$20 bottles of wine; $6.00 cocktail of the day
$3.00–$4.00 Portland's only "Build your own" Bloody Mary and mimosa bar at Sunday brunch!

**Atmosphere 3**
Totally striking architecture and design delights and captivates upon entrance, and draws you in wanting more – resplendent river views await! Ultra-contemporary with comfy couch pits, cocktail tables and soaring ceilings. Outside patio too.

Date visited: ____________ **My Rating:** ____________
Went with: ______________________________
Favorites: ______________________________
Not so much: ______________________________
Other comments: ______________________________
______________________________________________

# Bambuza

9

**Just off Willamette River**
3682 SW Bond Ave.
(503) 206-6330
www.bambuza.com

**Happy Hours**
4:00–6:00pm Mon–Sat

**Food Deals 3**
$2.00–$4.00
About a dozen delicious Vietnamese small plates like several salad rolls and spring rolls, skewers, soups, wontons, coconut shrimp and fresh salads.

**Drink Specials 3**
$3.00 NW bottled beers; $4.00 house wines
$5.00 select cocktails

**Atmosphere 2**
Colorful and bright, simple, quiet Asian bistro. Open room with hanging orange lanterns, green walls with bamboo stalks, lots of light from two walls of windows. Not on the water, but close enough to walk.

Date visited: __________ **My Rating:** __________
Went with: ____________________
Favorites: ____________________
Not so much: ____________________
Other comments: ____________________

# Beaches

9

**Columbia River (Vancouver)**
1919 SE Columbia River Dr.
(360) 699-1592
www.beachesrestaurantandbar.com

**Happy Hours**
3:00–6:00pm Daily; All night Monday★
9:00–11:00pm Tues–Sat; 9:00–10:00pm Sun

**Food Deals 3**
$1.40-$4.20
Huge menu with 23 items! First off, there's a brownie; also chipotle hummus, wings, taquitos, BBQ chicken pizza, mac & cheese, burgers, tots, fish & chips, rice bowls, and salads.

**Drink Specials 2**
$3.99 beer; $4.75 wines; $3.99 wells

**Atmosphere 3**
SO nice along the river here, but Happy Hour is in the inside bar area only. Overall, has a fun, but refined beach bar motif, wall-to-wall giant windows for river peeks and big stone fireplace.

Date visited: ___________ **My Rating:** ___________
Went with: ___________________________
Favorites: ___________________________
Not so much: _________________________
Other comments: ______________________
_____________________________________

# Cafe Murrayhill

9

**On cute little lake in Beaverton (off map)**
14500 Murray-Scholls Dr.
(503) 590-6030
www.cafemurrayhill.com

**Happy Hours**
3:00–6:00pm Daily

**Food Deals 3**
$5.00
Good-sized portions of Happy Hour faves: BLT or pork sliders, burgers, fried mushrooms or onion rings, hummus, calamari, crab cake or choice of unique pita "sandwiches."

**Drink Specials 2**
$4.00 beer; $5.00 house wines
Special Monday night deals

**Atmosphere 3**
It's totally pleasant in the summer by their little lake! Outdoor seating with lots of tables and colorful umbrellas. Nice café-style restaurant in a small strip mall. Skinny and long dining room with neutral woods and sherbet-colored walls.

Date visited: ____________ **My Rating:** ____________
Went with: ________________________________
Favorites: ________________________________
Not so much: ______________________________
Other comments: ___________________________
__________________________________________

# Five Spice

9

**Lake Oswego Map**
315 First St., Ste 201
(503) 697-8889
www.fivespicerestaurant.com

**Happy Hours**
3:00–6:00pm Daily ('til 5pm on outside deck)

**Food Deals 2**
$2.00–$12.00
About a dozen seasonal favorites with items like oysters on the half-shell, soup, fried squid, crab cakes, field greens, trio of tartares, beet salad.

**Drink Specials 3**
$5.00 selection of wines, cocktails and drafts; plus 1/2 off bottles of wine on Sundays

**Atmosphere 3**
Head upstairs to their lounge area for Happy Hour and sit outside if possible for views of the lake! Inside, it's pleasant as well, with Northwest-natural stylings, lots of light and huge windows. Relaxing fireplace with lounge area and couches.

Date visited: __________ **My Rating:** __________
Went with: ______________________________
Favorites: ______________________________
Not so much: ______________________________
Other comments: ______________________________

# Hayden's Lakefront Grill

10

**Tigard Map (Tualatin)**
8187 SW Tualatin
(503) 885-9292
www.haydensgrill.com

**Happy Hours**
11:00am–close Daily

**Food Deals 3**
$2.95–$9.95
Happy Hour starts at lunch! Bar classics turned up a notch, plus half sandwiches: super nachos, pepper bacon mac & cheese, teriyaki chicken bowl, beef medallions, Caesar, burgers, fries, plus salmon or tuna melt, reuben, French dip.

**Drink Specials 3**
$4.25 select draft; $5.00 house wines
$4.25 martinis

**Atmosphere 3**
Upscale and upbeat retro spin with color blocking and mod graphics. Good mix of private dining tables and more social cocktail area. Great stop when coming back from wine country! Happy Hour restricted to the bar area or partial patio seating.

Date visited: __________ **My Rating:** __________
Went with: ______________________________
Favorites: ______________________________
Not so much: ______________________________
Other comments: ______________________________

# Jantzen Beach Bar&Grill

10

**Columbia River**
909 N Hayden Island Drive
(503) 283-4466
www.redliontheriver.com

**Happy Hours**
3:00–6:00pm and 9:00–11:00pm Daily

**Food Deals 3**
$3.00–$6.00
Nice, well-rounded menu with items like grilled ciabatta, salads, burgers, calamari, hummus, dungeness crab cakes, clams, beef skewers.

**Drink Specials 3**
$4.00 drafts; $5.00 house red or white wines
$4.00 martini or cocktail of the day

**Atmosphere 3**
Wall-to-wall windows frame excellent river views! Large black & white photos reveal scenes of bygone glory days of Jantzen Beach Amusement Park. Enjoy Happy Hour seating anywhere in the understated, fine-dining restaurant or out on the long, outdoor patio. Fully remodeled and nicely appointed. Shenanigan's used to be next door.

Date visited: __________ **My Rating:** __________
Went with: ______________________________
Favorites: ______________________________
Not so much: ______________________________
Other comments: ______________________________
______________________________

# Lil Cooperstown

9

**Waterfront Map**
1831 SW River Dr; (503) 719-5394

Hillsboro: 2947 SE 73rd Ave; (503) 718-7513
Oregon City: 19352 Molalla Ave; (503) 305-6954
West Linn: 1817 Willamette Falls; (503) 655-1995

www.lilcooperstown.com

**Happy Hours**
3:00–6:00pm and 9:00pm–close Daily

**Food Deals 2**
$1.99–$4.99
About a 20 item list covering all the bases: wings, rings, nachos, burger, fish & chips, penne, tacos, quesadilla, pork sliders, salad soup, fries and more!

**Drink Specials 3**
$2.79–$5.29 domestics, micros and mondos!
$1.00 off all wines; $3.79 wells; $3.99 cocktails

**Atmosphere 3**
One of five locations, the brand-new Waterfront location is in the former Stanford's spot. Overall, the restaurant sides are decked out with full throttle sports memorabilia, but bar side decor (with Happy Hour) may be more for the B team.

Date visited: ____________ **My Rating:** ____________
Went with: ____________________________________
Favorites: ____________________________________
Not so much: __________________________________
Other comments: _______________________________
_______________________________________________

# Manzana's 10

**Lake Oswego Map**
305 1st St.
(503) 675-3322
www.manzanagrill.com

**Happy Hours**
4:00–6:00pm and 9:00pm–close Daily

**Food Deals 3**
$2.00–$6.00
Chicken quesadilla, citrus honey chicken wings, BBQ sandwich, hummus, Caesar, sliders, soup, seafood cakes, pork quesadilla, chimichanga.

**Drink Specials 3**
$1.00 off drafts; $4.00 red & white wine
$4.00 wells; $4.00 featured cocktails

**Atmosphere 3**
Mmmm... the rotisserie smell! Deep, dark, rich wooden booths and walls (new and modern). Big space attracts a crowd. Located right on the lake, but Happy Hour seating inside only. Part of the beloved Restaurants Unlimited Group.

Date visited: __________ **My Rating:** __________
Went with: ______________________________
Favorites: ______________________________
Not so much: ______________________________
Other comments: ______________________________
______________________________

# McCormick&Schmick's

Harborside Pilsner Room

10

**Willamette River**
0309 SW Montgomery
(503) 220-1865
www.mccormickandschmicks.com

**Happy Hours**
3:00–6:00pm and 9:00pm–close Daily
10:00pm–close Fri–Sat (in the summer)

**Food Deals 3**
$2.95–$5.95
A dozen or so items with a menu that changes a bit every month, with items like sliders, tacos, artichoke dip, wings, calamari, or hummus plate, but then you almost always have to get the famous cheeseburger and fries for only $3.95!

**Drink Specials 3**
$4.00 drafts; $5.00 wine; $6.00–$7.00 cocktails

**Atmosphere 3**
Gorgeous and stately restaurant overlooking the Willamette River! Impressive, traditional-style. Happy Hour inside, on bar side. Classy, but fun.

Date visited: ____________ **My Rating:** ____________
Went with: ________________________________
Favorites: ________________________________
Not so much: ______________________________
Other comments: ___________________________
___________________________________________

# Newport Seafood Grill

**Willamette River**
0425 SW Montgomery
(503) 227-3474
www.newportseafoodgrill.com

**Happy Hours**
3:00–6:00pm Daily; 9:00–10:00pm Fri–Sat

**Food Deals 3**
$3.00–$5.00
Extensive, cheap, and delicious menu with fish & chips, burger, chowder, calamari, shrimp tempura, tacos, pear and pecan salad, Cajun chicken tenderloins, prawns, Caesar, fries.

**Drink Specials 3**
$3.50 draft beer, wines and well drinks

**Atmosphere 3**
Formerly known as Marina Fish House, located right out over the river amidst the yachts, docks and ducks in the marina. This is one of the best places in Portland to kiss! Get there early and hope for one of the few spots available outside on the patio. Happy Hour is upstairs in bar area.

Date visited: ____________ **My Rating:** ____________
Went with: ______________________________
Favorites: ______________________________
Not so much: ______________________________
Other comments: ______________________________

# Red Lion Quay 9

**Columbia River (Vancouver)**
100 Columbia St.
(360) 750-4940
www.redlion.com

**Happy Hours**
4:00–7:00pm Daily; 9:00pm–close Sun–Thurs

**Food Deals 3**
$3.00–$6.00
Plentiful and cheap menu that changes monthly with 10-12 items like clams, clam chowder, salads, wings, sliders, burger, calamari.

**Drink Specials 3**
$3.00 drafts, $4.75 house wines ; $4.00 wells
1/2 priced bottles of wine all Wednesday

**Atmosphere 3**
Quay (pronounced "key") is in the Red Lion Hotel. Houseboat-like interior with dark oak wood everywhere, huge sailboat pulleys and thick ropes. River views, but more industrial looking as the I-5 bridge blocks things a bit.

Date visited: __________ **My Rating:** __________
Went with: ______________________________
Favorites: ______________________________
Not so much: ______________________________
Other comments: ______________________________
______________________________

# Rivershore Bar and Grill

9

**Willamette River / Oregon City**
1900 Clackamette Dr.
(503) 655-5155
www.rivershorerestaurant.com

**Happy Hours**
3:00–6:00pm and 8:00–9:00pm Daily

**Food Deals 2**
$2.95–$4.95
More than a dozen bar & grill items: potato skins, hummus, spinach & artichoke dip, wings, rings, bacon cheese tots, quesadillas, Caesar salad, BBQ ribs, cheeseburger, and bruschetta.

**Drink Specials 3**
$2.00 domestics; $4.00 house wines
$3.50 wells; $4.50 cocktail

**Atmosphere 3**
There's a wonderful outside deck here with a beautiful, wide view of the Willamette, and they even let you sit there for Happy Hour! Dinner may be in order, as the restaurant is very nice, but otherwise Happy Hour is in the more casual bar area. Check their website for info on poker, live music, karaoke, game days (70" screen), and other specials. Nice positioning for sunsets!

Date visited: ____________ **My Rating:** ____________
Went with: ______________________________
Favorites: ______________________________
Not so much: ____________________________
Other comments: __________________________
__________________________________________

# Riverview

10

**Sandy River / Troutdale**
29311 SE Stark
(503) 661-FOOD (3663)
www.yoshidariverview.com

**Happy Hours**
4:30–7:00pm Daily; All night Tuesday★

**Food Deals 3**
$2.00–$5.00
Nice mix of bar menu faves done gourmet-style and switched out seasonally: BBQ ribs, Caesar, chowder, sliders, calamari, wontons, spicy wings, sweet potato fries, and spicy cannellini spread.

**Drink Specials 3**
$4.00 beer; $5.00 wine; $4.00 wells
$5.00 martinis and cocktails

**Atmosphere 3+**
An absolutely gorgeous place! Fine dining with views of the Sandy River and surrounding forest. Happy Hour's bar area offers outdoor tables and is a perfect choice to hit after a Sunday Gorge hike (unless your shoes are muddy 'cause it's fancy here)! Frequent live music.

Date visited: __________ **My Rating:** __________
Went with: ______________________________
Favorites: ______________________________
Not so much: ______________________________
Other comments: ______________________________
______________________________________________

# Salty's

10

**Columbia River**
3839 NE Marine Drive
(503) 288-4444
www.saltys.com/portland

**Happy Hours**
4:00–6:00pm Mon–Fri

2012 Happy Hour of the Year!

**Food Deals 3**
$2.00–$9.00
Over a dozen superb menu items including a cup of award-winning seafood chowder (yum!), blackened salmon Caesar, fish & chips, oysters, chilled or coconut prawns, calamari, fish tacos, and the *best* bacon cheeseburgers around!

**Drink Specials 3**
$3.00 choice draft; $6.00 wine selections
$6.00 Margaritas, Bloody Mary, Salty Dog, Wildberry Martini, Drink of the Week

**Atmosphere 3+**
Fine-dining waterside restaurant; wall-to-wall giant windows and stellar outdoor deck; yacht club motif. Gorgeous scenery along the river, and a great place to watch the sunset!

Date visited: ____________ **My Rating:** ____________
Went with: ______________________________
Favorites: ______________________________
Not so much: ______________________________
Other comments: ______________________________
______________________________

# Soho Asian Fusion

10

**Just off Willamette River**
3500 SW River Parkway
(503) 467-7533
www.sohopdx.com.com

**Happy Hours**
4:30–6:00pm Mon–Fri; 8:30pm–close Daily

**Food Deals 3+**
$1.00–$6.00
Huge menu currently offers 40 tasty nibbles! 10 sushi items (rolls and nigiri); fried tofu, wings or calamari; miso soup, several salads, mixed tempura, veggie gyoza, sweet potato fries.

**Drink Specials 3**
$1.00 off drafts and wells; $5.00 wines
$3.00–$4.00 sake; $6.00 cocktails

**Atmosphere 3**
Large, open space with big, blocky sandstone bricks, giant TV screen, and silky, wavy, white back wall. Not on the water, but close enough to walk. Soho can be translated into the saying "when you smile, good things will happen."

Date visited: ____________ **My Rating:** ____________
Went with: ______________________________
Favorites: ______________________________
Not so much: ____________________________
Other comments: __________________________
__________________________________________

# Thirst

**Willamette River**
0315 SW Montgomery (RiverPlace)
(503) 295-2747
www.thirstwinebar.com

**10**

**Happy Hours**
3:00–6:00pm Tues–Sun

Top cover fave 2013

**Food Deals 3**
$2.00–$6.00
Delicious nibbles perfect with wine (plan and pair your choices): charcuterie and cheese plates, hot crab dip, baked brie or gnocchi, salads and seasonal soups.

**Drink Specials 3**
$2.50 beer; $5.00 select wine (try the $9.00 flight)
$5.50 cocktail of the day

**Atmosphere 3**
Right on RiverPlace Esplanade with huge windows and sidewalk seating for people and river-gazing; lovely lounge area with comfy couch and fireplace. A truly enjoyable wine bar, now with a separate NW wine tasting room!

Date visited: ____________ **My Rating:** ____________
Went with: ______________________________
Favorites: ______________________________
Not so much: ____________________________
Other comments: __________________________
_________________________________________

# Three Degrees 10

**Willamette River**
1510 SW Harbor Way (RiverPlace)
(503) 295-6166
www.threedegreesrestaurant.com

A Happy Hour favorite!

**Happy Hours**
3:00–6:00pm Daily

**Food Deals 3**
$2.00–$5.00
Menu covers basic demands in bar food with grilled cheese or a cheeseburger, plus some more healthy snacks like edamame, chicken satay, hummus plate or a mixed green salad.

**Drink Specials 3**
$4.00 drafts; $4.00 red or white wine
$4.00 select well cocktails

**Atmosphere 3**
Romantic upscale perfection; river view with lots of windows, cushy seats, and a cozy fireplace. Summer weather treats us to their outstanding outdoor deck. Free valet parking!

Date visited: ____________ **My Rating:** ____________
Went with: ______________________________
Favorites: ______________________________
Not so much: ______________________________
Other comments: ______________________________
______________________________________________

# Tippy Canoe

9

**Sandy River / Troutdale**
28242 E Historic Columbia Hwy.
(503) 492-2220
www.shirleysfood.com

**Happy Hours**
3:00–6:00pm and 9:00pm–close Sun–Thur

**Food Deals 3**
$3.00–$3.50
Half-off appetizers at bartop and whole bar area: BBQ beef, jalapeno poppers, wings, spinach artichoke dip, fried mushrooms, or a quesadilla. Or just split a GIANT sandwich (no HH discounts).

**Drink Specials 3**
$2.50 domestics; $3.50 micros
$4.50 wine; $3.75 wells

**Atmosphere 3**
Also known as Shirley's Tippy Canoe Bar & Grill on the Sandy River. Remodeled and re-opened in early 2009, it still retains the look and feel of a 1940's woodsy, riverside lodge. Enjoy the patio out back in the summer! Perfect location and vibe when coming back from a hike in the Gorge.

Date visited: __________ **My Rating:** __________
Went with: ______________________________
Favorites: ______________________________
Not so much: ______________________________
Other comments: ______________________________
______________________________

# Who Song & Larry's 9

**Columbia River (Vancouver)**
111 SE Columbia Way
(360) 695-1198

**Happy Hours**
2:00pm–close Mon–Thur★

**Food Deals 3**
$4.25–$6.00
99 cent "Taco Tuesdays" (2:00pm–10:00pm)
Big menu with BIG portions: taquitos, quesadillas, wings, guacka wacka mole, nachos supreme, sopes and tacos. Americanized Mexican food, but the price is right at Happy Hour.

**Drink Specials 3**
$3.00 domestics; $3.00 house wines
$3.00 wells; $3.00 margaritas

**Atmosphere 3**
Re-vamped and downplayed fiesta bar area with stucco walls, doorway arches, wood beams and carved, painted booths. Seating on outside deck with beautiful, breezy views of the river, made all the better with a boat drink in hand.

Date visited: __________ **My Rating:** __________
Went with: ______________________________
Favorites: ______________________________
Not so much: ______________________________
Other comments: ______________________________
______________________________

## The Deck www.thedeck.bz

**Columbia River** 33rd & Marine Dr.; (503) 283-6444

**Happy Hours** 12:00-6:00pm Daily★
Seasonal/Outdoor (mid-April – end of September)

**Food Deals 2** $2.00-$5.00 Bar eats with emphasis on seafarer's grub; shrimp, fish tacos, chili, nachos.

**Drink Specials 2** $2.50 domestic beers; $3.50 wells $6.00 blended margaritas, mojitos, daiquiris, coladas

**Atmosphere 3** Floating deck on the river (you'll feel it move)! Down the ramp from McCuddy's parking lot, past the harbor boats, to a slice of PDX paradise.

## Island Café www.islandcafepdx.com

**Hayden Island** 250 NE Tomahawk.; (503) 283-0362

**Happy Hours** 3:00-6:00pm Mon-Fri
Seasonal/Outdoor (mid-April – mid-October)

**Food Deals 2** $2.00-$5.00 Basic and limited pub grub

**Drink Specials 1** Daily beer specials

**Atmosphere 3** Totally tropical! Well, as much as you can get in Portland anyway. A favorite treasure that's worth fighting horrific traffic heading north on I-5.

## McMenamin's www.mcmenamins.com

**Columbia River (Vancouver)**
1801 S.E. Columbia River Dr.; (360) 699-1521

**Happy Hours** 3:00–6:00pm / 10:00pm–close Daily

**Food Deals 2** $2.00–$6.00 The usual suspects in the line-up of standard McMenamin's bar eats.

**Drink Specials 2**
$2.75–$3.25 drafts; $5.50–$6.50 wines; $3.50 wells
Specials on taster flights for both beer and wine

**Atmosphere 3**
An especially nice McMenamin's with an on-site brewery for brews with views. Traditional spin to the interior, but it's all about being *outside* at Happy Hour!

## Portland Sports Bar

**Willametter** 1811 SW River Dr,: (503) 222-2027
www.portlandsportsbarandgrill.com

**Happy Hours** 3:00–6:00pm Daily

**Food Deals 3** $3.00-$5.00 About a dozen menu items, many with some real substance: philly cheese steak, cheeseburger and fries, gyros, chicken coco bowl, polish dogs, salad, hummus, fries and wings.

**Drink Specials 3** $3.75 beers; $5.00 wines; $4.50 wells; $4.50 martinis (a very wide and fun variety)

**Atmosphere 2** It's a small place for a sports bar, but as such, it's a very nice one. Colorful jerseys hang from the ceiling, and several TVs in sight at all times.

## Sextant

**Columbia River** 4035 NE Marine Dr.; (503) 281-5944

**Happy Hours** All night specials

**Food Deals 1** Changing – Dinner-of-the-Day

**Drink Specials 2** Changing – $2.75 domestics and $3.75 micros are commonly specials; $3.50 wells

**Atmosphere 3** Prime-positioned outdoor deck right on the Columbia River, with view marred by chainlink fence (Why? Why?!). Inside is casual and only slightly nautical; Nice sunset vantage point!

# On the Columbia

(Limited or NO Happy Hour, or a bit far away)

• • • • • • • • • • • • • • • • • • •

## Full Sail Brewpub

**Hood River, OR**

506 Columbia St; (541) 386-2247

www.fullsailbrewing.com

*Big, high-up patio with great views of river and wind surfing. Fun pub inside and on-site brewing.*

## Hidden Bay

**Waterside Map (Portland)**

515 NE Tomahawk Island Dr; (503) 240-1871

*Casual, with elevated views of river and marina.*

## Joe's Crab Shack

**Waterside Map (Vancouver)**

101 SE Columbia Way; (360) 693-9211

www.joescrabshack.com

*Kind of a crazy chain with great views and deck.*

## Mark's on the Channel

**Scappoose, OR**

34326 Johnsons Landing Rd; (503) 543-8765

www.marksonthechannel.com

*Cute place out on the docks in a floating home.*

## Norma's Kitchen

**Waterside Map (Portland)**

12010 N Jantzen Dr; (503) 240-3447

www.normaskitchen.org

N'awlins down-home cooking with views of the moorage below, but from inside (no deck).

## Puffin Cafe

**Washougal, WA**

24 S "A" St; (360) 335-1522

www.puffincafe.com

Fun place out on the docks in a floating home.

## Simon's Cliff House

**Columbia Gorge Hotel (Hood River)**

4000 Westcliff Drive; (800) 345-1921

www.columbiagorgehotel.com

Fancy restaurant with views. Nice grounds to walk.

## Skamania's River Rock

**Stevenson, WA**

1131 SW Skamania Lodge Way; (800) 221-7117

www.skamania.com

Gorgeous scenery with river and gorge views.

## Windseeker Restaurant

**The Dalles, OR**

1535 Bargeway Rd; (541) 298-7171

www.windseekerrestaurant.com

Nice place, good food, beautiful gardens, and views!

*

**Gorgeous Columbia River VIEWS Wine Tastings!**

## Jacob Williams

**Wishram, WA**

3 Avery Rd (Hwy 14; (541) 645-0462

www.jacobwilliamswinery.com

## Memaloose

**Lyle, WA**

34 State St (Hwy 14);(360) 635-2887

www.winesofthegorge.com

## Maryhill

**Goldendale, WA**

9774 Highway 14; (509) 773-1976

www.maryhillwinery.com

# Downtown-West

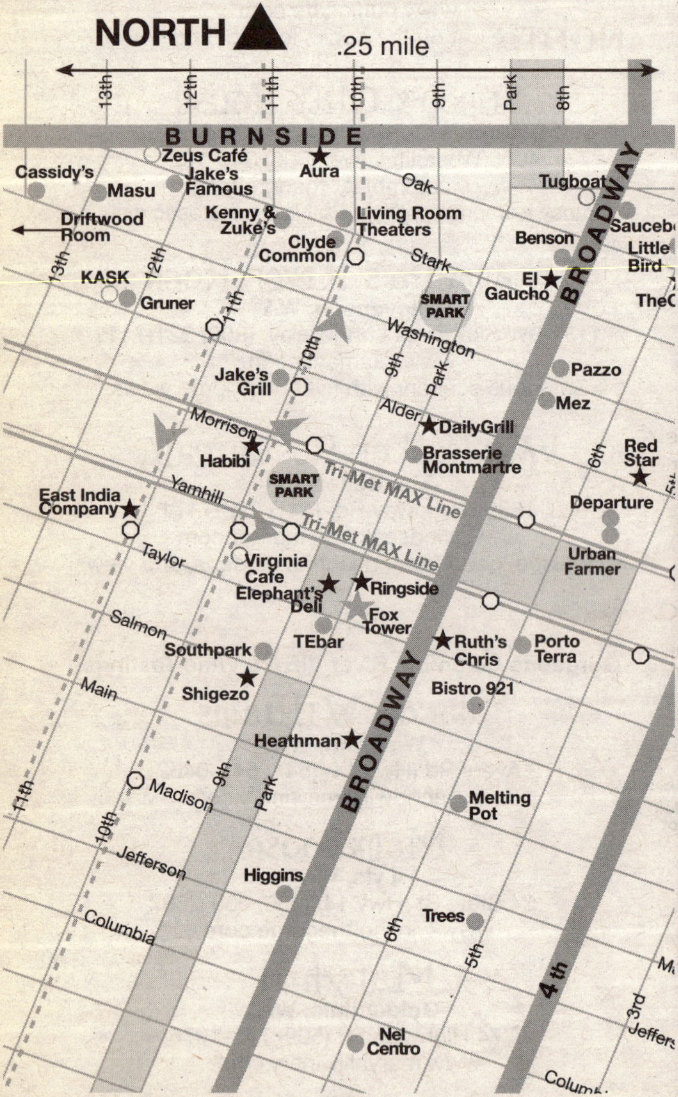

# Downtown-East

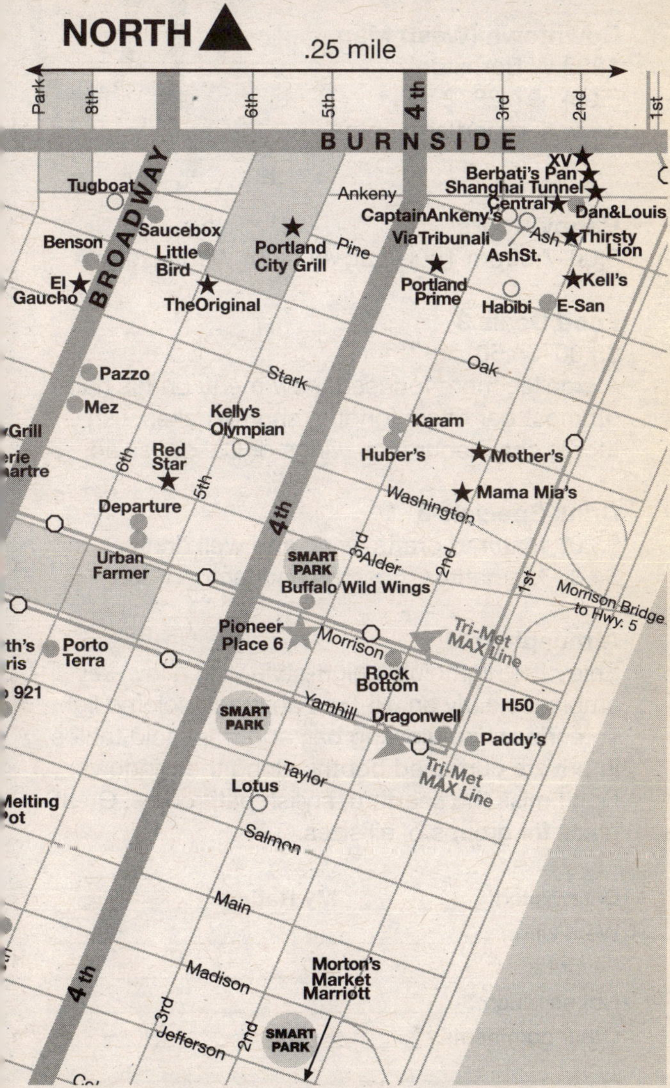

# Aura

10

**Downtown (West) Map**
1022 W Burnside
(503) 597-2872
www.auraportland.com

**Happy Hours**
5:00–7:00pm Thur–Sat; All night Wednesday★

**Food Deals 3**
$3.00–$4.50
A smaller, more focused, new menu brings half-off most bar bites: fondue, shrimp cakes, fish tacos, cheeseburgers, wings or Caesar salad.

**Drink Specials 3**
$3.00 featured drafts, wine and well drinks
$4.00 Margaritas, cosmos and lemondrops

**Atmosphere 3**
Enjoy the nightclub's high-style with a low-key ambiance early on. Hi-tech abstract, colored light screens, white glowing bar, and trapezoid tables in private curtained booths along the windows. Don't miss the see-thru, stylish bathrooms! Great place for groups of all sizes.

Date visited: ____________ **My Rating:** ____________
Went with: ______________________________
Favorites: ______________________________
Not so much: ______________________________
Other comments: ______________________________

# Benson Hotel

7

**Downtown (East) Map**
309 SW Broadway
(503) 228-2000
www.bensonhotel.com

**Happy Hours**
4:00–6:00pm and 9:00pm–close Daily

**Food Deals 1**
$10.00–$15.00
Not much of a Happy Hour focus – currently just $1.00 off all plates: cheese or charcuterie, Pacific NW/seafood plate, mezza or snack plates.

**Drink Specials 2**
$1.00 off all beer, wines and well drinks

**Atmosphere 3+**
Historic and Fancy with a capital "F," their Palm Court Bar in the hotel lobby offers the opportunity to dine in high-style at a great value. Their food is prepared by the award-winning London Grill! Perfect place to pretend you're Thurston or Lovey Howell. It's simply fabulous, dahling!

Date visited: __________ **My Rating:** __________
Went with: ____________________
Favorites: ____________________
Not so much: ____________________
Other comments: ____________________
____________________

# Brasserie Montmarte

10

**Downtown (West) Map**
626 SW Park Avenue
(503) 236-3036
www.brasserieportland.com

**Happy Hours**
★2:00-6:00pm and 9:00pm-mid Daily

A Happy Hour favorite

**Food Deals 3**
$2.00-$6.00
Insanely huge and delicious Happy Hour menu! About half-off 20 or so menu items with five kinds of flavored "frites" (duck fat with rosemary, pork belly w/tarragon, truffle fries, garlic aioli), salads, mac & cheese, French onion soup, and more!

**Drink Specials 3**
$2.00 Rainier; $4.00 wine; $11.00 carafe
$4.00 wells; $4.00-$10.00 cocktails

**Atmosphere 3**
The new owners have hit it out of the park! Rather than jazzing things up, they've toned things down on a more country-rustic note. Giant gold mirrors over the bricked back bar, checkerboard floors, white-washed walls, cozy booths, and candlelit.

Date visited: __________ **My Rating:** __________
Went with: ______________________________
Favorites: ______________________________
Not so much: ____________________________
Other comments: __________________________
__________________________________________

# Central

**Downtown (East) Map**
220 SW Ankeny
(503) 869-1445

**10**

A personal favorite!

**Happy Hours**
5:00–7:00pm Mon–Fri

**Food ★**
Unique, seasonal bar bites (5 at $4.00) and great full menu, but no extra discounts at Happy Hour. The chef was previously with Carlyle and Fenouil!

**Drink Specials 3+**
$1.00–$3.00 select beers; Ten $5.00 highballs
Very special drinks here! Definitely a leader in the very best craft cocktails in the city.

**Atmosphere 3+**
I have so much personal enthusiasm for this place! It was love at first sight, which immediately grew deeper upon the first sip. It's a small place, and potentially hard to find, and my experience (and love) could very well be different than yours. Unlike all the other entries in this book, this one is *not* an objective rating that judges their Happy Hour only, but I just have to say, IloveitIloveitIloveit!

Date visited: __________ **My Rating:** __________
Went with: ______________________________
Favorites: ______________________________
Not so much: ______________________________
Other comments: ______________________________
______________________________

# Clyde Common 10

**Downtown (West) Map**
1014 SW Stark
(503) 228-3333
www.clydecommon.com

**Happy Hours**
4:00–6:00pm Mon–Fri (until 5:00pm Sat–Sun)
11:00pm–close Mon–Sat (food only)

**Food Deals 3**
$3.00–$6.00
Dozen-item bar menu includes both unique and mainstream treats like popcorn, pickled veggies, burger, fries, grilled baguette, salad, and cookies.

**Drink Specials 3**
$3.50 drafts; $5.00 select wines
$5.00 fun and funky cocktails

**Atmosphere 3**
Big, open warehouse space like an unfinished, art school gallery. Rough wood floors, banged-up bar stools, stenciled signage, and butcher paper walls give it a working-man edge. Popular social scene with community table seating.

Date visited: ____________ **My Rating:** ____________
Went with: ______________________________
Favorites: ______________________________
Not so much: ______________________________
Other comments: ______________________________

______________________________

# Daily Grill

9

**Downtown (West) Map**
750 SW Alder
(503) 294-7001
www.dailygrill.com

**Happy Hours**
4:00–7:00pm Daily

**Food Deals 3**
$3.95–$4.95
Kobe beef "sidekick" sliders, seared ahi, hummus, mac & cheese, mini pot-pies, spinach-artichoke dip, calamari, quesadilla.

**Drink Specials 3**
$3.50 domestics; $4.00 drafts; $2.00 off wine
$5.50 wells; $5.00–$7.00 cocktails

**Atmosphere 3**
Newly remodeled bar is now accessible from both restaurant-side as well as hotel lobby, creating a more open, swanky feel with great art and Chihuly-inspired glass fixtures. Sit in front of the bartop fire and get online at one of the iPad stations. Or, go for one of the cozy chairs and put your feet up.

Date visited: ____________ **My Rating:** ____________
Went with: ______________________________
Favorites: ______________________________
Not so much: ____________________________
Other comments: __________________________
__________________________________________

# Departure

**10** ★ ★ ★

*A Happy Hour favorite*

**Downtown (East) Map**
525 SW Morrison; Rooftop
(503) 222-9996
www.departureportland.com

**Happy Hours**
4:00–6:00pm Mon–Sat

**Food Deals 3**
$3.00–$6.00
Mostly Asian-inspired menu with things like maki roll, edamame, samosas, wings, and calamari.

**Drink Specials 3**
$5.00 beer; $5.00 wine; $20 bottle of bubbly
$5.00 cocktails/sake of the day

**Atmosphere 3+**
It's a departure from Portland norm in every way! From the funky elevator entrance and Space-Mountain-style exit, you know you're someplace different. Warm weather offers three top-floor patio seating areas with stellar views of the city below and mountains in the distance. Website has spectacular photography for a pre-tour.

Date visited: ____________ **My Rating:** ____________
Went with: ______________________________
Favorites: ______________________________
Not so much: ______________________________
Other comments: ______________________________
______________________________________________

# Dragonwell 10

A Happy Hour favorite!

**Downtown (East) Map**
735 SW First Ave.
(503) 224-0800
www.dragonwellbistro.com

**Happy Hours**
★2:30–6:30pm Mon–Fri; 4:00pm–close Sun★
9:30–11:30pm Fri–Sat

**Food Deals 3+**
$1.00–$6.00
Phenomenal food! And 25+ choices! Amazing line-up of *everything:* General Tso's, orange, or sesame chicken; several versions of fried rice, lo mein, or salt & pepper dishes; several kinds of noodle dishes; salad or spring rolls, and more!

**Drink Specials 3**
$1.50 Sapporo; $5.00 red and white wine
$5.00 Happy Sake or Cocktail of the Day

**Atmosphere 3**
Serene, upscale restaurant with a wonderful mix of understated elegance, Asian simplicity and exceptional design. Bright by day, dark and intimate by night. Flexible and group seating.

Date visited: ____________ **My Rating:** ____________
Went with: ______________________________
Favorites: ______________________________
Not so much: ______________________________
Other comments: ______________________________
______________________________________________

# Driftwood Room 10

**Downtown (West) Map**
729 SW 15th Ave.
(503) 223-6311
www.hoteldeluxeportland.com

**Happy Hours**
★2:00–6:30pm and 9:30pm–close Daily
(Holidays not included)

A Happy Hour favorite

**Food Deals 3**
$4.00–$8.00
Outstanding menu with more than a dozen choices: grilled portobello mushroom or Oregon beef burgers, Caesar and mixed greens salads, mussels, mac & cheese, chicken chowder, fries.

**Drink Specials 3**
$4.00 daily draft; $6.00 wines
$20.00 bottle of wine (red or white)
$6.00 champagne cocktails

**Atmosphere 3+**
Off the very impressive grand lobby of the Hotel deLuxe, the Driftwood has a dark, discreet, and fancy ratpack appeal in a kidney-shaped, dimly-lit, wooden room with NW touches. LOVE it!

Date visited: ___________ **My Rating:** ___________
Went with: ______________________________
Favorites: ______________________________
Not so much: ______________________________
Other comments: ______________________________
______________________________________________

# East India Company 9

**Downtown (West) Map**
821 SW 11th Ave.
(503) 227-8815
www.eastindiacopdx.com

**Happy Hours**
5:00–7:00pm Mon–Sat

**Food Deals 3**
$3.00–$5.00
Expanded menu with old favorites and several new ones: eggplant dip, wings, fish fingerlings, veggie fritters, potato croquettes, spicy peanuts, channa chaat, bhel puri.

**Drink Specials 3**
$4.00 drafts; $5.00 house wine
$1.00 off all drinks; $6.95 specialty cocktails

**Atmosphere 2**
Nice enough overall, but the front bar decor and ambiance at Happy Hour pales in comparison to the dark, rich, romantic restaurant in back. But if you get a group of 6-8 together and call ahead, you can get a nice table in the restaurant. Otherwise, tables are made for 2-3 people up front in the bar.

Date visited: __________ **My Rating:** __________
Went with: ____________________
Favorites: ____________________
Not so much: ____________________
Other comments: ____________________
______________________________

# El Gaucho

9

**Downtown (East) Map**
319 SW Broadway
(503) 227-8794
www.elgaucho.com

**Happy Hours**
5:00–7:00pm Mon–Fri; 10:00pm–close Mon-Sat
★5:00pm-close Sun

**Food Deals 3**
$6.00–$18.00
Delicious menu items, however on the spendy side: steak w/frites, cheddar bacon burger, beef tenderloin kebabs, salad, and cheese plates.

**Drink Specials 3**
$4.00 select beer; $6.00 red or white wine
$6.00 cosmos

**Atmosphere 3**
Notably classy, classic steakhouse. Enjoy a memorable evening in their dramatic lounge. See a celebrity or just feel like one yourself. (Author note: I think they have the best steaks in the city! Worth the occasional splurge. BYOW corkage fee $20.00)

Date visited: ____________ **My Rating:** ____________
Went with: ________________________________________
Favorites: ________________________________________
Not so much: ______________________________________
Other comments: ___________________________________
___________________________________________________

# Elephant's Deli

8

**Downtown West**
877 SW Taylor St.
(503) 546-3166
www.elephantsdeli.com

Also at 812 SW Park; (503) 546-3166 But no HH

**Happy Hours**
5:00–7:00pm Mon–Fri; All day Sat–Sun

**Food Deals 2**
$3.00–$4.50
The whole menu has pretty low-prices, but special happy snack deals on fish tacos, garlic fries, quesadilla, and steak meatballs.

**Drink Specials 2**
$1.00 off drafts and wine

**Atmosphere 3**
Looks like a train station entrance on the outside, and a fast-food breakfast diner on the inside. Great people watching through the all-glass building, and very enjoyable outdoor plaza seating! In the summer, it's the place to be! And conveniently right by the movie theater.

Date visited: __________ **My Rating:** __________
Went with: ______________________________
Favorites: ______________________________
Not so much: ______________________________
Other comments: ______________________________
______________________________

# Grüner 9

**Downtown (West) Map**
527 SW 12th Avenue
(503) 241-7163
www.grunerpdx.com

**Happy Hours**
4:30–6:00pm Mon–Fri

**Food Deals 3**
$2.00-$5.00 (Plus an $11.00 burger)
Nibbles of Germany, Austria, Hungary, and Romania. Food here is funky, but top marks for being unique! Roasted pumpkin seeds, soup, salmon canapes, bratwurst, dumplings, grilled gruyere sandwich, charcuterie plate, cheeses, beet-pickled hard-boiled eggs (they're good!)

**Drink Specials 2**
$5.00 bottled beer; $6.00 red or white wine
$6.00–$7.00 array of theme cocktails

**Atmosphere 3**
Simple NW style and not a lot of flourish. Deep blue-gray walls, sleek woods and limited bar/ HH seating inside. Sidewalk Happy Hour allowed.

Date visited: ____________ **My Rating:** ____________
Went with: ______________________________
Favorites: ______________________________
Not so much: ____________________________
Other comments: _________________________
_________________________________________

# H5O Bistro

9 ★

**Downtown (East) Map**
50 SW Morrison
(503) 484-1415
www.h5obistro.com

**Happy Hours**
4:00–6:30pm and 9:00pm–close Mon–Sat;
★All day Sunday (noon–close)

**Food Deals 3**
$1.00–$4.00
They've done their Happy Hour homework well! A dozen favorite small plates, several salads, an awesome $5 burger and dessert! Oysters, deviled eggs, olives, popcorn, fries, arancini, meatballs, pork rilette, sirloin tips, salmon tartare.

**Drink Specials 2**
$1.00 off beer and wells; $8.00 wines

**Atmosphere 3+**
Ultra-mod with knock-out design: contrasts of geometric shapes in decor and plates; sleek, clean, and linear, yet inviting and friendly; open fireplace; stellar ambiance! Great for groups.

Date visited: ________ **My Rating:** ________
Went with: ____________________
Favorites: ____________________
Not so much: ____________________
Other comments: ____________________
____________________

# Heathman Hotel 8

**Downtown (West) Map**
1001 SW Broadway
(503) 241-4100
http://portland.heathmanhotel.com

**Happy Hours**
2:00pm–close Daily (bar menu)
4:00–6:00pm / 9:00pm–close Daily (drinks & burger)

**Food Deals 2**
$2.00–$7.00
All day Bistro menu with more than a dozen unique, gourmet samplings that change just a bit seasonally: Oysters, beet salad, grilled fig, crepes, cheese or meat plate, rissotto, salad, bruschetta. Plus HH burger special for $5.00.

**Drink Specials 2**
$6.00 house wines; $7.00 select cocktails

**Atmosphere 3**
Two traditional upscale rooms: the quiet, romantic Tea Court in back with giant, marble fireplace, and the well-stocked Marble Bar, very popular with the after-work crowd. A landmark since 1927.

Date visited: __________ **My Rating:** __________
Went with: ____________________
Favorites: ____________________
Not so much: ____________________
Other comments: ____________________

____________________

# Higgins

7

**Downtown (West) Map**
1239 SW Broadway
(503) 222-9070
www.higginsportland.com

**Happy Hours**
4:00–6:30pm Sun–Fri

**Food Deals 2**
$4.00–7.00 Bonus points for fancy food that changes every day. Minus points for offering only 2-4 choices as listed on the blackboard menu. It's Higgins though – rest assured it will be good.

**Drink Specials 2**
20% off drafts and wells; $5.00 house wines

**Atmosphere 2**
Happy Hour is served in the bar, which is a separate tap room, which isn't nearly as nice as the adjacent, elegant, and expensive restaurant. Old-school, excellent service with black tie wait-staff. Cool place to go.

Date visited: __________ **My Rating:** __________
Went with: ______________________________
Favorites: ______________________________
Not so much: ______________________________
Other comments: ______________________________
______________________________

# Huber's

★7

**Downtown (East) Map**
411 SW 3rd Ave.
(503) 228-5686
www.hubers.com

**Happy Hours**
4:00–6:30pm Daily; 9:30pm–close Daily

**Food Deals 3**
$1.95–$2.95
Giant menu with wide variety of appetizers with a good mix of options: turkey (sandwich, enchilada or quesadilla), wings, calamari, burger, salads, house-smoked salmon plate, shrimp cocktail, nachos, skewers, ahi, mussels, soup.

**Drink Specials 0**
Sadly, no drink specials (but consider those *really* low food prices!)

**Atmosphere 3**
Historic architecture and design; giant, domed, stained-glass ceiling; open tables and cozy booths make it a pleasant, warm meeting place. Watch the Spanish coffee "shows!" Portland's oldest restaurant, so it's very famous. Est.1879!

Date visited: __________ **My Rating:** __________
Went with: ______________________________
Favorites: ______________________________
Not so much: ____________________________
Other comments: __________________________
_________________________________________

# Jake's Famous Crawfish

8

**Downtown (West) Map**
401 SW 12th Ave.
(503) 226-1419
www.jakesfamouscrawfish.com

**Happy Hours**
3:00–6:00pm Daily; 9:00pm–close Sun–Thurs
10:00pm–close Fri–Sat

**Food Deals 3+**
$1.95–$4.95
16 items and outstanding, hearty sizes: Enjoy the ever-famous cheeseburger with fries only $3.95(!), or chicken sandwiches, fish tacos, calamari, gumbo, sushi rolls, salmon cake, wings.

**Drink Specials 1**
$6.50 cranberry sangria

**Atmosphere 3**
Old-school fun with traditional class; outdoor sidewalk dining. Considered one of the top seafood restaurants in the nation, Jake's has been a downtown landmark for more than 110 years. Location not to be confused with Jake's Grill (see next page).

Date visited: __________ **My Rating:** __________
Went with: ______________________________
Favorites: ______________________________
Not so much: ______________________________
Other comments: ______________________________
______________________________

# Jake's Grill

9

**Downtown (West) Map**
611 SW 10th Ave.
(503) 220-1850
www.jakesgrill.com

**Happy Hours**
3:00–6:00pm Mon–Fri; 9:30pm–close Mon–Thurs
★1:00–4:00pm Saturday; 10:00pm–close Fri–Sat
★3:00pm–close Sundays

**Food Deals 3+**
$2.95–$5.95
Changing menu of 10-12 items with outstanding, hearty sizes: wings, cheeseburger with fries, ribs, skewers, hummus, pot stickers, pizza, pork sliders, quesadilla, enchilada, gyoza, fish taco, skewers.

**Drink Specials 2**
$5.00 red or white wine
Four for $4.00 late night (rotating drink choices)

**Atmosphere 3**
Stately and traditional with convivial class; fancy, white jacket and bowtie servers; connected with impressive Governor Hotel. Wildly popular and like Jake's Famous, pretty much always packed.

Date visited: ____________ **My Rating:** ____________
Went with: ______________________________
Favorites: ______________________________
Not so much: ____________________________
Other comments: __________________________
__________________________________________

# Karam Lebanese

**Downtown (East) Map**
316 SW Stark
(503) 223-0830
www.karamrestaurant.com

A Happy Hour favorite!

**Happy Hours**
2:00–6:00pm Mon–Fri

**Food Deals 3+**
$2.50
Deals on the basics and some mysteries: falafel, hummus, baleela (ultra-yummy, warmed, almost fluffy hummus), the best taboule, feta, fries, veggie kibbee nayee, arnabeet mekle, kafta.

**Drink Specials 3**
$3.00-$4.00 select beer; $5.00 red or white wine
$5.00–$7.00 cocktail-of-the-day

**Atmosphere 3**
A low-key and serene respite from the hussle of the downtown streets. Hand-painted mural art depicting ancient ruins, carpeted floors and nice wooden tables. Good for groups. (Author note: Look up their online reviews on your favorite critique source – they are *all* quite full of stars!)

Date visited: ____________ **My Rating:** ____________
Went with: ________________________________________
Favorites: ________________________________________
Not so much: ______________________________________
Other comments: ___________________________________
___________________________________________________

# Kell's Irish Pub

7

**Downtown (East) Map**
112 SW 2nd Ave.
(503) 227-4057
www.kellsirish.com

**Happy Hours**
4:00–6:30pm Mon–Fri;
10:00pm–mid Mon–Thurs

**Food Deals 3**
$3.00–$5.00
Long-time, established menu includes favorites like Irish nachos, wings, BLTC, burger or sandwich with fries, quesadilla, oyster shooters, sweet potato fries, hummus.

**Drink Specials 0**
Sadly, no drink specials

**Atmosphere 3**
You know a good time is to be had by all at this infamous Portland Institution! Fun bar with an upbeat Irish vibe, traditional decor, and crinkled dollar bills covering the ceiling. This was the birthplace of the *Happy Hour Guidebook* (where I came up with the idea to do this book).

Date visited: ______________ **My Rating:** ______________
Went with: ______________________________
Favorites: ______________________________
Not so much: ______________________________
Other comments: ______________________________
______________________________

# Little Bird

**7**

**Downtown (East) Map**
219 SW 6th Ave.
(503) 688-5952
www.littlebirdbistro.com

**Happy Hours**
2:30-5:00pm Mon-Fri and 10:00pm-mid Daily

**Food Deals 1**
$4.00–$9.00
A total favorite of foodies with HH menu hosting a smaller version of the dinner menu with same prices on salads, sides, appetizers and desserts. So overall, not all too happy. You'll hear raves about the famous "Le Pigeon" burger for $12.

**Drink Specials 2**
$1.00 off draft beer
$6.00–$7.00 specialty cocktails

**Atmosphere 3**
Sweet petite space with both French charm and Parisian cool thrown in. Robins-egg light blue walls give it a mellow vibe, with giant antlers adding some edge. Upstairs, lofted dining area and outside sidewalk seating too. Le Pigeon owners.

Date visited: __________ **My Rating:** __________
Went with: ____________________
Favorites: ____________________
Not so much: ____________________
Other comments: ____________________

# Living Room Theaters

**Downtown (West) Map**
341 SW 10th Ave.
(971) 222-2005
www.livingroomtheaters.com

**Happy Hours**
4:00–6:00pm Mon–Fri

**Food Deals 2**
$4.00
Delicious, inexpensive and healthy movie food: Small menu of Spanish-style tortillas, mezza plate, pizza, chicken skewers. Plus a $5.00 burger.

**Drink Specials 3**
$3.00 select beer; $4.00 white or red wine
$5.00 ginger mojo, pomegranate martini, or Spanish coffee

**Atmosphere 3**
Sleek, urban/retro stylings with low tables, fuzzy pillows and glowing, backlit "mood" bar; enjoy top-quality high-def movies in recliners with drink in hand. Get on their email list – they show the most interesting movies here!

Date visited: ____________ **My Rating:** ____________
Went with: ______________________________
Favorites: ______________________________
Not so much: ____________________________
Other comments: __________________________
_________________________________________

# Mama Mia Trattoria

**Downtown (East) Map**
439 SW 2nd Ave.
(503) 295-6464
www.mamamiatrattoria.com

**Happy Hours**
4:00–7:00pm Mon–Sat
★All night Sunday (4:00–10:00pm)

Top cover fave 2013!

**Food Deals 3**
$2.00, $3.00, and $4.00
New owners have ramped up this long-time favorite Happy Hour with several options at each price point for an outstanding menu featuring 20+ items! Features the full range of pasta dishes, several salads, plus desserts! OUTSTANDING!!!

**Drink Specials 3**
$3.00 select beer; $5.00 wines; $5.00 cocktail
That's right – they've added great drink deals!

**Atmosphere 3**
Mama mia! Now that's Italian! Dripping in old world ambience with nearly 100 gilded mirrors, 20 chandeliers, red velvet, gilded frames, fancy white tablecloths, and romantic candlelight.

Date visited: __________ **My Rating:** __________
Went with: ____________________
Favorites: ____________________
Not so much: ____________________
Other comments: ____________________

# Market 10

**Downtown (East) Map**
200 SW Market St.
(503) 248-0004
www.market-pdx.com

**Happy Hours**
2:30–5:30pm Mon–Fri; 8:00pm-close Daily

**Food Deals 3**
$5.00
Unique and delightful gourmet bar bites with a market-driven menu that changes often. Choice of salads, fancied up waffle fries or cheese curds, and special crostinis. Great burgers!

**Drink Specials 3**
$4.00 beer; $4.00 house wine; $5.50 cocktail

**Atmosphere 3**
Lost lots the sweetness of Carafe, revamped with a stark and more contemporary, cosmopolitan look. Simple, stylish touches beautifully marrying glass and woods. Sit in the bar or enjoy that famous outdoor plaza seating.

Date visited: __________ **My Rating:** __________
Went with: ______________________________
Favorites: ______________________________
Not so much: ____________________________
Other comments: __________________________
_________________________________________

# Marriott Lobby Bar

8

**Downtown (East) Map**
1401 Southwest Naito Parkway
(503) 226-7600
www.marriott.com

**Happy Hours**
4:00–6:00pm Daily

**Food Deals 2**
$2.00–$6.00
Simple menu with 10 typical upscale bar items: hummus, hazelnuts, olives, edamame, rustic bread, charcuterie and cheese board, veggies, soup, chips & dip, pico de gallo & guacamole.

**Drink Specials 2**
$3.00 domestics; $5.00 featured wine

**Atmosphere 3**
Striking, very contemporary hotel lounge with community couch seating with television; big, central long bar table; and several quiet booths (plus the usual two- and four-tops). Their Truss restaurant is upstairs, but now mostly used for group events. Live music third Fridays.

Date visited: __________ **My Rating:** __________
Went with: ______________________________
Favorites: ______________________________
Not so much: ______________________________
Other comments: ______________________________
______________________________

# Masu

**Downtown (West) Map**
406 SW 13th Ave;
(503) 221-6278
www.masusushi.com

**Happy Hours**
3:00–6:00pm Daily; 10:00–11:00pm Mon–Thurs
10:00pm–mid Fri–Sat

**Food Deals 3+**
$3.00–$9.00
Possibly the best sushi in the city! And about half of it is half-off at Happy Hour! Nigiri and sushi maki rolls, ramen, Kobe beef burgers.

**Drink Specials 1**
$3.50 Sapporo

**Atmosphere 3**
Unique "retro-Asian" lounge; open and boxy with Jenga-style wood blocks covering the walls and back bar; stunning, colorful, hand-painted mural. Ultra cool!

Date visited: __________ **My Rating:** __________
Went with: ______________________________
Favorites: ______________________________
Not so much: ______________________________
Other comments: ______________________________
______________________________

# Melting Pot

9

**Downtown (West) Map**
1001 5th Ave. (entrance at 6th & Main)
(503) 517-8960
www.meltingpot.com

**Happy Hours**
4:00-6:30pm Mon–Fri

**Food Deals 3**
$3.00–$5.00 (plus $12.00 cheese fondues)
Big discounts on great food: several salad selections ($3.00 each); artichoke and spinach dip; shrimp cocktail; smoked salmon cheese ball; mushroom paté; lobster, shrimp and caviar cups.

**Drink Specials 3**
$3.00 draft beer; $5.50 red or white wine
$5.50 daily cocktail

**Atmosphere 3**
Subterranean entrance leads to clean and simple windowless batcave perfect for celebrating cold winter nights or escaping summer heat. More stark and sleek than romantic, but dark.

Date visited: __________ **My Rating:** __________
Went with: ______________________________
Favorites: ______________________________
Not so much: ______________________________
Other comments: ______________________________

# Mez

8

**Downtown East**
520 SW Broadway
(503) 552-2220
www.marriottportland.com

**Happy Hours**
4:00–6:00pm Daily

**Food Deals 2**
$4.00–6.00
Half-off their high-quality bar menu, but few options: house made chips, onion tanglers, tacos, caprese salad, brie & jam flatbread.

**Drink Specials 1**
$4.00 domestics; $5.00 house wine

**Atmosphere 3**
The very grand gallery-like mezzanine level of the Marriott. Rich dark woods, decorative moldings, and a rotating artist showcase set the stage for elegance. Or hang out in the beautiful lobby area. It's really quite pleasant!

Date visited: __________ **My Rating:** __________
Went with: ______________________________
Favorites: ______________________________
Not so much: ____________________________
Other comments: __________________________
_________________________________________

# Morton's

9

Downtown (East) Map
213 SW Clay St
(503) 248-2100
www.mortons.com

A Happy Hour favorite!

**Happy Hours**
4:45–6:30pm and 9:00pm–close Sun–Fri

**Food Deals 3**
$6.00–$7.00
They've really quite outdone themselves – steak lovers, rejoice! You'll get a platter of four steak sandwiches, three 5" high slider burgers or four salad wedge bites; crab cakes, artichoke dip, house-made potato chips, or ahi tuna tacos.

**Drink Specials 2**
$5.50 drafts; $7.00 red and white wines
$8.00 martinis (on the spendy side, but good!)

**Atmosphere 3**
Enjoy the dark, rich ambiance in the bar area of this top-notch, manly-man steakhouse near the Keller Auditorium. Small bar area will fill up fast, so grab a table early.

Date visited: ____________ **My Rating:** ____________
Went with: ______________________________
Favorites: ______________________________
Not so much: ______________________________
Other comments: ______________________________
______________________________

# Mother's

9

**Downtown (East) Map**
212 SW Stark
(503) 464-1122
www.mothersbistro.com

**Happy Hours**
3:00–7:00pm Tues–Fri

**Food Deals 2**
$3.00
Fried ravioli, chicken quesadilla, mini-burgers, deviled eggs, hummus plate, chopped liver, and little teenie weenies.

**Drink Specials 3**
$3.00 microbrew pints; $6.00 wines
$5.00 array of infused cocktails

**Atmosphere 3**
Their "Velvet Lounge" bar area steps back in time and looks much like a wealthy, Southern grandmother's home. Ornate gilded mirrors, chandeliers, and flocked wallpaper everywhere.

Date visited: __________ **My Rating:** __________
Went with: ______________________________
Favorites: ______________________________
Not so much: ______________________________
Other comments: ______________________________
______________________________

# Nel Centro

10

**Downtown (West) Map**
1408 SW 6th Avenue
(503) 484-1099
nelcentro.com

**Happy Hours**
4:00–6:00pm Daily

A Happy Hour favorite!

**Food Deals 3**
$4.00–$7.00
New and expanded, seasonal menus from one of Portland's most respected kitchens: delicious gourmet-style pizza, lamb burger or meatballs, mussels, soup, pork slider, calamari, and salads.

**Drink Specials 3**
$4.00 drafts; $5.00 house wines and prosecco
$5.00 featured cocktail or well drinks

**Atmosphere 3**
One of the most enjoyable patios in town where you can enjoy Happy Hour too! Next to the Hotel Modera with mod, contemporary courtyard and long fire pits. Inside, the decor is sleek and stylish, with a giant open bar and globe lights.

Date visited: __________ **My Rating:** __________
Went with: ______________________________
Favorites: ______________________________
Not so much: ______________________________
Other comments: ______________________________
______________________________

# The Original 10

**Downtown (East) Map**
300 SW 6th Ave.
(503) 546.2666
www.originaldinerant.com

**Happy Hours**
4:30–6:00pm Mon–Fri

**Food Deals 3**
$2.00–$6.00
A dozen or so American diner food items with some Happy Hour oddities: chex mix, pickled veggies, chicken salad, scotch eggs, ribs, poutine, hotdogs, poppycock popcorn, and pie!

**Drink Specials 3**
$3.00 drafts; $4.00 wines; $5.00 punch/cocktails

**Atmosphere 3**
Very mod, retro and contemporary restaurant/ diner (aka "dinerant"). Amazingly giant, floor-to-ceiling, wall-to-wall windows that are two stories high, and run the length of the building. Sleek interior blends downtown, city-cool with the charm of 1950s greasy spoon lunch counters.

Date visited: ____________ **My Rating:** ____________
Went with: ______________________________
Favorites: ______________________________
Not so much: ______________________________
Other comments: ______________________________
______________________________

# Pazzo

**Downtown (East) Map**
627 SW Washington
(503) 228-1515
www.pazzo.com

9 ★

**Happy Hours**
3:00–6:00pm Daily

**Food Deals 2**
$4.00–$7.00
Simple, mostly Italian-style bar eats: artisan-cured meat plates, manicotti, salad, brick oven pizzas, hero subs, spiced nuts, and olives.

**Drink Specials 3**
$4.00 drafts; $5.00 house wines; $4.00 wells

**Atmosphere 3**
The PazzoBAR side of Pazzo's Ristorante is stately and traditional in tone, rather than countryside Italian. It hosts a low-key and popular after-work bar scene.

Date visited: ____________ **My Rating:** ____________
Went with: ______________________________
Favorites: ______________________________
Not so much: ______________________________
Other comments: ______________________________
______________________________________________

# Portland City Grill

**Downtown (East) Map**
111 SW Fifth Ave., 30th Floor
(503) 450-0030
www.portlandcitygrill.com

**Happy Hours**
4:00–7:00pm and 9:00pm–close Mon–Sat
4:00pm–close Sunday★

A Happy Hour favorite!

**Food Deals 3+**
$4.25–$9.25
About a dozen or so high-quality and beautifully-presented apps like salmon cakes, spring rolls, Caesar, gorgonzola cheese fries, California roll, bacon cheeseburger, Pacific oysters, spicy basil chicken, seared fresh salmon, plus their famous steak & frites and kung pao calamari.

**Drink Specials 3**
$5.25 beer and special cocktails; $6.25 wines

**Atmosphere 3+**
Get there early and try to get a window seat! Enjoy amazing views of the our city, river, hills, Mt. Hood, sunsets, and occasional full moons. Giant central bar, full walls of windows, raw timber beams, marble cocktail tables, and live music. Impressive!

Date visited: __________ **My Rating:** __________
Went with: ______________________________
Favorites: ______________________________
Not so much: ______________________________
Other comments: ______________________________
______________________________

# Portland Prime 10

**Downtown (East) Map**
121 SW 3rd Ave.
(503) 223-6200
www.portlandprime.net

**Happy Hours**
3:00–6:30pm Mon–Fri; 1:30–5:00pm Sunday

**Food Deals 3**
$5.00
Prime bar menu offers a wide array of tasty apps: sampler charcuterie and fromage plate, hummus veggie plate, shrimp salad, beef sliders, quesadilla, calamari, wings, chopped salad, and pizza.

**Drink Specials 3**
$5.00 drafts; $6.00 house wines
$6.00 wells and signature cocktails

**Atmosphere 3**
Located in Embassy Suites – enter through the lobby as it's majestic! Rich mahogany woods and private booth seating; enjoy elegant restaurant dining on the cheap! Several hi-def TVs.

Date visited: __________ **My Rating:** __________
Went with: ______________________________
Favorites: ______________________________
Not so much: ____________________________
Other comments: _________________________
_________________________________________

# Red Star Tavern 10

**Downtown (East) Map**
503 SW Alder
(503) 222-0005
www.redstartavern.com

**Happy Hours**
4:00–8:00pm Daily★

**Food Deals 3**
$3.00–$6.00
New menu with about a dozen bar bites: popcorn, poppers, spicy pork stew, mixed nuts, crispy tofu, ceviche, brushetta, grilled cheese, and burgers. They'll switch things up occasionally, to varying degrees of deliciousness and success.

**Drink Specials 3**
$4.00 beer; $4.00 wines; $4.00 wells
$5.00 cocktails

**Atmosphere 3**
Romantic and upscale with just a touch of rustic charm, interesting street-scape viewing, and big booth options for some serious lounging. Nice!

Date visited: ____________ **My Rating:** ____________
Went with: ______________________________
Favorites: ______________________________
Not so much: ______________________________
Other comments: ______________________________

______________________________________________

# Ringside Fish House

10

**NW/Nob Hill Map**
838 SW Park Ave. (Fox Tower)
(503) 227-3900
www.ringsidefishhouse.com

**Happy Hours**
3:00pm–7:00pm and 9:00pm-close Daily
★3:00–11:00pm Sunday

A Happy Hour favorite!

**Food Deals 3+**
$1.25–$4.75
Big menu of 12 or so items: steak bites (YUM!), Caesar salad, BBQ chicken slider, burger, chips, jambalaya, oysters, crabcake sandwich, fish tacos, clam chowder, salmon rillettes or tartine.

**Drink Specials 3**
$1.00 off drafts; $2.00 off wine or cocktails

**Atmosphere 3**
The temporary relocation of their steakhouse brought us a whole new Ringside! Contemporary, upscale, toned-down, interior with Happy Hour in bar area only. Illuminated, colorful ceramic fish and giant whale bone decorate the walls.

Date visited: __________ **My Rating:** __________
Went with: ______________________________
Favorites: ______________________________
Not so much: ______________________________
Other comments: ______________________________
______________________________

# Ruth's Chris 10

A Happy Hour favorite

**Downtown (East) Map**
850 SW Broadway
(503) 221-4518
www.ruthschris.com

**Happy Hours**
4:00–7:00pm Sun-Fri

**Food Deals 3**
$7.00
Seven high-quality apps like seared ahi tuna, prime sliders, 1/2 pound prime burger, lobster roll, beef tenderloin skewers, steak sandwich.

**Drink Specials 3**
$3.00 domestics; $7.00 red or white wine
$7.00 select cocktails

**Atmosphere 3**
This new and upgraded location gives us a wonderful and *bright*, richly-appointed, fine-dining steakhouse. Enjoy a very affordable, fancy evening out when you go here for their Happy Hour. Big cheers to the good life!

Date visited: ____________ **My Rating:** ____________
Went with: ______________________________
Favorites: ______________________________
Not so much: ____________________________
Other comments: __________________________
__________________________________________

# Saucebox

10

**Downtown (East) Map**
214 SW Broadway
(503) 241-3393
www.saucebox.com

**Happy Hours**
4:30–6:30pm Mon–Fri; 5:00–6:30pm Sat-Sun

A Happy Hour favorite!

**Food Deals 3**
$1.00–$5.00
Huge menu of about 20 mostly Asian-inspired fusion dishes, that impresses every time: crispy brussel sprouts, miso soup, taro chips, papaya salad, pad thai, salad, spring, or hand rolls, pork noodle, squash curry, and the best burgers!

**Drink Specials 3**
$3.00 select beer; $5.00 wine; $4.00 saké
$5.00 daily cocktail; $5.00 boxcar or daiquiri

**Atmosphere 3**
Big and open, boxy, saucy lounge; chocolate-browns and greys; looming giant art murals with personality overlook the entire room. Upstairs and sidewalk dining too. Cool bathroom entrance!

Date visited: __________ **My Rating:** __________
Went with: ______________________________
Favorites: ______________________________
Not so much: ______________________________
Other comments: ______________________________

# Shigezo

9

**Downtown (West) Map**
910 SW Salmon
(503) 688-5202
shigezo-pdx.com

**Happy Hours**
4:00pm–close Sun-Thur (Sun 2:00–close) ★
4:00–6:00pm and 9:00pm–close Fri–Sat

**Food Deals 3**
$1.00–$5.00
Giant 20+ item menu with an array of hand rolls and sushi rolls, salads, ceviche, wings, squid, miso soup, salmon carpaccio, tofus, and more.

**Drink Specials 3**
$5.00 drafts (22 oz.); $5.00 wines or sake
$2.00 off specialty cocktails

**Atmosphere 3**
There's something about the place that really seems authentic like you're in Japan. Happy Hour is on the more casual bar side of Shigezo, the first U.S. outpost of TKS Group, a 100-restaurant chain based in Tokyo. Big fish mural, lots of hanging paper lanterns, and character stamps.

Date visited: ___________ **My Rating:** ___________
Went with: ______________________________
Favorites: ______________________________
Not so much: ____________________________
Other comments: _________________________
_________________________________________

# Southpark

8

**Downtown (West) Map**
901 SW Salmon
(503) 326-1300
www.southparkseafood.com

**Happy Hours**
3:00–6:00pm Daily

**Food Deals 2**
$3.00–$8.00
Special Happy Hour menu with about 9 menu items at discounted prices: olives, pork belly, calamari, pate, flatbread, burger, fries.

**Drink Specials 2**
$5.00 red, white or sparkling wines
$4.00 glass of sangria ($10.00 carafe)

**Atmosphere 3**
Southpark has been a perennial favorite of many a Portlander, myself included. It just works on so many levels. Be aware that it's more of a bar than a romantic wine-date place and that it can get crowded. Outstanding wine selection.

Date visited: __________ **My Rating:** __________
Went with: ______________________________
Favorites: ______________________________
Not so much: ______________________________
Other comments: ______________________________

______________________________

# Tasting East

9

**Downtown (West) Map**
909 SW Park
(503) 243-5991
www.tastingeast.com

**Happy Hours**
4:00–7:00pm and 9:00pm–close Daily

**Food Deals 2**
2.95-$3.95
Declared low Happy Hour prices regular menu, plus a small HH menu of several special options like sesame balls, tempura veggies, hummus, maki.

**Drink Specials 3**
$4.00 drafts; $5.00 house wines; $3.00 saké
$5.00 select cocktails; Rotating specials

**Atmosphere 3**
TE:bar is the bar side of the new Tasting Room, formerly Dragonfish. Old and dark, wood planks cover the walls, bar, tables, and pillars, giving the place a kind of Asian street scene essence. Artistic and mod paper lanterns, low street level views, and big centrally located square bar.

Date visited: __________ **My Rating:** __________
Went with: ____________________
Favorites: ____________________
Not so much: ____________________
Other comments: ____________________
____________________

# Urban Farmer 10

A Happy Hour favorite!

**Downtown (East) Map**
525 SW Morrison
(503) 222-4900
www.urbanfarmerrestaurant.com

**Happy Hours**
3:00–6:00pm and 10:00pm–close Daily

**Food Deals 3** $2.00–$8.00
Giant new menu with over 20 items! Farm-fresh NW delights and seasonal updates, and changing options from the earth, ocean and range – plus several desserts! Chicken pops, bangers & mash, sliders, burgers, ribs, skewers, oysters, shrimp, deviled eggs, pork, and soup (but no salads).

**Drink Specials 3**
$5.00 drafts; $6.00 house wines
$5.00 cocktail of the day

**Atmosphere 3**
Absolutely stunning! The number one decor award winner! Truly a Portland stand-out in the giant, cavernous atrium of the Hotel Nines with cozy, mini-atrium seating areas. Ultra-modern style with subtle rustic touches. Coolest at night!

Date visited: ____________ **My Rating:** ____________
Went with: ________________________________
Favorites: ________________________________
Not so much: ______________________________
Other comments: ____________________________
____________________________________________

# Via Tribunali 7

**Old Town Map**
36 SW 3rd Ave.
(503) 548-2917
www.viatribunali.net

**Happy Hours**
4:00–6:00pm and 10:00pm–close Daily

**Food Deals 2**
$5.00
Choose from three tasty wood-fired pizzas (pepperoni, cheese or marinara), antipasto plate, or chocolate nutella calzone dessert.

**Drink Specials 2**
$3.00 select draft; $8.00 house wine carafe
$5.00 well drinks

**Atmosphere 2**
Small and skinny bar room with old-time charm, super-high ceiling, and upstairs mezzanine. A second, somewhat cozier area in back and sidewalk seating in the thick of some of Portland's weirdest action. Across from VooDoo Donuts at the end of the outdoor plaza on Ankeny Street.

Date visited: ___________ **My Rating:** ___________
Went with: ___________
Favorites: ___________
Not so much: ___________
Other comments: ___________

___________

## Berbati's www.berbati.com

**Downtown East** 231 SW Ankeny; (503) 248-4579

**Happy Hours** 4:00–7:00pm Daily; 3:00–8:00pm Sun★

**Food Deals 3** $3.00–$5.00 New, big menu! Four kinds of gyros, Greek salad, tzatziki or feta dip, rings, rings, calamari, hummus, soup, chicken souvlaki.

**Drink Specials 3** $2.00–$3.00 drafts; $3.00 wells $5.00 special "sinful" cocktails

**Atmosphere 2** Greek arches over doors, faux-aged walls, funky Aladdin lamps, cool, copper-studded floor, and original artwork. Outdoor patio seating.

## Bistro 921

**Downtown West** 921 SW 6th Ave; (503) 220-2685 www.bistro-921.com

**Happy Hours** 3:30-6:00pm & 9:00-10:00pm Mon–Fri

**Food Deals 2** $3.00–$6.00 Bar food basics like wings, sliders, salad, coconut shrimp, fries, quesadilla, calamari.

**Drink Specials 0** No drink deals

**Atmosphere 2** In the Hilton near the Schnitz. Nice restaurant area, but Happy Hour in the Bistro Bar only. Enter through the glamorous lobby and restaurant.

## Buffalo Wild Wings See page 229.

**Downtown East** 327 SW Morrison; (503) 224-1309

## Cassidy's www.cassidysrestaurant.com

**Downtown West** 1331 SW Washington; (503) 223-0054

**Happy Hours** 4:00–6:00pm & 10:00pm–2:00am Daily

**Food Deals 3** $6.50 Big, full-size servings of items like several salads, soups, burgers, pizzas, calamari, chicken fried pork belly, grilled portobello sandwich.

**Drink Specials 0** Sadly, no HH drink specials

**Atmosphere 2** Inside an old, historic building with lots of character on the inside too (and it's perfectly positioned behind the Crystal Ballroom).

## Dan & Louis' Oyster Bar

**Downtwn East** 208 SW Ankeny; (503) 227-5906
www.danandlouis.com

**Happy Hours** 4:00–6:00pm Mon–Fri

**Food Deals 2** $2.50-$7.50 Oyster bakes, fish tacos, fries, wings, Caesar, fish & chips, oysters (12 for $20).

**Drink Specials 0** Sadly, no drink specials

**Atmosphere 2** Happy Hour is in the bar area of this historic Old Town restaurant. Unique space with small-town, East-Coast, casual, crabbing charm. Cozy, candlelit, ship-like hideaway that's loaded with portside personality. Best at night (but that's after HH).

## E-San Thai www.e-santhai.com

**Downtown East** 133 SW 2nd; (503) 223-4090
North location: 8233 North Denver Ave; (503) 517-0683

**Happy Hours** 2:30–6:00pm and 9:00–10:00pm Daily

**Food Deals 3** $2.50–$4.00 A whopping 18 Thai basics: egg rolls, wontons, shrimp, an array of satays, pad thai, salads, tom kha soup, chicken skewers, and more.

**Drink Specials 3** $2.00 Drafts(!); $4.00 well drinks

**Atmosphere 2** Casual, comfortable, colorful Thai restaurant without any over-the-top styling, but up-top dining space for the huge crowds flooding in at lunch.

## Habibi

**Downtown Map** 221 SW Pine; (503) 459-4441
—and —1012 SW Morrison; (503) 274-0628
www.habibirestaurantpdx.com

**Happy Hours** All day Daily 11:00am–close

**Food Deals 2** $1.00–$4.99 Over 20 Syrian-Lebonese appetizer items cover all the basics and more.

**Drink Specials 1** Some, and they change. Ask...

**Atmosphere 2** Two locations and conveniently just blocks from everything downtown. Casual restaurants very popular at lunchtime. Very personable owner.

## Kenny & Zuke's

**Downtown West** 1038 SW Stark; (503) 222-3354
www.kennyandzukes.com

**North/NE Map** 2376 NW Thurman; (503) 954-1737
www.kzsandwichworks.com

**Happy Hours** 3:00–6:00pm Mon–Fri

**Food Deals 2** $1.00 off bagel and classic sandwiches and bagel dogs. Big enough to share!

**Drink Specials 1** $1.00 off draft beers

**Atmosphere 3** A real New York deli in Portland, with a twist of being fresh and clean, bright and upbeat, retro and modern at the same time.

## Leaky Roof www.theleakyroof.com

**Downtown (off map)**
1538 SW Jefferson St; (503) 222-3745

**Happy Hours** 3:30–6:00pm Mon–Fri

**Food Deals 2** $2.95–$5.50 Cheap, nice, and tasty pub food (may vary seasonally): A dozen items including Irish stew, burgers, hummus plate, risotto, wings, quesadillas (three kinds), tacos, calamari.

**Drink Specials 2** $1.00 off beer; $4.00 wine; $3.50 wells

**Atmosphere 2** Very cozy Irish pub, especially on a dark, cold night! Traditional, forest green walls, open fireplace and wooden booths and tables.

## Paddy's www.paddys.com

**Downtown (East) Map** 65 SW Yamhill; (503) 224-5626

**Happy Hours** 4:00–6:30pm/10:00pm–2:00am Daily

**Food Deals 3** $5.00–$6.00 Expanded bar menu, now with *nine* kinds of flavored mac & cheese! Also hummus, pork or corned beef sliders, nachos, poppers, calamari, shepherd's pie, wings, Guinness chili fries, hush puppies.

**Drink Specials 1** $3.50 Trumer pils; $4.00 wells

**Atmosphere 3** Warm, upscale Irish pub with a very impressive turn-of-the-century bar stacked sky-high with spirits of all sorts. Seasonal sidewalk seating.

## Porto Terra www.portoterra.com

**Downtown West** 830 SW 6th Ave.; (503) 944-1090

**Happy Hours** 3:30–6:00pm / 9:00–11:00pm Mon–Fri

**Food Deals 3** $2.00–$5.00 They've stepped things up a notch with more than a dozen apps: chips, salads, gnocchi, calamari, mac & cheese, pizza, burgers (meat or veggie), wings, and olives.

**Drink Specials 0** $5.00 house red or white wine

**Atmosphere 3** Hilton hotel bar with Tuscan countryside modern motif; an upscale, contemporary slice of Italy.

## Shanghai Tunnel Lounge

**Downtown East** 211 SW Ankeny; (503) 220-4001

**Happy Hours** 5:00–7:00pm Daily

**Food Deals 3** $2.00–$6.00 Yummy pot stickers, quesadillas, chips, veggie or chuck burgers, fries.

**Drink Specials 3** $1.00 off draft beers
$5.00 wine; $2.00 off wells

**Atmosphere 2** Built over the underground Shanghai tunnels; painted murals and simple Asian touches. Sidewalk Happy Hour.

## Thirsty Lion Pub

**Old Town Map** 71 SW 2nd Ave.; (503) 222-2155
www.thirstylionpub.com

**Happy Hours** 3–7pm Mon–Fri; 9:00pm-close Daily

**Food Deals 2** $2.95–$4.95 Scotch eggs, fries, Caesar, edamame, potato cakes, Reuben, pork, or burger sliders, nachos, calamari, and soft pretzel fondue.

**Drink Specials 2**
$3.00 domestics; $4.00 daily pints/wine; $3.00 wells

**Atmosphere 2** Neighborhood English Pub theme, being more new, yuppie and huge. Food, spirits, ales, live music, and sports on several TVs.

# West Café

**Downtown Map** 1201 SW Jefferson; (503) 227-8189
www.westcafepdx.com

**Happy Hours** 4:00-9:00pm/close Mon-Sat

**Food Deals 2** $2.00-$6.00 Extensive menu of fresh, gourmet and unique items (snacks, soups, salads, sliders, veggie dishes, skewers, dips, salsas, sauces).

**Drink Specials 1** $1.00 off beer and wine

**Atmosphere 3** They do lunch, dinner and brunch and fit somewhere between being a nice restaurant and cozy café. Elegant touches mix with diner styles. Live jazz (see calendar), and good facebook info.

# XV (15) www.xvpdx.com

**Old Town Map** 15 SW 2nd Ave; (503) 790-9090

**Happy Hours** 4:00–7:00pm Daily

**Food Deals 2** $2.00–$5.00 Big selection of good cheapies: yam fries, buffalo sliders, tacos, satay, mac & cheese, salads. $3.00 off pizzas too.

**Drink Specials 3** $1.00 PBRs all day; $3.00 drafts $4.00–$5.00 wine; $3.00 wells; $5.00 cocktails

**Atmosphere 2** Black and more black; regular bar area, but cool restaurant/candlelit lounge in adjacent room. Couches line the wall for kicking back. Crowded late-night.

# NW / Nob Hill

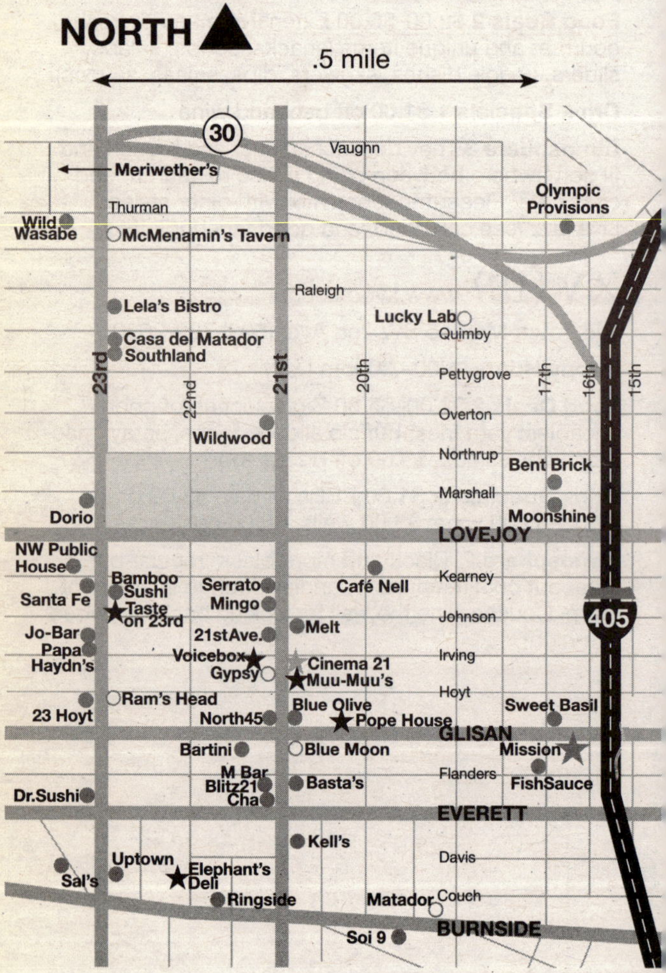
NORTH
.5 mile
30
Vaughn
Meriwether's
Thurman
Wild Wasabe
McMenamin's Tavern
Olympic Provisions
Raleigh
Lela's Bistro
Lucky Lab
Quimby
Casa del Matador
Southland
23rd
22nd
21st
20th
Pettygrove
17th
16th
15th
Overton
Wildwood
Northrup
Bent Brick
Marshall
Dorio
Moonshine
LOVEJOY
NW Public House
Bamboo Sushi
Santa Fe
Taste on 23rd
Serrato
Mingo
Café Nell
Kearney
Johnson
405
Jo-Bar
Papa Haydn's
21st Ave.
Melt
Voicebox
Gypsy
Cinema 21
Muu-Muu's
Irving
Ram's Head
Hoyt
23 Hoyt
North45
Blue Olive
Pope House
Sweet Basil
GLISAN
Bartini
Blue Moon
Mission
M Bar
Blitz21
Cha
Basta's
Flanders
FishSauce
Dr.Sushi
EVERETT
Kell's
Davis
Uptown
Sal's
Elephant's Deli
Ringside
Matador
Couch
BURNSIDE
Soi 9

# Pearl

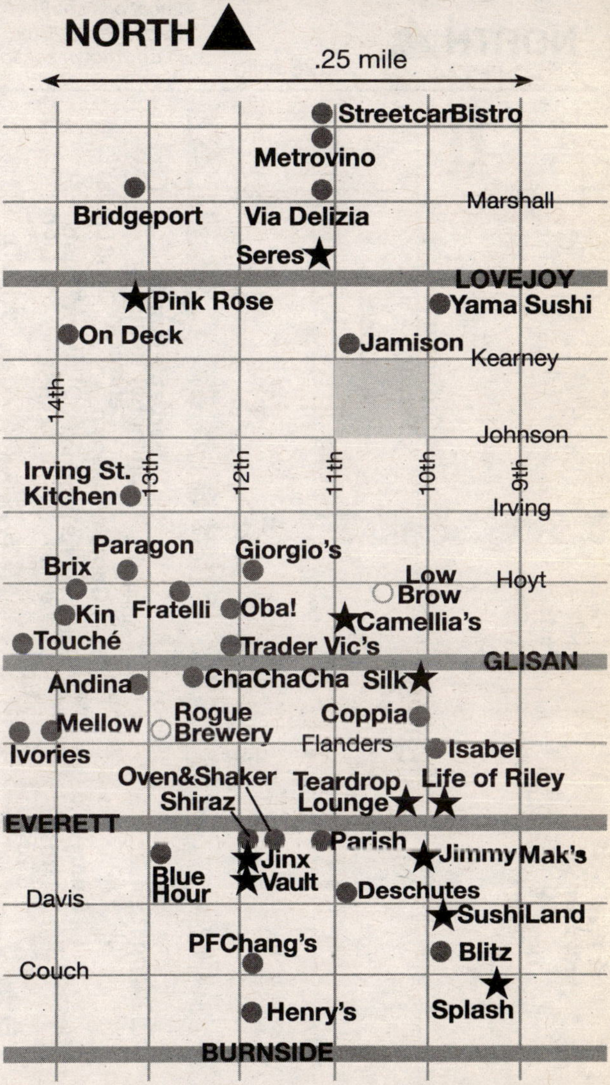
NORTH
.25 mile
StreetcarBistro
Metrovino
Bridgeport
Via Delizia
Marshall
Seres
LOVEJOY
Pink Rose
Yama Sushi
On Deck
Jamison
Kearney
14th
Johnson
Irving St. Kitchen
13th
12th
11th
10th
9th
Irving
Paragon
Giorgio's
Brix
Low Brow
Hoyt
Kin
Fratelli
Oba!
Camellia's
Touché
Trader Vic's
GLISAN
Andina
ChaChaCha
Silk
Mellow
Rogue Brewery
Coppia
Ivories
Flanders
Isabel
Oven&Shaker
Shiraz
Teardrop Lounge
Life of Riley
EVERETT
Parish
Jinx
Vault
Blue Hour
Jimmy Mak's
Davis
Deschutes
SushiLand
PFChang's
Blitz
Couch
Henry's
Splash
BURNSIDE

# Old Town

*Locations south of Burnside are listed in downtown section.*

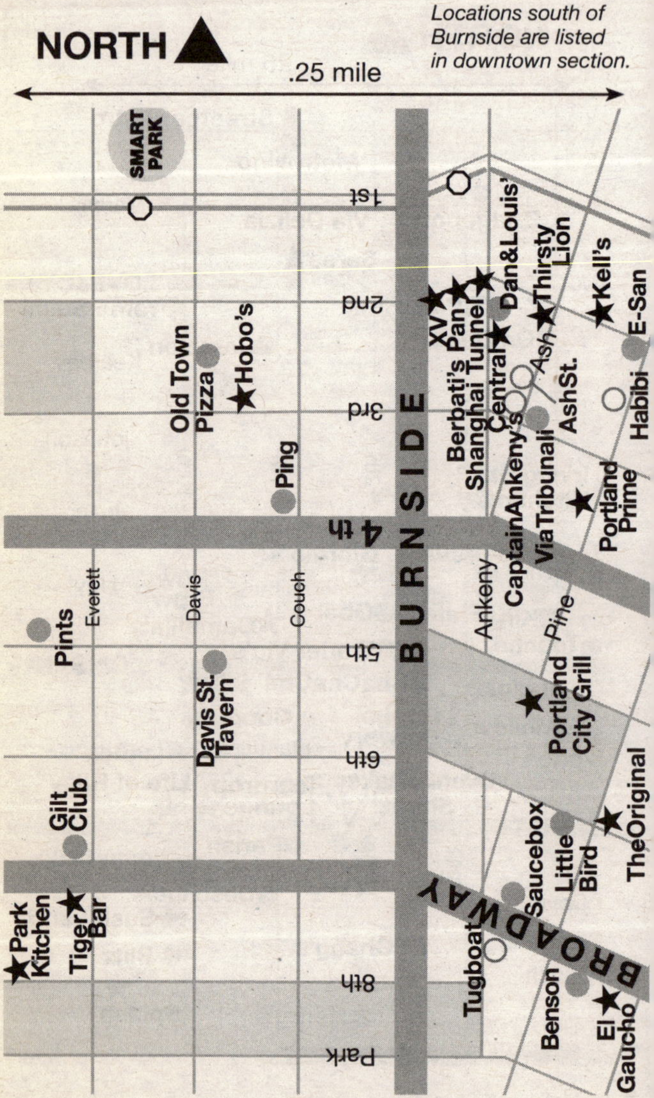

# 23 Hoyt

10

**NW/Nob Hill Map**
529 NW 23rd Ave.
(503) 445-7400
www.23hoyt.com

**Happy Hours**
4:00–6:30pm Daily
9:00–10:30pm Fri–Sat

**Food Deals 3**
$1.00–$8.00
One or two items at each price point with seasonal menu including cheeseburger, salad, steak bites, flatbreads, mushroom ragu, and dare I say the best deviled eggs in the city!

**Drink Specials 3**
$4.50 drafts; $5.00 select wines
$6.00 specialty cocktails

**Atmosphere 3**
Sleek, stylish and soaring inside with lofted seating overlooking the bar area. Very cool design, yet remains warm and inviting. Stellar!

Date visited: ____________ **My Rating:** ____________
Went with: ______________________________
Favorites: ______________________________
Not so much: ______________________________
Other comments: ______________________________
______________________________

# Andina

8

**Pearl Map**
1314 NW Glisan
(503) 228-9535
www.andinarestaurant.com

**Happy Hours**
4:00–6:00pm Daily

**Food Deals 2**
Skewers Sm $5 / Med $10 / Lrg $20
Choose from kebobs (chicken, beef heart, or grilled octopus), $7.00 beet salad or $1.50 raw bar oysters. Low on choices, hence a deceptively lower score here, but a top PDX place! Just go full-throttle and go for dinner.

**Drink Specials 2**
$6.00 house wines; $6.75 specialty cocktails

**Atmosphere 3**
One of Portland's most renowned restaurants and a most active Happy Hour bar scene. High, wooden-beamed ceilings, copper-topped tables, painted stucco walls, fireplace.

Date visited: ____________ **My Rating:** ____________
Went with: ______________________________
Favorites: ______________________________
Not so much: ______________________________
Other comments: ______________________________

# Bamboo Sushi 10★

**NW/Nob Hill Map**
836 NW 23rd Ave; (971) 229-1925

310 SE 28th Ave; (503) 232-5255
www.bamboosushipdx.com

**Happy Hours**
4:00–6:00pm Mon–Fri

**Food Deals 3**
$1.00–$6.00
The food at Bamboo Sushi is soooo goood! To list in plain English: house-pickled veggies, seafood pancake, seaweed salad, mushrooms, salad, veggie tofu crisped noodles, grilled peppers, plus nigiri set, daily hand rolls, and veggie rolls.

**Drink Specials 3**
$3.00 Sapporo; $4.00 wine; $4.00–$7.00 sake

**Atmosphere 3**
NEW! Very similar in layout and overall style to original location in SE Portland. Serene and cozy with focus on sustainability and Japanese simplicity. Natural, neutral woods, pillows on bench seating and fascinating artwork.

Date visited: ____________ **My Rating:** ____________
Went with: ________________________________
Favorites: ________________________________
Not so much: ______________________________
Other comments: ___________________________
____________________________________________

# Bar Mingo

9

**NW/Nob Hill Map**
811 NW 21st Ave
(503) 445-4646
www.barmingonw.com

**Happy Hours**
4:00–6:00pm Daily

**Food Deals 3**
$6.00
Expanded menu delivers a nice field green salad, cheese and meat plates, manilla clams, calamari, baked polenta, or lamb meatballs and the ever-elusive and delicious goat cheese in spicy tomato sauce with bruschetta!

**Drink Specials 2**
$5.00 beer (kind of... two PBRs); $5.00 wines
$5.00 daily martinis or bellinis

**Atmosphere 3**
Big in size and style with modern, Italian design and some groovy West Elm touches. Warm, harvest tones with cool, giant wooden doors imported from Italy. Several pillowy conversation pits. Outdoor sidewalk seating at HH.

Date visited: ____________ **My Rating:** ____________
Went with: ______________________________
Favorites: ______________________________
Not so much: ____________________________
Other comments: __________________________
__________________________________________

# Bartini

10 ★

**NW/Nob Hill Map**
2108 NW Glisan
(503) 224-7919
www.bartinipdx.com

**Happy Hours**
4:00–6:30pm and 9:30pm–close Daily
4:00pm–close Sunday and Monday★
9:30pm–close Fri-Sat (food only)

**Food Deals 3**
$3.00–$7.00
Literally 25 gourmet choices, plus fondue: three kinds of salads, ahi tuna pork or chicken sliders; crab cakes; coconut shrimp, shrimp tacos, several flatbreads and satays, burgers, soup, hummus, pork tacos, mashed potato martini.

**Drink Specials 3**
Half-off signature martinis (full menu of 80!)

**Atmosphere 3**
Black, black and more black; small & intimate martini lounge; best appreciated after sunset. Truly a classic and all-time fave of so many fans! Sidewalk seating at Happy Hour.

Date visited: __________ **My Rating:** __________
Went with: ______________________________
Favorites: ______________________________
Not so much: ______________________________
Other comments: ______________________________
______________________________

# Bent Brick

9

**Pearl Map**
1639 NW Marshall
(503) 688-1655
www.thebentbrick.com

**Happy Hours**
5:00–6:30pm Tues–Sat

**Food Deals 3**
$3.00 or new $25.00 chef's trio
Follows the trending, funky-fresh, Northwest foodie thing with seasonal variety but only a few items like green beans, salmon poofs, pickle plate, scallop tartare, or country ham rillettes.

**Drink Specials 3**
$3.00 tall boys; $5.00 house wines
$5.00 select cocktails

**Atmosphere 3**
Rustic and warm with brick walls (but of course) and an upscale angle on a neighborhood tavern. It's not a big place, and there's a well-designed waiting/lounge area at the entrance with a cool, artsy wooden "tree" to sit beneath. Park Kitchen chef/owner (and James Beard Award nominee).

Date visited: __________ **My Rating:** __________
Went with: ____________________
Favorites: ____________________
Not so much: ____________________
Other comments: ____________________

# Blitz 21

**8**

**Nob Hill/Northwest Map**
305 NW 21st Ave.
(503) 208-3227
www.blitzbarpdx.webs.com

**Happy Hours**
3:00–6:00pm and 9:00pm-close Daily

**Food Deals 2**
$1.95–$4.95
All the top bar standards like sliders, burgers, skewers, SW wrap, fish & chips, chips & salsa, cheese fries, hummus and YAY! Totchos!

**Drink Specials 3**
$2.50 domestics; $3.50 micros
$4.50 house wines; $3.00 wells

**Atmosphere 2**
A new Blitz added this year – a nice and casual sports bar on 21st (hence the name). Brick red walls, with a mix of booth, bar, cooshy, and cocktail table seating. Lots of TVs for watching sports, and lots of light during daytime hours.

Date visited: __________ **My Rating:** __________
Went with: ______________________________
Favorites: ______________________________
Not so much: ______________________________
Other comments: ______________________________

______________________________________________

# Bluehour

**10★**

**Pearl Map**
250 NW 13th Ave.
(503) 226-3394
www.bluehouronline.com

**Happy Hours**
4:00–6:30pm Mon–Fri; 5:00–6:30pm Sat-Sun

**Food Deals 3**
$1.00–$5.00
Wow! They're happier than ever with a super-extensive menu with about 15 items like lamb sliders, pasta with mushrooms, burgers, rings, pizzetta, ribs, cheese or charcuterie boards.

**Drink Specials 3**
$4.00 draft beers; $6.00 house wines
$20 select bottle wine; $6.00 specialty cocktails

**Atmosphere 3+**
Impressive lofted interior; very well-designed—a Portland standout! Trés trendy and active scene (can be a touch loud). Happy Hour side-walk patio dining allowed—and totally enjoyed! Ultra cool lighting effects at night. LOVE it!

Date visited: __________ **My Rating:** __________
Went with: ____________________
Favorites: ____________________
Not so much: ____________________
Other comments: ____________________
____________________

# Blue Olive

9

**NW/Nob Hill Map**
500 NW 21st Ave; (503) 528-2822
and 2712 NE Alberta (503) 206-6168
www.blueolivepdx.com

**Happy Hours**
3:00pm–close Sun–Thurs
3:00-6:00pm and 9:30pm-close Fri–Sat

**Food Deals 2**
$2.50–$7.00
About 20 Mediterranean appetizers including hummus, baba ghanouj, feta, prawns, calamari, chicken kabobs, dolmathes, burger, salad, soup. Smaller menu at more casual Alberta location.

**Drink Specials 3**
$4.00 pints and bottles; $5.00 red or white wine or sangrias; $5.50 wells; $7.50 cocktails

**Atmosphere 3**
Refined, mellow space with neutral palette, large screen TV, and ornate empty frames hanging over the bar. Formerly Virgo & Pisces.

Date visited: ___________ **My Rating:** ___________
Went with: ___________
Favorites: ___________
Not so much: ___________
Other comments: ___________

# Brix

10

**Downtown (East) Map**
1338 NW Hoyt
(503) 943-5995
www.brixtavern.com

**Happy Hours**
3:00–6:30pm and 9:30pm-mid Daily
★All night Monday

**Food Deals 3**
$2.95-7.95
A wide array of seasonal variations of gastropub food: sliders, ribs, soups, salads, wings, yummy Brix chips, cheddar fries, burger, tacos, pizza.

**Drink Specials 3**
$1.00 off drafts (or try one of 30 cans of beer)
$1.00 off wine; $4.00 cocktails (nice, wide array)

**Atmosphere 3**
A welcomed new sportsbar/restaurant/lounge in the Pearl's old Olea space. The front half is very social with brick walls, extra-long bar, and chalkboard menu. Back half hosts the dining crowd and has a couple of pool tables too. Plus, an elevated private loft space for small groups.

Date visited: __________ **My Rating:** __________
Went with: ______________________________
Favorites: ______________________________
Not so much: ______________________________
Other comments: ______________________________
______________________________

# Café Nell

10

A Happy Hour favorite!

**NW/Nob Hill Map**
1987 NW Kearney
(503) 295-6487
www.cafenell.com

**Happy Hours**
3:00–6:00pm Mon–Fri; 4:00–10:00pm Sat ★

**Food Deals 3**
$1.00–$7.00
Big, diverse menu with about 15 items like soups, mixed greens salad, oyster shooters, mac & cheese, catfish nuggets, tacos, or spaghetti bolognese They also serve a great brunch and lunch daily!

**Drink Specials 3**
$2.00 select beer; $5.00 wine; $5.00 bubbles or champagne cocktails; $5.50 martinis/cocktails

**Atmosphere 3**
Cute, little hidden gem tucked away on a quiet tree-lined street. A welcoming brasserie both day and night. Tiny Parisian-style bar with big cushy couch and cafe windows opening to the outside. The kind of place you could stay all day into the night!

Date visited: ____________ **My Rating:** ____________
Went with: ______________________________
Favorites: ______________________________
Not so much: ______________________________
Other comments: ______________________________
______________________________________________

# Camellia Lounge

9

**Pearl Map**
510 NW 11th Ave.
(503) 221-2130
www.teazone.com

**Happy Hours**
4:00-7:00pm Daily; 2:00pm-close Sun★

**Food Deals 2**
$5.00–$6.00
A number of discounted café goodies: black bean burger, Caesar salad, chipotle bacon shrimp tacos, red potato skins, or a turkey panini.

**Drink Specials 3**
$4.00 drafts; $5.00 house wines
$3.00 wells $5.00 unique, signature cocktails

**Atmosphere 3**
Pass through the super-cute Tea Zone Café to discover a tucked-away, speakeasy secret: the Camellia Lounge! Cozy, candlelit charm in the bar/lounge in back. Store and tea scene in front.

Date visited: __________ **My Rating:** __________
Went with: ______________________________
Favorites: ______________________________
Not so much: ____________________________
Other comments: __________________________
_________________________________________

# Casa Del Matador

**NW/Nob Hill Map**
1438 NW 23rd Ave.; (503) 228-2855
**Lloyd Center Map**
2424 East Burnside; (503) 719-5757
www.matadorseattle.com (small local chain)

**Happy Hours**
4:00–6:00pm & 10:00pm–1:00am Daily

**Food Deals 3**
$5.00
Four kinds of quesadillas, choice of six tacos, and even more: nachos, habanero or garlic prawns, soups, chili, salad, spicy wings or calamari.

**Drink Specials 0**
No drink specials, but know that they have over 96 varieties of tequila!

**Atmosphere 3**
A handsome and sexy interior worthy of the title "Matador" greets you upon entering! Stunning, wrought iron artistry, gilded mirrors and rustic stucco walls. A stand-out space with compelling, centrally located, circular fireplace.

Date visited: ____________ **My Rating:** ____________
Went with: ____________
Favorites: ____________
Not so much: ____________
Other comments: ____________

# Cha

10

A Happy Hour favorite!

**NW/Nob Hill Map**
305 NW 21st Ave.
(503) 295-4077
www.chaportland.com

**Happy Hours**
3:00–6:00pm Daily; 10:00–11:00pm Fri–Sat
★Sit at the bartop for Happy Hour all the time!

**Food Deals 3+**
$5.00–$9.00
More than a dozen unusual, gourmet (delicioso), authentic Mexican specialties! Tacos, torta, two ceviches, empanadas, enchiladas, beef tartare, burgers, nachos, burrito, or corn mesa cakes.

**Drink Specials 3**
$3.50 beer; $5.50 wine
$5.50 sangria; $5.50 margarita of the day

**Atmosphere 3**
Same owners as Cha Cha Cha, but Nob Hill's version is quite refined and elegant overall. Big, open space with cool, artsy, white divider and rough, lofty touches. Fun outside patio!

Date visited: ____________ **My Rating:** ____________
Went with: ______________________________
Favorites: ______________________________
Not so much: ____________________________
Other comments: __________________________
__________________________________________

# Coppia

9

**Pearl Map**
417 NW 10th Avenue
(503) 295-9536
www.coppiaportland.com

**Happy Hours**
4:00-6:00pm Tues–Sat

**Food Deals 2**
$6.00–$8.00
Limited selections, but fresh and tasty, and paired with wine: risotto, soups, salad, and artisan cheese or salami and fruit plates.

**Drink Specials 3**
$2.00 off any wine and cocktails; Wine flights too!

**Atmosphere 3**
This is the former Vino Paradiso, rebranded to better emphasize focus on food. The interior changed a bit, but is more refined and cozy now. Three seating areas provide different staging for rotating gallery art. Owned by Pink Martini vocalist and percussionist, Timothy Nishimoto.

Date visited: ____________ **My Rating:** ____________
Went with: ________________________________________
Favorites: ________________________________________
Not so much: ______________________________________
Other comments: ___________________________________
___________________________________________________

# Davis Street Tavern

9

**Old Town Map**
500 NW Davis Street
(503) 505-5050
www.davisstreettavern.com

**Happy Hours**
4:00–6:00pm Mon–Fri; Sat-Sun 3:00-5:00pm

**Food Deals 3**
$1.50–$9.00
Stepped-up bar menu includes oysters and mussels, fish tacos, salads, duck wings, cauliflower tempura, olives, beef or pork sandwiches, mac & cheese, and steak frites.

**Drink Specials 2**
$4.00 beer; $5.00 wines

**Atmosphere 3**
Full of light and Old Town warehouse character, this warm and classy tavern makes for a most perfect spot to congregate and satiate. Brick walls, soaring wood-beamed ceilings, wooden z-shaped bar and giant medieval chandeliers.

Date visited: ____________ **My Rating:** ____________
Went with: ______________________________
Favorites: ______________________________
Not so much: ____________________________
Other comments: __________________________
__________________________________________

# Dr. Sushi & BBQ

10

A Happy Hour favorite!

**NW/Nob Hill Map**
333 NW 23rd Ave.
(971) 279-4022
www.drsushibbq.com

**Happy Hours**
4:00–6:00pm Mon–Sat

**Food Deals 3** $5.00
Selected nigiri and maki are 50% off all day. Plus, a special HH menu of 16 delights will round out everything you'd want to eat, with several kimchi-based specialties, lots of stir-fry, plus chicken, pork, or beef on sizzling platters.

**Drink Specials 3+**
$2.50–$4.00 beers; $2.50 wines and select saké
$6.00 wide array of cocktails

**Atmosphere 3**
It's an under-the-radar place, with kind of a funny name, but rest assured that Dr. Sushi takes his Happy Hour seriously! The restaurant is pleasant, refined, and understated, with attention to design in furniture choice, lighting, paint, and moldings. Great group space!

Date visited: __________ **My Rating:** __________
Went with: ______________________________
Favorites: ______________________________
Not so much: ______________________________
Other comments: ______________________________

______________________________

# Elephant's Deli

9 ★

**NW/Nob Hill Map**
115 NW 22nd Ave.
(503) 299-6304
www.elephantsdeli.com

**Happy Hours**
5:00–7:00pm Mon–Sat

**Food Deals 2**
$3.95
Nice little array of eats like pizza, fondue, buffalo chicken meatballs, and mahi mahi. Plus a whole, Whole Foods-like deli with desserts too.

**Drink Specials 3**
$3.50 drafts, $4.00 wines, $6.00 cocktail

**Atmosphere 3**
It's a super-cute, little, urban bar tucked inside a quaint, but modern, country store. Eat and shop, drink and bring home good wine, and grab gourmet to go! Fun outdoor deck too. It's really quite a unique place for Happy Hour!

Date visited: ____________ **My Rating:** ____________
Went with: ______________________________
Favorites: ______________________________
Not so much: ______________________________
Other comments: ______________________________
______________________________________________

# Fish Sauce

10

**NW/Nob Hill Map**
407 NW 17th Ave
(503) 227-8000
www.fishsaucepdx.com

**Happy Hours**
4:30-6:00pm Mon–Sat

**Food Deals 3**
$2.00-$8.00
Draper Valley wings, tenderloin beef rolls, salad and crispy rolls, sugarcane shrimp, grilled corn, ribs, or salad, all beautifully presented with artful garnishes. Also $2.00 off banh mi sandwiches.

**Drink Deals 3**
$4.00 drafts, $4.00 sake; $5.00 wines
$6.00-$7.00 signature cocktails

**Atmosphere 3**
Think Asian and reclaimed wood. The space is intimate and inviting, with beautiful, knotty finished tables, including a super-long, central communal table. Lighting fixtures made from pallets, interesting white chalk murals on black walls, and large, nicely done outside patio.

Date visited: __________ **My Rating:** __________
Went with: ______________________________
Favorites: ______________________________
Not so much: ____________________________
Other comments: __________________________

______________________________________________

# Fratelli

9

**Pearl Map**
1230 NW Hoyt
(503) 241-8800
www.fratellicucina.com

**Happy Hours**
5:00–6:00pm and 9:00pm–close Daily

**Food Deals 3**
$4.00–7.00
Tasty pizzettes and small plates are only slightly discounted from regular prices: four styles of pizzettes (mostly veggie options); fried risotto balls, bruschetta, penne, mixed green salad.

**Drink Specials 3**
$2.00–3.00 drafts; $6.00 red or white wine
$4.00 wells; $6.00 cello drops

**Atmosphere 3**
Now fully Fratelli Restaurant – Bar Dué closed and will be used as a private party/event space. Happy Hour is at the bar of the incredibly charming and romantic Italian restaurant, so it works out to enjoy a higher "cute" factor!

Date visited: ___________ **My Rating:** ___________
Went with: ______________________________
Favorites: ______________________________
Not so much: ______________________________
Other comments: ______________________________

# Gilt Club

10

Top cover fave 2013!

**Old Town Map**
306 NW Broadway
(503) 222-4458
www.giltclub.com

**Happy Hours**
5:00–6:30pm Mon–Fri

**Food Deals 3**
$2.00–$5.00
An already impressive menu, now made larger. A good mix of fancy and fun: spicy deviled eggs, pork rinds, fritto misto, mixed olives, spicy chicken pops, salad, pork belly, and frito pie!

**Drink Specials 3**
$2.50 Stellas; $5.00 wine
$5.00 appletini or Moscow mule

**Atmosphere 3**
Yes, it IS most luscious! Plushness abounds with deep red walls and velvet drapes with gold touches & sexy curves galore. WAY swanky! Very creative touches and overall surroundings. Famously featured in first episode of "Portlandia!"

Date visited: ____________ **My Rating:** ____________
Went with: ______________________________
Favorites: ______________________________
Not so much: ____________________________
Other comments: __________________________
_________________________________________

# Giorgio's

**10**

A Happy Hour favorit

**Pearl Map**
1131 NW Hoyt
(503) 221-1888
www.giorgiospdx.com

**Happy Hours**
5:00–6:30pm Tues–Fri

**Food Deals 3**
$3.00–$10.00
One of the most highly-rated Italian restaurants in town! Happy Hour doesn't quite offer the cheapest prices, but the food is top-notch: grilled octopus, several salads, mixed olives or nuts, soup, paninis, meat and cheese plates.

**Drink Specials 3**
$4.00 beer of the day; $5.00–$7.00 wines
$5.00 cocktail of the day

**Atmosphere 3**
It's a low-key, off-the-radar place that's been around since July 2000. Simple, European café style with black & white tiled floors, dark wood tables, and a long, copper-topped bar.

Date visited: ______________ **My Rating:** ______________
Went with: ______________
Favorites: ______________
Not so much: ______________
Other comments: ______________

# Irving St. Kitchen

10

**Pearl Map**
703 NW 13th Ave.
(503) 343-9440
www.irvingstreetkitchen.com

**Happy Hours**
4:30–6:00pm Daily

**Food Deals 2**
$5.00–$7.00
Unique menu items totally matching the theme and food changes almost weekly: olives, spiced nuts, jambalaya, poutine, pork belly with waffles and egg, beignets, wings.

**Drink Specials 3**
$2.00 PBRs (with $2.00 whisky back)
$6.00 house wines; $5.00 specialty cocktails

**Atmosphere 3**
Trendy and rustic with TONS of character and attention to design details. Named Willamette Week's "Best New Restaurant" in its 2010 Reader's Choice Poll. Lots of nice little nooks and separate seating areas throughout.

Date visited: ___________ **My Rating:** ___________
Went with: ________________________________________
Favorites: ________________________________________
Not so much: ______________________________________
Other comments: ___________________________________
___________________________________________________

# Isabel

9

**Pearl Map**
330 NW 10th
(503) 222-4333
www.isabelscantina.com

**Happy Hours**
5:00–6:30pm Daily

**Food Deals 3**
$2.00 off appetizers
Isabel's Cantina cookbook features "bold Latin flavors from the New California kitchen," as does her Happy Hour food which may change a bit seasonally: lettuce wraps, wontons, plantains with carnitas, grilled veggies, dragon potatoes.

**Drink Specials 3**
$4.00 beer; $4.00 wines; $4.00 sangria
$5.00 specialty cocktails

**Atmosphere 2**
Located inside a small, fishbowl-ish building made almost entirely of glass walls; minimalist interior with high ceilings, gray carpet, orange chairs and nice, big seasonal outdoor plaza patio.

Date visited: __________ **My Rating:** __________
Went with: ____________________
Favorites: ____________________
Not so much: ____________________
Other comments: ____________________

____________________

# Ivories

9

**Pearl Map**
1435 NW Flanders
(503) 241-6514
www.ivoriesjazz.com

**Happy Hours**
4:00–6:00pm Daily; ★All day Tuesday

**Food Deals 3**
$2.00-$6.00
About a dozen bar eats with a few twists: penne pasta, calamari, burger, grilled cheese, wings, Southwest chicken twister, chicken w/avocado and swiss, wontons, fries, or a pork sandwich.

**Drink Specials 3**
$3.00 drafts; $2.00 off wine; $3.00 wells

**Atmosphere 3**
Jazz Club in the Pearl, that's not too fancy, but quite nice. It's a big, loft-like space with a stage, and can feel a little funny being more empty early on. If you stop in later for a drink, be aware that cover charges can go into effect as there is live music there and some are big names (including the friendly owner, Jim Templeton).

Date visited: ____________ **My Rating:** ____________
Went with: ______________________________
Favorites: ______________________________
Not so much: ______________________________
Other comments: ______________________________

______________________________

# Jamison's

8

**Pearl Map**
900 NW 11th St.
(503) 972-3330
www.jamisonpdx.com

**Happy Hours**
3:00–5:00pm Daily (This must change, right?!)

**Food Deals 2**
Good but pricey, and always changing with things like three-buck nuts and $9.00 for choice of three flatbreads or a salad or cheese plate.

**Drink Specials 3**
$4.00 beer; $6.00 wines; $6.00 house cocktails

**Atmosphere 3**
Gorgeous design! Very different than the former space, Fenouil. Still with an upper-crust look, but in a very manly and rustic tone. The outside patio overlooks Jamison square and fountain, and you can sit there for Happy Hour, or anywhere else in the restaurant. Inside, it's gray suede and muted, rough woods, brown leather chairs, a "living wall", and a kick-ass fireplace.

Date visited: ____________ **My Rating:** ____________
Went with: ______________________________
Favorites: ______________________________
Not so much: ______________________________
Other comments: ______________________________
______________________________

# Jimmy Mak's

8

**Pearl Map**
221 NW 10th Ave
(503) 295-6542
www.jimmymaks.com

**Happy Hours**
5:00–6:30pm Mon–Fri

**Food Deals 1**
10% off appetizer, salad, and dinner menu. A different kind of Happy Hour... I could be down with more like 30% off, but can't give many points for trying too hard. Still fun to dine here though.

**Drink Specials 3**
$1.00 off beer ($2.75 domestics; $3.50–$4.25 micros); $5.00 wine; $3.50 well cocktails

**Atmosphere 3**
Be an early bird and enjoy Jimmy Mak's swanky jazz club finery complete with thick, brilliantly illuminated, red velvet curtains, dark & cushy booth seating, and tiny candlelit cocktail tables. And while you're there, play some free pool too!

Date visited: __________ **My Rating:** __________
Went with: ______________________________
Favorites: ______________________________
Not so much: ______________________________
Other comments: ______________________________
______________________________

# Jo-Bar

10

**NW/Nob Hill Map**
715 NW 23rd Ave.
(503) 222-0048
www.papahaydn.com/r/6/Jo-Bar

**Happy Hours**
3:00–6:00pm Daily; also last hour before closing

**Food Deals 3**
$1.00–$7.00
Expanded menu with 17 items: the famous Jo Burger, fries, homemade sweet potato chips, Cobb salad, fondue, French onion soup, steamed clams, pizza, mac & cheese, wings, olives, nuts.

**Drink Specials 3+**
$4.00 beer; $5.50 house wines
$5.00-$6.00 cocktails (10 selections)

**Atmosphere 3**
Deep red and olive walls, stunning entry flower display, original art, huge iron chandelier, open stone wood oven and rotisserie, full front windows, outdoor sidewalk seating. Casually chill, yet nice.

Date visited: ____________ **My Rating:** ____________
Went with: ______________________________
Favorites: ______________________________
Not so much: ______________________________
Other comments: ______________________________
______________________________

# Kell's Brewpub

8

**Nob Hill/Northwest Map**
305 NW 21st Ave.
(503) 208-3227
www.kellsbrewpub.com

**Happy Hours**
4:00–6:30pm Mon–Fri; 10:00pm–close Mon–Thurs

**Food Deals 3**
$3.00–$5.00
Irish nachos, wings, BLTC, burger or sandwich with fries, quesadilla, oyster shooters, sweet potato fries, hummus.

**Drink Specials 0**
Sadly, no drink specials

**Atmosphere 3**
A whole new Kell's – inside and out – with an on-site brewery! Bit by bit, they're playing around with introducing all kinds of new fun. The inside of this version of Kell's is brand-new and not all that Irish-y, but still with dark wood booths. More brews on their way day-by-day...

Date visited: ____________ **My Rating:** ____________
Went with: ______________________________
Favorites: ______________________________
Not so much: ____________________________
Other comments: __________________________
__________________________________________

# Kin

9

**Pearl Map**
524 NW 14th Ave.
(503) 228-4546
www.kinpdx.com

**Happy Hours**
5:00–6:00pm Tues–Fri

**Food Deals 3**
$4.00–$6.00
Very unique "globally influenced Asian cuisine inspired by local ingredients": springrolls, grilled Japanese eggplant, spicy potstickers, wontons, asian pastrami slider, and several yakitoris.

**Drink Specials 3**
$3.50 draft beer; $5.00 select wines
$6.00 cocktail of the day (award-winning!)

**Atmosphere 3**
This is the former Holden's space with new owner and chef, Kevin Shikami, formerly a *Food & Wine* "Best New Chef." Cozy, loft-style space with paper artwork adding gallery-style flair. Outside seating and open, garage-style door.

Date visited: ____________ **My Rating:** ____________
Went with: ______________________________
Favorites: ______________________________
Not so much: ____________________________
Other comments: __________________________
_________________________________________

# Lela's Bistro

6

**NW/Nob HillMap**
1524 NW 23rd Ave.
(503) 719-4744
www.lelasbistro.com

**Happy Hours**
4:00–7:00pm Tues–Fri

A Happy Hour favorite!

**Food Deals 0**
$4.25–$7.95
The food is so good here, but alas, currently, there are no food discounts at Happy Hour. Menu items won't break the bank though, and this place is still "page-worthy" and you need to go!

**Drink Specials 2**
$1.00 off beer, wine and cocktails

**Atmosphere 3**
This might be your new second home if you live anywhere nearby! Part coffeeshop in tone (counter service), with bench seats and café tables set up in what would be the living and dining room of this welcoming, old house.

Date visited: ____________ **My Rating:** ____________
Went with: ________________________________
Favorites: ________________________________
Not so much: ______________________________
Other comments: ___________________________
___________________________________________

# Mellow Mushroom

8

**Pearl Map**
1411 NW Flanders
(503) 224-9019
www.mellowmushroom.com

**Happy Hours**
3:00-6:00pm Daily

**Food Deals 2**
$2.00–$5.00
Tiny menu with garlic knots, pesto bread, Caesar salad, pizza slider, or sampling of bruschetta with capri salad, or wings and meatball combo.

**Drink Specials 2**
$3.00 well drinks; $4.00 Boilermaker; plus other special daily drink deals

**Atmosphere 3**
Retro-modern-lounge-y with a lot of grooviness going on. Vinyl swivel seats, orange plastic chairs, open kitchen, and wall-to-wall paneling. Half-walls and funky 70s dividers segment out the large, open room. Cool vibe.

Date visited: __________ **My Rating:** __________
Went with: ____________________
Favorites: ____________________
Not so much: ____________________
Other comments: ____________________

# Meriwether's 10

A Happy Hour favorite!

**NW/Nob Hill Map**
2601 NW Vaughn
(503) 228-1250
www.meriwethersnw.com

**Happy Hours**
3:00-6:00pm Daily

**Food Deals 3+**
$3.00–$12.00
OMGWOW! 16 "Pantry Board" items to mix and mingle and another 11 sandwiches and such! Seasonal deliciousness like soup, chickpea fries, olives, crab deviled eggs, several salads, cauliflower gratin, fries, burger, butternut squash and goat cheese pizza, and bacon-wrapped dates.

**Drink Specials 3**
$3.00 bottles; $3.50 drafts; $5.00 select wine

**Atmosphere 3+**
Built on the site of the 1905 World's Fair. Their historic and stately interior exudes a warm and hospitable countryside inn quality. Impressive! Incredibly cozy in the winter. Gorgeous deck out back, but not available for Happy Hour.

Date visited: ___________ **My Rating:** ___________
Went with: ______________________________
Favorites: ______________________________
Not so much: ______________________________
Other comments: ______________________________
______________________________________________

# Metrovino

10

A Happy Hour favorite!

**Pearl Map**
1139 NW 11th Ave
(503) 517-7778
www.metrovinopdx.com

**Happy Hours**
4:00–6:00pm Mon–Fri

**Food Deals 3**
$1.00–$9.00
Delicious and seasonally fresh NW, but on the pricey side. Menu changes with the seasons: beet salad, confit chicken wings, tempura, bread or charcuterie plate, plus $10 cheeseburger.

**Drink Specials 3**
$5.00 select red, white or bubbles
$5.00 daily cocktails

**Atmosphere 3**
Contemporary and sleek restaurant/wine bar that would hold its own in NYC. More than 80 wines by the glass, made possible by their ultra-cool enomatic wine system. Built green with recycled and fully recyclable carpets, reclaimed wood and salvaged materials. Gorgeous.

Date visited: ____________ **My Rating:** ____________
Went with: ______________________________
Favorites: ______________________________
Not so much: ______________________________
Other comments: ______________________________
______________________________

# North 45

9

**NW/Nob Hill Map**
517 NW 21st Ave.
(503) 248-6317
www.north45pub.com

**Happy Hours**
4:00–6:00pm Daily; All night on Mondays★

**Food Deals 3**
$3.00–$6.00
Ten tasty appetizers like calamari, green beans, wings, mac & cheese, sliders, salads, chicken flautas, and pommes frites (yum!)

**Drink Specials 2**
$3.50 pints of draft pilsner; $5.00 house wines
$4.00 wells; $5.50 "Patio-Rita"

**Atmosphere 3**
A rich, but homey feel to their travelers-themed bar with framed maps and vacation photos. Very cozy inside/huge patio beer garden in back – which is tented and heated in the winter.

Date visited: __________ **My Rating:** __________
Went with: ____________________
Favorites: ____________________
Not so much: ____________________
Other comments: ____________________

____________________

# Oba!

★ 10

**Pearl Map**
555 NW 12th Ave.
(503) 228-6161
www.obarestaurant.com

**Happy Hours**
4:00–6:30pm Daily; 4:00pm–close Sundays★
9:00pm–close Mon–Thurs; 10pm-close Fri-Sat

**Food Deals 3** A Happy Hour favorite
$4.50–$7.00
A forever classic! Giant menu of deliciousness (careful – you'll easily leave too full): pork, fish or chicken baja tacos, nachos, corn cakes with Yucatan pork, grilled sweet corn, plus Salbut' and Choripan (don't ask – just get it :-)

**Drink Specials 3**
$4.00 selected beer; $5.00 house wine
$6.50 flavored Margaritas; $6.00 mojitos

**Atmosphere 3**
Colorful, Latin-American-style with a festive and trendy scene. Golden and terra cotta walls, pillars and white sparkly tree lights. Outdoor sidewalk dining. "The kind of place you need to hit before confession."

Date visited: __________ **My Rating:** __________
Went with: ____________________
Favorites: ____________________
Not so much: ____________________
Other comments: ____________________
____________________

# Oven & Shaker 6

**Pearl Map**
1134 NW Everett
(503) 241-1600
www.ovenandshaker.com

**Happy Hours**
2:30–4:00pm Daily; 10:00pm–mid Sun–Thurs

**Food Deals 3**
$7.00–$10.00
Phenomenally delicious wood-fired pizza, as brought to us by Cathy Whims of Nostrana (Four-time James Beard nominee). About half-off several pizza styles with unique, gourmet spins. A couple of fresh and healthy salads too.

**Drink Specials 0**
Sadly, no drink discounts

**Atmosphere 3**
Rough, exposed woods cover the place with rustic urban charm. An ultra-long bar (45-feet) dominates one full wall, with windows open to the street along the front. It may be more of a late lunch than a Happy Hour given the 4:00pm end-time, but being enormously popular and delicious, it's nice they offer a break. It's great late!

Date visited: __________ **My Rating:** __________
Went with: ____________________
Favorites: ____________________
Not so much: ____________________
Other comments: ____________________

# Papa Haydn

10

**NW/Nob Hill Map**
701 NW 23rd Ave.; (503) 228-7317

Sellwood 5829 SE Milwaukee; (503) 232-9440
(Similar menu 3–6pm Mon–Thur /3–5pm Fri–Sat)
www.papahaydn.com

**Happy Hours**
3:00–6:00pm Mon–Fri

**Food Deals 3**
$2.00–$7.00
A Portland favorite since 1983, they finally do a most excellent, high-quality Happy Hour! Good size menu with French onion soup, salad, burger, cheese plate, pizza, clams, fried chickpeas, fries, croque monseur or madam (with turkey).

**Drink Specials 3**
$4.00 drafts; $5.50 wines and wells
$5.00–$6.00 signature cocktails

**Atmosphere 3**
Everything cute in traditional design is represented and ties together beautifully: buttercream walls, upholstered seats, paned glass, thick moldings, stripes and harlequin patterns, and carpeting. Well-known reputation for delicious desserts!

Date visited: ____________ **My Rating:** ____________
Went with: ______________________________
Favorites: ______________________________
Not so much: ____________________________
Other comments: __________________________
__________________________________________

# Paragon

9

**Pearl Map**
1309 NW Hoyt
(503) 833-5060
www.paragonrestaurant.com

**Happy Hours**
4:00–6:00pm Daily

**Food Deals 2**
$5.00
Short list of bar menu items that changes seasonally with items like onion rings, spicy peanuts, fritters, pork & black bean tostadas, sliders, hummus.

**Drink Specials 3**
$3.00–$4.50 drafts; $6.50 house wines
$6.50 house infusions, drops or coolers

**Atmosphere 3**
A forever-favorite in the Pearl finally started Happy Hour! Open-air in the summer = fresh breezes, fun, and excellent views of the Pearl parade outside. Contemporary Northwest style with big open bar, chill music, and bar mirrors overhead to reflect the good-looking crowd.

Date visited: __________ **My Rating:** __________
Went with: ______________________________
Favorites: ______________________________
Not so much: ______________________________
Other comments: ______________________________
______________________________

# Parish

**Pearl Map**
231 NW 11th Ave.
(503) 227-2421
www.theparishpdx.com

**Happy Hours**
3:00-6:00pm Daily

**Food Deals 3**
$3.00–$6.00
Select oysters on the half shell (several kinds, be sure to stick to the HH ones for the discount); grilled shrimp, corn, or chicken hearts; plus wedge salad, burger, sausage, soft boiled eggs.

**Drink Specials 3**
$2.00 Trumer pils; $6.00 house wine or sparkling
$4.00 well drinks

**Atmosphere 3**
An oyster bar in the Pearl. I like it! Then add in a New Orleans spin with spicy creole taster plates and super cute decor? I'm a devoted follower! Beautiful design with soft blue-greys, dark woods, and Martha Stewart-worthy signage and slightly churchy room dividers.

Date visited: ____________ **My Rating:** ____________
Went with: ______________________________
Favorites: ______________________________
Not so much: ______________________________
Other comments: ______________________________
______________________________

# Park Kitchen

9

**Old Town Map**
422 NW 8th Ave
(503) 223-7275
www.parkkitchen.com

**Happy Hours**
5:00–7:00pm Daily

**Food Deals 3**
$8.00
Seasonal changes with 10 or so Americana-nouveau small plates like chickpea fries, soups, terrine of the day, garden lettuces, feta and radish salad, flank steak, and cod fritters. One of the best restaurants, but ya gotta pay for it.

**Drink Specials 3**
$5.00 drafts; $5.00 wine; $5.00 cocktails

**Atmosphere 3**
Cute and cozy bistro across from the park with café tables outside, but sadly, Happy Hour go-ers are relegated to the bar. Don't worry – you'll still experience the sweet, subdued, almost-country respite inside.

Date visited: ____________ **My Rating:** ____________
Went with: ________________________________________
Favorites: ________________________________________
Not so much: ______________________________________
Other comments: ___________________________________
___________________________________________________

# PF Chang's

10

**Pearl Map**
1139 NW Couch
(503) 432-4000

Tigard 7463 SW Bridgeport Rd; (503) 430-3020
Hillsboro (Tanasbourne)
19320 NW Emma Way; (503) 533-4580
www.pfchangs.com

**Happy Hours** 3:00-6:00pm Daily

**Food Deals 3**
$3.00–$6.00
Big, extensive list of appetizers: Several dim sum dumplings, wraps and wontons, plus traditional street fare like ahi tuna crisps, ribs, and rolls.

**Drink Specials 3**
$2.75-$3.25 beers; $5.00-$6.00 wine
$4.00 wells; $5.00-$6.00 cocktails

**Atmosphere 3**
An Emperor's Palace appearance, complete with huge stone lion sculptures and artistic modern lighting effects. Sit and enjoy the beauty of the restaurant (kids are welcome) or the bar.

Date visited: __________ **My Rating:** __________
Went with: ______________________________
Favorites: ______________________________
Not so much: ____________________________
Other comments: __________________________

# Ping

9

**Old Town Map**
102 NW 4th Ave
(503) 229-7464
www.pingpdx.com

**Happy Hours**
2:00–5:30pm Tues-Sat; 9:00–10:00pm Tues–Thur

**Food Deals 3**
$2.00–$7.00
Big menu with lots of choices and delicious food! Chicken, beef and lamb satay, Thai salad, kobawayshi dogs, pork buns, pickled cucumber salad, plus chicken, prawn, or potato skewers.

**Drink Specials 3**
$3.00 drafts (20 oz.); $4.00 select saké or wells
$4.00–5.00 house specialty cocktails

**Atmosphere 2**
Long and low, front-and-center bar in front of the open kitchen gives Ping an old American diner look. Antique Chinese metal beverage signs and hanging paper sculptures start to add the Asian twist. Too bright at Happy Hour time.

Date visited: __________ **My Rating:** __________
Went with: ______________________________
Favorites: ______________________________
Not so much: ______________________________
Other comments: ______________________________
______________________________

# Pink Rose

9

**Pearl Map**
1300 NW Lovejoy
(503) 482-2165
www.pinkrosepdx.com

**Happy Hours**
4:00-7:00pm and 10:00pm–mid Tues-Fri

**Food Deals 3** $3.00-$6.00
New menu that may vary somewhat seasonally: pork w/cheese fries, butter lettuce or brussel sprouts salad, stuffed mushrooms, bacon-wrapped dates, chips & dip, and grilled cheese.

**Drink Specials 3**
$3.00 select draft; $5.00 wines; $5.00 cocktail

**Atmosphere 3**
A few years ago, this was the all-new, ultra-hip SoLo Lounge. It's lost some edge and is softer now, but still retains a dark, underground, clubby look and feel. The upstairs deck is lovely in the summer, with its pink umbrella tables, torches, heat lamps, potted plants and the elevated view of Lovejoy street passer-bys and traffic.

Date visited: __________ **My Rating:** __________
Went with: ______________________________
Favorites: ______________________________
Not so much: ______________________________
Other comments: ______________________________

# Pope House

**10** ★

**NW/Nob Hill Map**
2075 NW Glisan
(503) 222-1056
www.popehouselounge.com

**Happy Hours**
4:00–7:00pm Daily; ★All day Sunday

**Food Deals 3**
$3.00–$5.00
Yes! Frito Pie! Plus a big and delicious array of several kinds of paninis, fritters, pulled pork quesadilla, mac & cheese, and deviled eggs.

**Drink Specials 3**
$3.50 drafts; $5.00 house wines; $3.50 wells
$5.00 Southern-style cocktails; $4.00 whiskeys

**Atmosphere 3**
This wonderful, old Victorian exudes welcoming southern hospitality, warmth, and charm, especially at night. Several parlor-like dining/drinking rooms, social central bar, and lots and lots of whiskey to boot! Still vaguely remembered fondly as the old Brazen Bean.

Date visited: ____________ **My Rating:** ____________
Went with: ____________
Favorites: ____________
Not so much: ____________
Other comments: ____________

____________

# Ringside Steakhouse 7

**NW/Nob Hill Map**
2165 NW Burnside
(503) 223-1513
www.ringsidesteakhouse.com

**Happy Hours**
9:30pm–close Daily and 4:00–5:30pm Sun

**Food Deals 3+**
$2.25–$4.75
A forever favorite menu: steak bites (YUM!), potato skins, prime rib sandwich, crabcakes, clams, burger, Caesars, oysters, calamari, jo-jos, mussels, satay, quesadilla, and meatballs.

**Drink Specials 0**
Sadly, no drink specials

**Atmosphere 3**
Back to basics and the beloved, old-school, lounge remains pretty much intact! Renovation didn't really change things all too much (behind the scenes re-do excluded). You'll love the place – dimly-lit, super-cozy interior, and wrap-around bartender pit. Since 1944. Wow.

Date visited: __________ **My Rating:** __________
Went with: ______________________________
Favorites: ______________________________
Not so much: ____________________________
Other comments: _________________________
_________________________________________

# Sal's Famous Italian

9

**NW/Nob Hill Map**
33 NW 23rd Place
(503) 467-4067
www.salskitchen.com

**Happy Hours**
3:30–5:30pm Daily

**Food Deals 3**
$5.00
Delicious samplings of all the most popular dishes: polenta, caprese or Caesar salad, burgers, spaghetti, pizza, butternut squash ravioli.

**Drink Specials 3**
$3.00 beer; $5.00 house wine
$4.00 well drinks; $7.00 featured cocktails

**Atmosphere 3**
Hip and quaint old-world Italian trattoria with gorgeous, faux wall treatments and walls of classic framed pictures. Sweet space inside, but in strip mall.

Date visited: ____________ **My Rating:** ____________
Went with: ______________________________
Favorites: ______________________________
Not so much: ______________________________
Other comments: ______________________________
______________________________________________

# Seres

10

**Pearl Map**
1105 NW Lovejoy
(971) 222-7327
www.seresrestaurant.com

**Happy Hours**
3:00–7:00pm Mon–Sat; All night Tues★

Top cover fave 2013!

**Food Deals 3+**
$3.00–$6.00
More than 20 cravable, high-quality, fresh and organic Pan Asian delights brings everything under the sun: Mongolian lamb, General Tso's chicken, Cantonese crispy prawns, spring or salad rolls, wonton soup, lo mein, salt & pepper calamari, prawns w/ snow peas, and pork dishes.

**Drink Specials 3**
$3.00 drafts; $5.00 wines
$6.00 signature cocktails

**Atmosphere 3**
Pearlesque loft-style with Far East reserve. High-end but friendly and comfortable. Lofty loft space with full, floor-to-ceiling windows; natural tones and tables; gorgeous hanging tile art pieces.

Date visited: ____________ **My Rating:** ____________
Went with: ________________________________________
Favorites: ________________________________________
Not so much: ______________________________________
Other comments: ___________________________________
___________________________________________________

# Serratto

10

A Happy Hour favorite!

**NW/Nob Hill Map**
2112 NW Kearney
(503) 221-1195
www.serratto.com

**Happy Hours**
4:00–6:00pm Daily

**Food Deals 3+**
$4.00–$6.00
Some of the best food around, at Happy Hour and beyond! Positively stellar menu items (13): stone oven pizzas (my personal favorite for Happy Hour), spicy rigatoni, flame-broiled burgers, salad, calamari, hummus, deviled eggs, stuffed peppers, French onion soup, and pommes frites.

**Drink Specials 3**
$3.00 drafts; $5.00 red or white house wine
$5.00 cocktail specials and wells

**Atmosphere 3**
Happy Hour is in their more casual "Vineria" which is only slightly Italian in ambiance, but extremely pleasant and even romantic.

Date visited: ____________ **My Rating:** ____________
Went with: ______________________________________
Favorites: ______________________________________
Not so much: ____________________________________
Other comments: _________________________________

# Shiraz

10

A Happy Hour favorit

**Pearl Map**
1140 NW Everett
(503) 821-7500
www.shiraz-grill.com

**Happy Hours**
3:00–6:00pm Mon–Sat

**Food Deals 3+**
$3.00–$8.00
Giant menu of absolutely delicious food! Sample Mediterranean and Persian specialties galore with several wood-fired pizzas, different kinds of kabobs, gyros, and wings, plus many basics like hummus, baba ghanoush, falafel, fries and *more!*

**Drink Specials 3**
$4.00-$5.00 drafts; $5.00 house wines
$5.00 cocktail specials

**Atmosphere 3**
Modern space with small café tables and a long, glowing bar. Wall-size, colorful street scene graphics at far end of long room that formerly housed Everett St. Bistro. The Iranians call Shiraz the city of poets, gardens, wine, and flowers.

Date visited: ____________ **My Rating:** ____________
Went with: ____________
Favorites: ____________
Not so much: ____________
Other comments: ____________

____________

# Silk

10

**Pearl Map**
1012 NW Glisan
(503) 248-2172
www.silkbyphovan.com

**Happy Hours**
4:00–6:30pm Mon–Sat

**Food Deals 3**
$4.00–$7.00
Enjoy a large variety of delicious Vietnamese mini-dinners including salad rolls, crispy rolls, hoisin ribs, chicken curry, lemongrass chicken, baguettes, wings, pho, and crazy noodles.

**Drink Specials 3**
$4.00 Kirin beer, $6.00 specialty cocktails
$5.00 red or white wine ($20.00 bottles)

**Atmosphere 3**
White and natural borderline-retro decor blends contemporary hard lines with silky flow. It's totally mod, gorgeous, and romantic. Enjoy the illuminated and mesmerizing, white "flowing" wall!

Date visited: ____________ **My Rating:** ____________
Went with: ______________________________
Favorites: ______________________________
Not so much: ______________________________
Other comments: ______________________________
______________________________________________

# Soi 9

10 ★

**NW/Nob Hill Map**
1914 W. Burnside
(503) 894-9153
www soi9pdx.com

**Happy Hours**
4:30–6:30pm Daily

**Food Deals 3+**
$1.50–$5.00
GIANT menu of Thai treats like grilled chicken or eggplant in coconut sauce, calamari, wings, salad and spring rolls, skewers, wontons, and several rice and noodle bowls. Delicious food!

**Drink Specials 3**
$3.25 beer; $5.00 red or white wine
$5.00 specialty cocktails (i.e. guava margarita)

**Atmosphere 3**
Center-city-retro-zen! Contemporary and colorful, it seems a little fast-foodish upon entrance, but give it a chance, come in and stay awhile, and you'll soon mellow out and switch gears. Try it soon – it's one of those "hidden gems."

Date visited: __________ **My Rating:** __________
Went with: ______________________________
Favorites: ______________________________
Not so much: ____________________________
Other comments: _________________________
_________________________________________

# Southland Whiskey Kitchen

6

**NW/Nob Hill Map**
1422 NW 23rd Ave.
(503) 224-2668
www.southlandwhiskeykitchen.com

**Happy Hours**
3:30–6:00pm Daily

**Food Deals 0**
$3.00–$4.00
No extra food deals at Happy Hour, but you can create your own from their "Sides" menu with 15 items like mac & cheese, coleslaw, baked potato, cornbread, salt & vinegar potato chips, collard greens, grit stix, beans, rings, or fries.

**Drink Specials 2**
$1.00 off beer, wine, and wells

**Atmosphere 3**
Southern style for the Pacific Northwest, right out of a Texas roadhouse, but new and beautiful. Wood parquet walls with a striking zigzag design. Hanging wagonwheel lights and exposed brick add to the charm. Same owners as Casa del Matador.

Date visited: __________ **My Rating:** __________
Went with: ______________________________
Favorites: ______________________________
Not so much: ______________________________
Other comments: ______________________________
______________________________

# Streetcar Bistro 8

**Pearl Map**
1101 NW Northrup
(503) 227-2988
www.streetcarbistro.com

**Happy Hours**
3:00-6:00pm and 10:00pm-mid Daily

**Food Deals 2**
$3.00-$8.00
About 10 items of all sorts that vary seasonally, with slight discounts from regular prices: salad, soup, pretzel, meatball sandwich, burger, cheese or charcuterie board, mac & cheese, half BLT, grilled shellfish.

**Drink Specials 1**
$4.00 shots of Jack or Jamison
Beer and scotch taster flights

**Atmosphere 3**
Sleek modern look in cool new bistro. Muted white pine woods, white leather boxy chairs, and a big bar with about 30 illuminated taps. Nice lounge area with couches and fireplace.

Date visited: __________ **My Rating:** __________
Went with: ______________________________
Favorites: ______________________________
Not so much: ______________________________
Other comments: ______________________________
______________________________

# Sweet Basil

9

**NW/Nob Hill Map**
1639 NW Glisan
(503) 473-8758
www.sweetbasilor.com

**Happy Hours**
5:00–7:00pm Daily; ★5:00–9:00pm Sunday

**Food Deals 3**
$2.50–$4.75
YUM! Lots of delicious Thai specials: OMG crab rolls, wraps, tofu/veggie or beef salads, wings, crab rangoon, satay, gyoza, and wontons.

**Drink Specials 3**
$3.00 all beer; $2.00 off glasses of wine
$5.00 cocktail of the night

**Atmosphere 2**
Originally opened as Sweet Basil, then took on a name change to Oasisba along with a facelift, and now back to Sweet Basil. Always the same owners. Very colorful and fun, but just a touch off the beaten path, so keep it in mind!

Date visited: __________ **My Rating:** __________
Went with: ______________________________
Favorites: ______________________________
Not so much: ______________________________
Other comments: ______________________________

# Taste on 23rd

**NW/Nob Hill Map**
2285 NW Johnson
(503) 477-7238
www.tasteon23rd.com

**Happy Hours**
4:00–7:00pm Daily (closed Tuesdays)

**Food Deals 2**
$2.00–$6.00
Light bites to taste and nibble while you sip: grilled bread, spiced nuts, warm olives, deviled egg trio, truffle popcorn, or a salami or cheese plate. Oh! And prosciutto-wrapped dates too!

**Drink Specials 2**
$4.00 select beer; $2.00 off glasses of wine
$5.00 select wines (the good stuff)

**Atmosphere 3**
Wine bar, small plates and bottle shop housed in a sweet green home on 23rd Ave. Up a half-flight of stairs in a long room with refined, traditional style. Dark woods, cream walls, windows to the street, and pleasant outside patio dining.

Date visited: __________ **My Rating:** __________
Went with: ______________________________
Favorites: ______________________________
Not so much: ____________________________
Other comments: __________________________

# Teardrop Lounge 9

**Pearl Map**
1015 NW Everett
(503) 970-8331
www.teardroplounge.com

**Happy Hours**
4:00–7:00pm Mon–Fri

**Food Deals 2**
$3.00–$6.00
Always-changing the line-up with a couple of gourmet items like pear & arugula sandwich or a sugar snap pea salad; plus a couple of little snacks like a pickle plate or marinated olives.

**Drink Specials 3**
$5.00-$7.00 wine specials
$5.00–$6.00 specialty weekly cocktails (2-3)

**Atmosphere 3**
Attention to detail in every aspect of design almost brings a tear to my eye... It's gorgeous every step of the way from the bartenders and their magical mixology (the real focus), to the industrial chic and very cool decor. LOVE it!

Date visited: __________ **My Rating:** __________
Went with: ______________________________
Favorites: ______________________________
Not so much: ______________________________
Other comments: ______________________________
______________________________

# Touché

10 ★

**Pearl Map**
1425 NW Glisan
(503) 221-1150
www.touchepdx.com

**Happy Hours**
4:00-6:30pm and 10:00pm–close Daily
(Fri–Sat 3:00pm start time and 11:00pm–close)
★All day Sunday (4:00pm–2:30am)

**Food Deals 3**
$2.50–$6.50
Big menu and big servings! Gyros (chicken, lamb or veggie), wood-fired pizzas, salads, Mediterranean platter, spaghetti bolognese, lasagna, burger with fries, tiramisu(!), and more!

**Drink Specials 3**
$1.00 off drafts; $3.00 wells
$5.00 wines (choice of four)

**Atmosphere 3**
Happy Hour anywhere in the gorgeous restaurant downstairs, upstairs in the semi-stately pool hall, or out on the wonderful new patio(s)! Grand staircase entrance and six nice, full-size tables. Great for both stylish pool boys and true sharks.

Date visited: __________ **My Rating:** __________
Went with: ______________________
Favorites: ______________________
Not so much: ______________________
Other comments: ______________________

# Trader Vic's

10

**Pearl Map**
1203 NW Glisan; (503) 467-2277
www.tradervicspdx.com

**Happy Hours**
4:00–6:30pm and 10:00pm-close Mon–Fri
★All day Sunday (2:00pm–close)

**Food Deals 3**
A personal favorite!
$5.00
Tiki tidbits and plenty of "pupus": char sui pork, spicy calamari, spring rolls, Korean tacos, sliders, edamame, spiced fries and Shanghai Caesar.

**Drink Specials 3**
$1.00 off drafts and wells; $5.00 wine
$5.00 mai tais and signature tropical cocktails

**Atmosphere 3+**
A Polynesian piece of paradise in the Pearl! Refined, tropical, tiki elegance mixed with fun, fascination, and fire. It's fully enchanting and magical! Thatched ceilings and walls, bamboo and carved wooden masks everywhere, and a social, central tiki bar with themed cocktailware everywhere. Full walls of windows open to the street.

Date visited: __________ **My Rating:** __________
Went with: ____________________
Favorites: ____________________
Not so much: ____________________
Other comments: ____________________

# Uptown Billiards Club

10 A Happy Hour favorite!

**NW/Nob Hill Map**
120 NW 23rd Ave.
(503) 226-6909
www.uptownbilliards.com

**Happy Hours**
4:00–6:30pm Tues–Sat

**Food Deals 3+**
Half-price, 20-item bistro menu! Choose from six sandwiches/burgers, several soups and salads, five kinds of pizzas, and several bistro items.

**Drink Specials 3**
$3.00-$4.00 drafts; $5.00-$6.00 wines
$4.25–$6.00 cocktails ($1.00 off all of them)

**Atmosphere 3**
Totally different in the pool hall classification with its upscale class and elegence, spruced up in 2010. There's a nice, big room for playing pool, a gorgeous wooden bar, a small dining room and a private, tucked-away billiards room.

Date visited: ____________ **My Rating:** ____________
Went with: ____________________________________
Favorites: ____________________________________
Not so much: __________________________________
Other comments: _______________________________
______________________________________________

# Vault Martini

10

**Pearl Map**
226 NW 12th Ave.
(503) 224-4909
www.vault-martini.com

**Happy Hours**
4:00–7:00pm Daily; ★All day Sunday

A Happy Hour favorite!

**Food Deals 3**
$3.00-$6.00
A small menu of good drinking accompaniments like a charcuterie or cheese plate, bread and oil, olives, dolmas, caprese salad or bacon-wrapped dates. Order several items and share.

**Drink Specials 3+**
$3.00 Stellas; $5.00 house wines; $3.00 wells
$5.00 select cocktails (17 included at Happy Hour, but ask to see the full menu of 80+!)

**Atmosphere 3**
An absolute stand-out in Portland, and a classic, very classy bar not to be missed – and visited often. Gorgeous space with a fireplace, several lounge areas with very comfortable seating, and fine design and beauty everywhere you look.

Date visited: __________ **My Rating:** __________
Went with: ______________________________
Favorites: ______________________________
Not so much: ______________________________
Other comments: ______________________________
______________________________

# Via Delizia

7

**Pearl Map**
1105 NW Marshall
(503) 225-9300
www.viadelizia.com

A Happy Hour favorit

**Happy Hours**
3:00–6:00pm Sun–Fri

**Food Deals 2**
$4.00–$6.00
Good portions and great food! Bruschetta, salads, ravioli, spaghetti alla bolognese, pork panini, and several flatbreads (steak, chicken or caprese). Be sure to save room for the gelato!

**Drink Specials 0**
Sadly, no drink deals, but low prices at all times.

**Atmosphere 3**
A giant tree dominates overhead and creates a pleasant patio piazza scene inside. Hanging tree lights, stone walls, an arched wooden doorway and shutters on windows help transport you to Italy. Cozy little Italian streetside café!

Date visited: ____________ **My Rating:** ____________
Went with: ____________________________
Favorites: ____________________________
Not so much: ____________________________
Other comments: ____________________________
____________________________________________

# Voicebox Karaoke

10

**NW/Nob Hill Map**
2112 NW Hoyt
(503) 303-8220
www.voiceboxpdx.com

**Happy Hours**
4:00–7:00pm Thurs–Sun ($4.00/hr. Karaoke)
Tuesdays – $10.00 covers your karaoke cost!
★Wednesdays – All night Happy Hour

A Happy Hour favorite!

**Food Deals 3**
$1.00 off all menu items
New, unique, Asian-focused menu with lots of snacks and small plates: soba noodles, chicken or tofu banh mi, quesadillas, sandwiches, pizza.

**Drink Specials 3**
$1.00 off all beer, wine, saké, and saké cocktails ($3.00 micros, $5.00 house wines)

**Atmosphere 3**
Rent private "boxes" and never stop singing (or laughing as the case may be—it's a blast!). High-style space-age Japanese pop decor with Pander Bros. art, ultramod hanging lamps and high-def big-screen TVs. It's a super-happy place!

Date visited: ____________ **My Rating:** ____________
Went with: ______________________________
Favorites: ______________________________
Not so much: ______________________________
Other comments: ______________________________
______________________________________________

# Wild Wasabe 7

**NW/Nob Hill Map**
2330 NW Thurman
(503) 242-6404
www.wildwasabe.com

**Happy Hours**
3:00–5:00pm Mon–Fri

**Food Deals 3**
$1.00–$4.00
Several options at each price point including ten kinds of rolls (California, tuna, salmon, shrimp, etc.), plus a number of appetizers like miso soup, egg rolls, gyoza, and a couple of salads.

**Drink Specials 0**
Sadly, no drink specials.

**Atmosphere 3**
A tucked-away Japanese Bistro that's not too wild at all, but rather serene and refined in decor and attitude. Big open space with giant windows along the front. Keep your eye on this immediate neighborhood for more new and recent newcomers. It's growing...

Date visited: ____________ **My Rating:** ____________
Went with: ____________
Favorites: ____________
Not so much: ____________
Other comments: ____________

# Wildwood

7

**NW/Nob Hill Map**
1221 NW 21st Ave.
(503) 248-9663
www.wildwoodrestaurant.com

**Happy Hours**
4:30–6:30pm Mon–Fri (Bar and patio only)

**Food Deals 1**
$2.00–$3.00
A few light munchies to match your thirst: fries, truffled popcorn, onion rings, french fries or maybe some fried Corona beans. "No Somm Sundays" – no corkage fees on Sunday night!

**Drink Specials 3**
$2.00–$3.00 beer; $5.00 select wine
$5.00 choice of 12 signature cocktails

**Atmosphere 3**
As Northwest good as it gets, but in an understated way. Small bar area with stone, slate, wood, and gridded windows. Enjoy the patio outside at Happy Hour! Summer brings Tuesday and Thursday outdoor BBQs (early dinner hours).

Date visited: __________ **My Rating:** __________
Went with: ______________________________
Favorites: ______________________________
Not so much: ______________________________
Other comments: ______________________________
______________________________

# Wilfs

7

**Pearl (off map)**
800 NW 6th Avenue (Union Station)
(503) 223-0070
www.wilfsrestaurant.com

**Happy Hours**
5:30–7:00pm Tues–Fri

**Food Deals 3**
$3.50–$6.00
Half-off limited seasonal bar menu items like French onion soup, calamari, bread pudding, pizza, salads, or white bean dip.

**Drink Specials 0**
Sadly, no drink specials

**Atmosphere 3**
A beautiful, top-notch Portland classic that falls off the radar, but has a great Happy Hour! Enjoy a fancy evening out in their classy jazz lounge, then stick around to hear some live music later. Truly a special place when you're in the mood for a wonderful night!

Date visited: __________ **My Rating:** __________
Went with: ______________________________
Favorites: ______________________________
Not so much: ______________________________
Other comments: ______________________________

______________________________

# Yama Sushi

9

**Pearl Map**
926 NW 10th Ave.
(503) 841-5463
www.yamasushiandsakebar.com

**Happy Hours**
5:00–6:30pm Mon–Thur

**Food Deals 3**
$2.00-$6.00
A dozen small hot plates (two ramen dishes, homemade gyoza, calamari, shrimp tempura, edamame, yakitori chicken, and more); and six sushis (four rolls – California, spicy or crunch-spicy tuna, or salmon), plus sushi – tempura salmon or tempura snapper.

**Drink Specials 2**
$3.00 Japanese small beers; $4.00 house wines
$4.00–$7.00 sakés

**Atmosphere 3**
Nice place with front lounge and dining room divider of old pieces from a Japanese xylophone. Full sushi bar acoss the back, and a long dining area with two rows of tables, cushioned chairs.

Date visited: ____________ **My Rating:** ____________
Went with: ____________________________________
Favorites: ____________________________________
Not so much: __________________________________
Other comments: ________________________________
________________________________________________

## 21st Avenue Bar & Grill

**NW/Nob Hill Map** 721 NW 21st Ave; (503) 222-4121

**Happy Hours** 3:00–6:00pm Mon–Fri (Drink specials) Open–6:00pm Daily (Food deals)

**Food Deals 2** $3.50 Tons of bar food cheapies like mac & cheese, nachos, totchos, salads, spring rolls, quesadilla, veggie curry – and fried twinkie sundae!

**Drink Specials 2** $1.50 PBR; $2.50 micros and wells

**Atmosphere 2** Dive bar without too much character, but with a secret, surprisingly cute back patio area!

## Basta's Trattoria

**NW/Nob Hill Map** 410 NW 21st Ave; (503) 274-1572 www.bastastrattoria.com

**Happy Hours** 5:00-6:30pm; 10:00pm-close Daily

**Food Deals 2** No extra discounts at happy hour, just the regular bar menu with about 12 unusual samplings with seasonal updates. Check out owner, Chef Marco Frattaroli's, new SE place, Cibo.

**Drink Specials 2** $1.00 off all beers; $2.00 off glass of any wine; $6.00 well cocktails

**Atmosphere 2** Cool mural paintings; kidney shapes and velvet drapes; outdoor sidewalk seating.

## Blitzbar Pearl

**Pearl Map** 110 NW 10th Ave; (503) 222-2229 www.blitzbarpdx.net

**Happy Hours** 3:00–6:00pm and 9:00pm-close Daily

**Food Deals 2** $1.95–$4.95 Similar menu as other Blitzes

**Drink Specials 3** $2.00 domestics; $3.00 micros $5.00 house wines; $3.00 wells

**Atmosphere 2** Sporty, designed-on-a-dime collegiate feel with game room. Tables and booths surrounding one big central bar, spanning two rooms. Outdoor patio seating. Head to the downstairs level.

## Cha Cha Cha www.chachachapdx.com

**Pearl Map** 1208 NW Gilsan; (503) 221-2111

**Happy Hours** 3:00–6:00pm Daily

**Food Deals 3** $4.00 Nice array of homemade Mexican: tostadas, fish tacos, quesadillas, burritos, salads.

**Drink Specials 2** $3.00 beer; $5.00 wine
$4.75 Margaritas (unique and tasty!)

**Atmosphere 2** There are now eight ChaChaChas! Convenient location in the heart of the Pearl, but decor and vibe are very casual for this part of the city. Colorful and vibrant with sidewalk seating too.

## Daily Café www.dailycafe.net

**NW/Nob Hill Map** 902 NW 13th Ave; (503) 242-1916

**Happy Hours** 3:30–6:00pm Mon–Fri

**Food Deals 2** $2.00–$5.00 About 10 standards that cover all the bases, plus a daily dessert! Caesar salad, pickle plate, veggie slider, fritto, fries, pasta, ice cream.

**Drink Specials 2** $3.50 drafts; $1.00 off 1/2 liter wine

**Atmosphere 2** It seems more like a breakfast or lunch spot than a place to go for drinks, but it's location, service, food, low prices, and café-style freshness often fit the bill for a refreshing visit.

## Dorio www.dorionw.com

**NW/Nob Hill Map** 1037 NW 23rd Ave; (503) 219-0633

**Happy Hours** 3:00–6:00pm Mon–Sat

**Food Deals 2** Good samplings of tasty Greek food: tyropites (phyllo dough triangles of cheese), hummus plate, skewers, tzatziki, feta and olives.

**Drink Specials 3** $2.00 domestics; $3.00 micros
$4.00 wines; $4.00 wells; $6.00 martinis

**Atmosphere 2** A kind of urban Greek bistro. It's an L-shaped room, so it's a somewhat awkward use of space, but fine in the front area if you think of it as a bar. Big windows with just a little charm.

## Hobo's www.hobospdx.com

**Old Town Map** 120 NW 3rd Ave.; (503) 224-3285

**Happy Hours** 4:00–7:00pm Sun–Fri

**Food Deals 2** $3.00–$4.00 Classic pub grub done well: calamari, fish tacos, buffalo hot wings, oyster shooters, cheese fries, quesadilla, and mac & cheese.

**Drink Specials 2** $1.00 off beer and wells

**Atmosphere 3** Beautiful, turn-of-the-century, old Portland charm; positioned directly over the haunted Shanghai Tunnels and the starting point for the ghostly Portland Underground Tours.

## Jinx Lounge www.jinxlounge.com

**Pearl Map** 232 12th Ave.; (503) 922-0178

**Happy Hours** 4:00–7:00pm Mon–Sat; 9:30pm–close Tues–Thur; ★All night Mondays

**Food Deals 3** $3.00–$6.00 About a dozen appetizers and really good food! Menu changes somewhat with Thai-focused treats like mussels, wontons, potstickers, curry, pad thai, coconut prawns, tom yum soup.

**Drink Specials 3**
$3.00 Stellas or PBR; $5.00 house wines;
$3.00 wells; $5.00 select cocktails (must-see menu!)

**Atmosphere 3** Laid-back, retro vibe and decor without being over the top. Deep red walls adorned with funky artwork and fabulous flea market finds.

## Life of Riley

**Pearl Map** 300 NW 10th Ave.; (503) 224-1680

**Happy Hours** 4:00–7:00pm Daily ★All day Sunday

**Food Deals 2** $3.00–$7.00 Tasty basics like buffalo wings, fries, kettle chips, sliders, tofu tacos, oysters.

**Drink Specials 2** $2.00 domestics; $3.00 drafts (good tap list!); $1.00 off wine, wells, cocktails

**Atmosphere 2** Large and open navy-colored room; semi-retro, semi-Irish decor. Rare, ultra-casual option in contrast to other Pearl restaurants.

## Melt www.meltportland.com

**NW/Nob Hill Map** 716 NW 21st Ave.; (503) 295-4944

**Happy Hours** 2:00pm–close Mon–Sat

**Food Deals** $3.00–$6.00 Big deals on their 20+ item appetizer menu with salads, sliders, soups and more.

**Drink Specials** $4.25 drafts; $5.00 cocktails

**Atmosphere** New owner gilded/golded up the joint and continues the all-day Happy Hour tradition. Central bar/service station. Popular place! Sidewallk HH.

## Moonshine Kitchen

**Pearl Map** 1020 NW 17th Ave.; (503) 943-2780 www.moonshinekitchen.com

**Happy Hours** 2:00–6:00pm Mon–Fri

**Drink Specials 2** $3.50 drafts; $3.00 wells

**Food Deals 0** No Happy Hour discounts, but food is good and cheap. Giant and GREAT $7.00 burgers!

**Atmosphere 2** New-ish, super-casual corner tavern. Old ceramic moonshine bottles adorn the high shelves, and deep into the nighttime darkness, the whole place really shines. Be aware that it's a loud bar...

## Muu-Muu's www.muumuus.net

**NW/Nob Hill Map** 612 NW 21st Ave.; (503) 223-8169

**Happy Hours** 3:00–7:00pm Daily

**Food Deals 2** $4.00-$7.00 BIG small plates menu with a bit of *everything!* Spicy wings, pork tacos, wasabi tuna, salads, calamari, hummus plate, steak bites, potstickers, fish & chips, satay, ribs, tacos.

**Drink Specials 3** $2.00 PBRs; $3.50 wells & micro-brews; $4.00 well martinis

**Atmosphere 2** Chill, traveler's-style bar with black tin ceiling tiles, orange hanging lights, velvet drapes, giant urn lamps, and tiny bubble lights.

## Northwest Public House

**NW/Nob Hill Map** 2327 NW Kearney; (503) 228-5553
www.northwestpublichouse.com

**Happy Hours** 3:00–6:00pm and 9:00pm–close Daily

**Food Deals 2** $5.00 Hot wings, Lugan special (potato cake), salad, spicy hummus. Great food quality, variety, and prices on regular menu. Lots of gluten-free fare!

**Drink Specials 3** $3.00 cans/draft beers; $5.00 wine
$4.00 wells; $5.00 Moscow Mule

**Atmosphere 3** Cute! It's really a house, made into a pub, and made to feel like home. Nice outdoor decks both upstairs and down, and plenty of big-screen TVs.

## On Deck Sports

**Pearl Map** 910 NW 14th Ave.; (503) 227-7020
www.ondecksportsbar.com

**Happy Hours** 3:30–6:30pm Mon–Fri; 9:00pm–mid Daily
Note: No HH during Ducks or Beavers games

**Food Deals 2** $2.00–5.00 16 item bar menu: nachos, Caesar, chicken strips or burgers w/fries, taquitos, chips & salsa, pork, beef or turkey sliders, hummus.

**Drink Specials 2** $2.75 domestics; $3.75 micros
$4.00 wines; $3.50 wells; $4.00 flavored Smirnoff

**Atmosphere 3** Really as nice as a sports bar can be: wall-to-wall windows; hi-tech wavy black ceiling tiles; hi-def TVs. Outdoor deck gets even better at night!

## Santa Fe www.santafetaqueria.com

**NW/Nob Hill Map** 831 NW 23rd Ave.; (503) 220-0406

**Happy Hours** 3:00–6:00pm and 9:00pm–close Daily

**Food Deals 2** $3.75–$5.75 Big menu of 15 items covering all the Mexican and texmex basics.

**Drink Specials 3** $.50 off drafts; $5.00 wine
$3.75 wells; $4.75 Margaritas

**Atmosphere 2** A popular, neighborhood watering hole. Good for trivia and outdoor sidewalk seating. Sit anywhere in the restaurant. Good for families too.

## Splash Bar www.splashbarpdx.com

**Pearl Map** 904 NW Couch; (503) 893-5551

**Happy Hours** 5:00–7:00pm Tues-Sat; ★All night Wed
Drink deals 'til 10:00pm

**Food Deals 2** $2.00 off Burgers, sliders, and all the bar food basics, plus several great (and giant) salads. Daily $5.00 fish & chips and $1.00 Taco Tuesdays.

**Drink Specials 2** $3.00 select micro and domestics
$4.00 wines; $3.50 wells; plus rotating nighlty specials

**Atmosphere 2** Formerly Candy, now a decked out Margaritaville nightclub, with a customized VW bus converted into a shot bar. Surf stuff hanging everywhere it possibly can, with a lifesize Captain Morgan statue overseeing the central, high-energy dance floor.

## Sushi Land (Marinepolis)

**Pearl Map** 138 NW 10th Ave; (503) 546-9933
www.sushilandusa.com

**Happy Hours** 5:00–7:00pm Daily

**Food Deals 2** $1.50 off larger size special rolls (4)

**Drink Specials 3** $1.00 off drafts; $4.00 wine
$3.50 wells; $5.00 select cocktail

**Atmosphere 2** An upstairs bar awaits – eye-level with the black ceiling ductwork, you'll overlook the diner below. Simple, but nice enough at night.

Remember to check our website every once in a while for changes and closures.

**www.happyhourguidebook.com**

And please let us know if you see information that needs changing.

*See Alberta map next page*

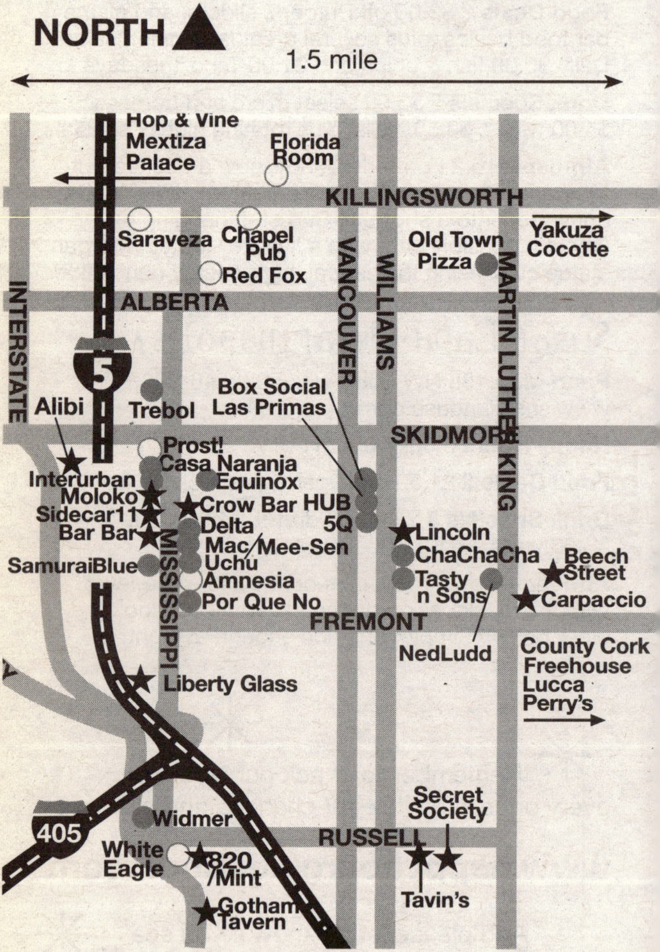

# Alberta & Fremont

*Note: Streets do not align.*

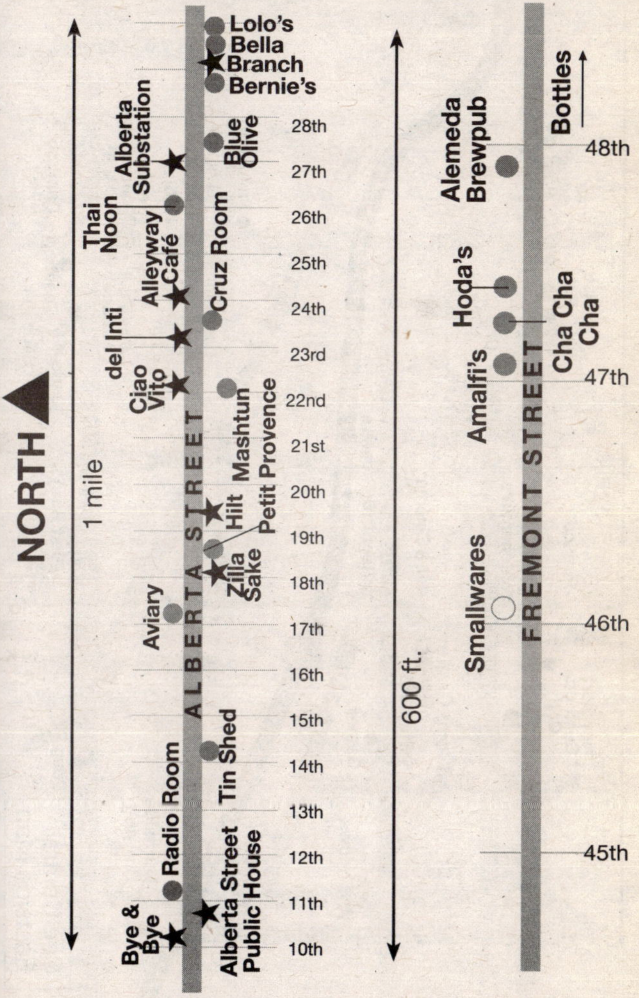

# Lloyd Center-ish

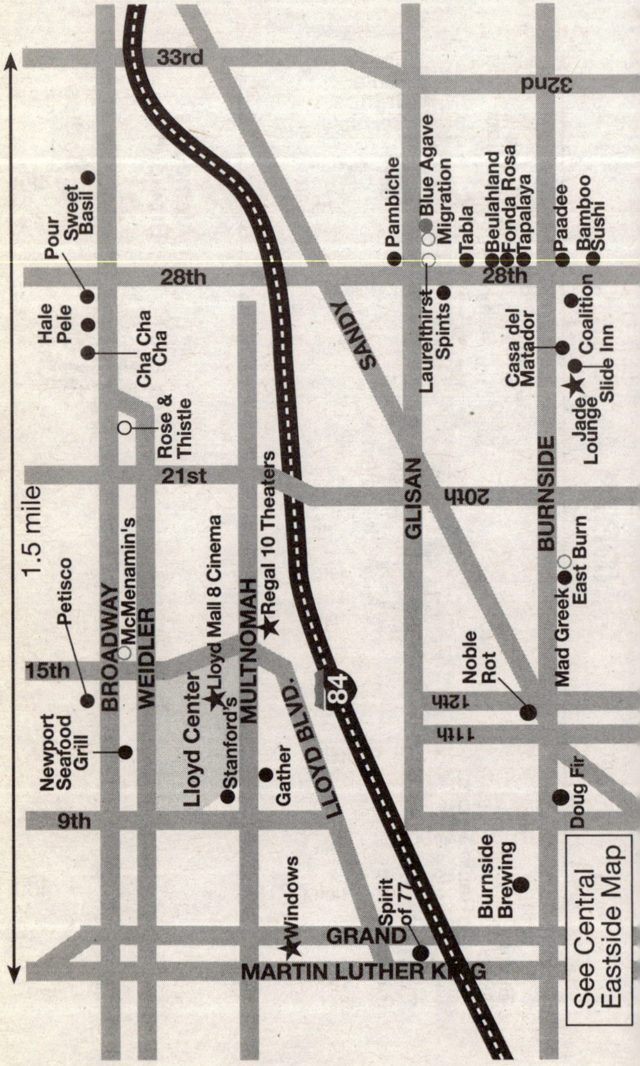

# Alberta Substation 8

**Alberta Map**
2703 NE Alberta
(503) 284-4491
www.albertasubstation.com

**Happy Hours**
4:00–7:00pm Daily; All night Monday

**Food Deals 2**
$3.50–$5.50
Sportsbar pub fare with just a touch of flair: Korean tacos, oyster shooters, garlic herb fries, salad, hummus, nachos, mac & cheese, Buffalo chicken sliders, and Louisiana hot links.

**Drink Specials 2**
$3.50 Dos Equis; $4.00 drafts; $5.00 house wine
$4.00 wells; $5.00 Back 9 cocktail

**Atmosphere 3**
Formerly Siam Society – Big city, award-winning design in artfully renovated old power station. Happy Hour is anywhere in the restaurant or out on their peaceful, outdoor patio. New bar struggling with an identity crisis, but expect the best with pub specialist new owners from North 45.

Date visited: ____________ **My Rating:** ____________
Went with: ______________________________
Favorites: ______________________________
Not so much: ______________________________
Other comments: ______________________________

______________________________

# Amalfi's ★ 10

**Fremont Map**
4703 NE Fremont St.
(503) 284-6747
www.amalfisrestaurant.com

**Happy Hours**
4:00–6:00pm Tues-Fri; 3:00pm–6:00pm Sat-Sun
9:00pm-close Tues-Sun

Happy Hour of the Year 2011

**Food Deals 3**
$3.00-$4.00
Enjoy over a dozen zesty Italian eats: pizzas, pastas, shrimp scampi, soup, bruschetta, prawns, plus caprese, Caesar and Greek salads.

**Drink Specials 2**
$3.00 Coors Light; $5.00 house red or white wine

**Atmosphere 3**
For more than 50 years, Amalfi's has served up some of Portland's best Italian food, and is still to this day, a much-beloved icon. Comfy yet contemporary, romantic and still social. Table-top fireplaces both inside and out. Great patio!

Date visited: ____________ **My Rating:** ____________
Went with: ______________________________
Favorites: ______________________________
Not so much: ______________________________
Other comments: ______________________________
______________________________

# Aviary

10

**Alberta Map**
1733 NE Alberta
(503) 287-2400
www.aviarypdx.com

**Happy Hours**
5:00–7:00pm Mon-Fri

**Food Deals 3**
$2.00-$6.00
You are in for a treat! Happy Hour is taken up a notch with a very unique and eclectic, seasonal menu with items like tempura pumpkin, summer squash fritters, brussel sprout nachos, or oysters. Check out the dinner menu before biting on HH!

**Drink Specials 3**
$3.00 drafts; $5.00 house wines
$5.00 wells; $6.00 daily cocktail specials

**Atmosphere 3**
Happy Hour is inside all the way in the back in the very cool, dark and cozy bar area, or outside out front on the plaza style, street-side patio. One of Portland's top "chef-driven" restaurants!

Date visited: __________ **My Rating:** __________
Went with: ______________________________
Favorites: ______________________________
Not so much: ______________________________
Other comments: ______________________________
______________________________

# Bamboo Sushi 10

**Northwest/Nob Hill Map**
836 NW 23rd Ave; (971) 229-1925

**Lloyd Center Map** 310 SE 28th; (503) 232-5255
www.bamboosushi.com

**Happy Hours**
4:00–6:00pm Mon–Fri (4:30 start SE location)

**Food Deals 3** $1.00–$7.00 Bamboo Sushi has some of the best sushi in town! Nigiri set, inari, daily hand rolls, vegetable roll, spicy albacore and NW Philly rolls. Non-sushi items too: truffled potatoes, salad, mushrooms, veggie tempura, salmon, brisket, grilled beef flank.

**Drink Specials 3**
$3.00 drafts; $4.00 wine; $4.00–$7.00 sake

**Atmosphere 3**
Both restaurants are quite similar in layout and overall style. Serene and cozy with focus on sustainability and Japanese simplicity. Dark browns, tans and white; carpeted with patterned pillows on bench seating and origami fish art.

Date visited: ____________ **My Rating:** ____________
Went with: ______________________________
Favorites: ______________________________
Not so much: ______________________________
Other comments: ______________________________

# Bar Lolo

9

**Alberta Map**
2940 NE Alberta St
(503) 288-3400
www.barlolo.com

**Happy Hours**
4:30–6:30pm Tues–Fri; ★All night Wed
10:00pm–close Tues–Fri (drinks only)

**Food Deals 2**
$4.00–$6.00 ($2.00 off)
Unique Spanish nibbles like spiced meatballs, chicken skewers, calamari, empanadas, sliders.

**Drink Specials 3**
$3.50 drafts; $5.00 house wines; $4.00 sangria
$5.00 Margaritas

**Atmosphere 3**
Upscale tapas bar; big, open room with floor-to-ceiling windows along Alberta Street; simple style with neutral tones and chalkboard menus. Originally called Lolo (new owners).

Date visited: ____________ **My Rating:** ____________
Went with: ______________________________
Favorites: ______________________________
Not so much: ______________________________
Other comments: ______________________________
______________________________________________

# Bernie's Southern Bistro

9

**Alberta Map**
2904 NE Alberta
(503) 282-9864
www.berniesbistro.com

**Happy Hours**
4:00–6:00pm Tues–Sun

**Food Deals 3**
$4.00
Gourmet southern samplers including Po' Boys, fried green tomatoes, bread pudding, veggie salad, sweet potato fries, mac & cheese, fried pickles, meatloaf sandwich, hush puppies.

**Drink Specials 2**
$5.00 house wines; $5.00 cocktail specials

**Atmosphere 3**
Serene and outstanding outdoor garden patio, and they even let you sit outside for Happy Hour. Absolutely lovely! Simple, fine-dining, romantic interior. Casual bar.

Date visited: ____________ **My Rating:** ____________
Went with: ______________________________
Favorites: ______________________________
Not so much: ____________________________
Other comments. __________________________
__________________________________________

# Blue Agave

10 ★

**Lloyd Center-ish Map**
2828 NE Glisan
(503) 206-85421

**Happy Hours**
5:00–6:30pm Daily

**Food Deals 3**
$4.00-$6.00
Really great food here! About 20 tapas with salads, empanadas, ceviches, flank steak, Spanish omelette, chicken, pork, garlic shrimp, stuffed mushrooms, fried squid, and desserts!

**Drink Specials 3**
$4.00 beer; $5.00 house wine; $5.00 Margarita
$7.00 flavored Margaritas and lots of cocktails

**Atmosphere 3**
Garage style space partially shared with the courtyard/patio of Migration Brewing. Roll-up doors, floor-to-ceiling windows, light wood tables, terra cotta walls, illuminated bar back, blue floral lamps. Front bar and side restaurant.

Date visited: ____________ **My Rating:** ____________
Went with: ______________________________
Favorites: ______________________________
Not so much: ____________________________
Other comments: _________________________
_________________________________________

# Box Social

10

A Happy Hour favorite!

**NE Map**
3971 N Williams
(503) 288-1111
www.bxsocial.com

**Happy Hours**
4:00–6:00pm Daily: 11:00pm–close Sun–Thurs

**Food Deals 3**
$2.00–$5.00
Small menu, but it's one worth repeating often! Parmesan popcorn, field greens salad, hummus plate, spinach spread, and a craveable grilled cheese sandwich served with *yummy* tomato soup.

**Drink Specials 3**
$4.00 drafts; $4.00 house wine
$4.00 select wells; $6.00 signature craft cocktails

**Atmosphere 3**
Light, cool and contemporary by day; dark, sizzling, and seductive by night. The Box Social bills itself as a friendly and relaxing "drinking parlour". Fresh, urban style with a welcoming, neighborhood feel. Exquisite cocktailing!

Date visited: ____________ **My Rating:** ____________
Went with: ________________________________
Favorites: ________________________________
Not so much: ______________________________
Other comments: ___________________________
___________________________________________

# Buffalo Wild Wings

8

**Lloyd Center**
1200 NE Broadway
(503) 432-8179
www.buffalowildwings.com

EIGHT locations throughout Portland:

**Cascade Station** 9810 Cascades Pkwy; (503) 281-0351
**Downtown** 327 SW Morrison; (503) 224-1309
**Hazel Dell (Vancouver)** 7704 NE 5th; (360) 597-3486
**Beaverton** 11995 SW Beav-Hills Hwy; (503) 352-9503
**Wood Village** 22849 NE Glisan; (503) 328-9475
**Hillsboro** 2219 NW Allie; (503) 645-9424
**Tualatin** 8505 SW Tualatin Sherwood; (503) 486-5295

**Happy Hours**
3:00-6:00pm Mon-Fri /9:00pm–close Daily

**Food Deals 2** $3.00 Ten top bar bites

**Drink Specials 3**
$1.00 off beer (decent line-up of microbrews)
$3.00 wine; $3.50 select cocktails (three)

**Atmosphere 2**
Sporty, collegiate atmosphere that's good clean fun for everyone; hi-def TVs *everywhere*.

Date visited: __________ **My Rating:** __________
Went with: ______________________________
Favorites: ______________________________
Not so much: ______________________________
Other comments: ______________________________
______________________________

# Carpaccio

9 ★

**North/NE Map**
3500 NE MLK Jr Bvd.
(503) 972-4252
www.carpacciotrattoria.com

**Happy Hours**
4:00–8:00pm Mon–Fri

**Food Deals 3**
$4.00-$6.00
Nice big menu! More than a dozen Italian small plates like Caesar or Mediterranean salads, clams, shrimp, mussels, calamari, chicken marsala, ciabatta with tomato, steak and cheese, or goat cheese and sauce, plus other pastas.

**Drink Specials 2**
$3.00–$4.00 beer; $5.00 house wines
$4.00 wells

**Atmosphere 3**
Formerly the space occupied by Belly, and quite similar in look. Happy Hour is at the bar only, but it's all quite open to the restaurant. Friendly and comfortable, fresh, new and contemporary. Big wall of wine at entry in bar. Sidewalk patio.

Date visited: ____________ **My Rating:** ____________
Went with: ______________________________
Favorites: ______________________________
Not so much: ______________________________
Other comments: ______________________________
______________________________

# Casa Naranja

9

**NE/Mississippi Map**
4205 N Mississippi
(503) 459-4049
www.casanaranjapdx.com

**Happy Hours**
4:00–6:00pm Tues–Sun; 10:00pm–close Tues–Sat

**Food Deals 2**
$4.00–$7.00
Seasonal menu rotates (it's not Mexican food as the name may lead you to think): bruschetta, salads, calamari, spicy wings, meatballs, burgers.

**Drink Specials 3**
$2.00 PBR tall boys; $1.00 off drafts
$1.00 off house wines; $3.75 wells

**Atmosphere 3**
Super cute, very orange two-story Victorian house. Homey touches inside with original artwork, candles and fresh flowers; but it's all about the front, back, and side deck and patio areas complete with tiki torches and umbrellas.

Date visited: __________ **My Rating:** __________
Went with: ______________________________
Favorites: ______________________________
Not so much: ____________________________
Other comments: __________________________
__________________________________________

# Ciao Vito

**10**

**Alberta Map**
2203 NE Alberta
(503) 282-5522
www.ciaovito.net

**Happy Hours**
5:00–7:00pm Daily; 9:00-10:00pm Daily (food)

**Food Deals 3**
$5.00–$7.00
Wow! Giant array of 15 or so seasonal, mostly Spanish-influenced menu items: beef & potato or Moroccan lamb croquettes, garlic prawns, pork belly sandwich, octopus carpaccio, fried quail egg on toast, potato bravas, skirt steak.

**Drink Specials 3**
$3.00 pints; $5.00 wines
$5.00–$7.00 specialty cocktails

**Atmosphere 3**
Classic elegance with warmth and style, nice neighborhood welcoming feel with bright and funky mural on outside side wall.

Date visited: ____________ **My Rating:** ____________
Went with: ________________________________________
Favorites: ________________________________________
Not so much: ______________________________________
Other comments: ___________________________________
___________________________________________________

# Cocotte

10

**Northeast (off map)**
2930 NE Killingsworth
(503) 227-2669
www.cocottepdx.com

**Happy Hours**
9:00pm-close Tues-Sat; ★5:00pm-close Sun-Mon
5:00–6:30pm Tues–Sat (HH on Drink deals only)

A Happy Hour favorite!

**Food Deals 3**
$3.00-$5.00-$8.00
Big changes with a BIG menu of 20 or so joyeux small plates: pork belly banh mi, crepes, soups, creamy polenta, baked brie, spring greens, +++!

**Drink Specials 2**
$1.00 off drafts and house cocktails; $5.00 wines
$5.00 apertifs (with a lengthy list to choose from)

**Atmosphere 3**
Trés cute! Sweet and cozy little corner café with a wall of paned windows/doors that open to the street, thick floor length curtains, Country-French decor and accents, and fresh flowers. A great word to know, "Cocotte" essentially means cute little hen/honey/love/stewpan.

Date visited: ____________ **My Rating:** ____________
Went with: ______________________________
Favorites: ______________________________
Not so much: ______________________________
Other comments: ______________________________
______________________________

# Equinox

10

**North/NE Map**
830 N Shaver St
(503) 460-3333
www.equinoxrestaurantpdx.com

**Happy Hours**
4:00–6:00pm Tues–Fri (plus Mondays in summer)

**Food Deals 3**
$3.00–$6.50
Menu with about a dozen items. Varies with the seasons with unique items like chickpea crepe, beets and bleu, duck confit sliders, seasonal salad, mushroom bites, fettuccine, calamari, soup, truffle fries, or delicious cheese burger.

**Drink Specials 3**
$3.00 drafts; $5.00 wine; $4.00 wells
$5.50 specialty cocktails

**Atmosphere 3**
Enter through their delightful front patio (where you can enjoy Happy Hour, weather permitting). Inside, it's warm and woody throughout with old, rough wood floors, natural wood tables, and paneled half-walls. Skylight and garage door.

Date visited: ____________ **My Rating:** ____________
Went with: ________________________________________
Favorites: ________________________________________
Not so much: ______________________________________
Other comments: ___________________________________
__________________________________________________

# Firehouse

9

**North/NE (off map)**
711 NE Dekum
(503) 954-1702
www.firehousepdx.com

**Happy Hours**
5:00–6:00pm Daily

**Food Deals 3**
$3.00–$11.00
Delicious but limited and somewhat pricey menu. Items like a roasted beet salad, wood-fired pizza, meatballs, and fried cauliflower.

**Drink Specials 2**
$3.50–$4.00 select drafts; $5.00 wines

**Atmosphere 3**
A very cool building from the outside and in, and on its own triangular block. Firehouse 29 from the early 1900s has been renovated with lots of sweat and dreams and now houses one of the city's cutest Happy Hour places. Smokin' patio allows Happy Hour dining!

Date visited: __________ **My Rating:** __________
Went with: ______________________________
Favorites: ______________________________
Not so much: ____________________________
Other comments: __________________________
__________________________________________

# Fonda Rosa

9

**Lloyd Center-ish Map**
108 NE 28th Ave.
(503) 235-3828

**Happy Hours**
4:30–6:00pm Tues–Sun

**Food Deals 3**
$3.00–$6.00
Solid neighborhood fave! Spinach w/goat cheese tacoyos, ceviche or veggie tostadas, beet and avocado salad, chicken torta, and tasty tacos with chicken, meat or salmon.

**Drink Specials 3**
$3.00 drafts; $5.00 wine selections;
$5.00-$6.00 Margarita or cosmo; $6.00 sangria

**Atmosphere 2**
Simple in style with two bars; the narrow room is flanked by windows along 28th for lots of light and has a diner/coffeeshop feel by day, lounge by night.

Date visited: __________ **My Rating:** __________
Went with: ____________________
Favorites: ____________________
Not so much: ____________________
Other comments: ____________________

# Gather

9

**North/NE Map**
1000 NE Mulnomah
(503) 331-4943
www.gatherportland.com

**Happy Hours**
4:00–6:00pm Mon–Fri

**Food Deals 3**
$2.50–$7.50
A full half-off their seasonal bar menu, offering several gluten-free choices like quinoa-crusted chicken, wings, mussels and hazelnuts. Also burgers, grilled cheese, pork sliders or calamari.

**Drink Specials 3**
$4.00 drafts, house wines, wells, and margaritas

**Atmosphere 3**
Wide open to the lobby, but get a little past that and there are several nice seating areas. Modern space with a flair for Northwest taste and style. Recycled boards from an old Jim Beam distillery, giant log beams overhead, and a cool fireplace. Great location for movie at Lloyd Center! Free parking validation (two hours).

Date visited: ____________ **My Rating:** ____________
Went with: ________________________________
Favorites: ________________________________
Not so much: ______________________________
Other comments: ___________________________
___________________________________________

# Gotham Tavern

9

**North/NE Map**
2240 N Interstate
(503) 517-9911
www.gothamtavern.com

**Happy Hours**
4:00–7:00pm and 9:00pm–close Mon-Sat

**Food Deals 3**
$3.00-$4.00
Big and tasty menu: steak & cheese, red corn tortilla, onion battered green beans, wings, pepperjack quesadilla or nachos, artichoke dip w/ sun-dried tomatoes, burger, shrimp, edamame.

**Drink Specials 2**
$2.00 Sessions, PBR, and Bud; $1.00 off drafts and wells; Other occasional nightly specials

**Atmosphere 3**
Amazing, artistic woodwork divides bar from dining room and if you're lucky, you'll get a rare opportunity to drink and dine inside your own private egg (see for yourself). Outside HH too. Prime location for Rose Quarter pre-show fun!

Date visited: __________ **My Rating:** __________
Went with: ______________________________
Favorites: ______________________________
Not so much: ____________________________
Other comments: _________________________

# Hale Pele

7

**Central Eastside Map**
2733 NE Broadway
(503) 662-8454
www.halepele.com

**Happy Hours**
5:00–6:00pm Mon–Sat

**Food Deals 1**
$5.00
Really just one chef's special plate (such as the kimchi dog, pork fried rice, chao tom, etc.).

**Drink Specials 2**
$3.00 beer; $2.00 off tiki drinks and craft cocktails

**Atmosphere 3**
Now owned by master mixologist, Blair Reynolds, of B.G. Reynolds exotic syrups fame. It's the old Thatch all shined up, and now with a full kitchen behind the scenes. Still a mecca for every tiki aficionado, decorated with extreme personality and true respect and aesthetic of 50s/60s-style tiki lounge. Big tiki Gods, blowfish lights and a fun back tiki hut for groups (or just two).

Date visited: ____________ **My Rating:** ____________
Went with: ______________________________
Favorites: ______________________________
Not so much: ____________________________
Other comments: __________________________
_________________________________________

# Hoda's

8

**North/NE Map**
4727 NE Fremont
(503) 688-5577
Southeast 3401 SE Belmont; 503-236-8325
www.hodas.com

**Happy Hours**
2:30–5:30pm Monday–Friday

**Food Deals 2**
$3.00–$5.00
Short but tasty and traditional menu: hummus, tabouleh bites, fried spicy potatoes, baby kafta burgers, falafel plate, feta salad, and delicious zaatar and spinach pies.

**Drink Specials 3**
$3.00 beer; $4.00 wines; $5.00 specialty cocktail

**Atmosphere 2**
Very simple little café spot. Cozy, open room with tile floors and a small corner bar area. Per their website, in Arabic, "Hoda" means enlightenments and many use the word to exchange friendly, warm wishes with one another. This Fremont location is new this year, while the more authentic Belmont location was opened in 1999.

Date visited: ____________ **My Rating:** ____________
Went with: ________________________________
Favorites: ________________________________
Not so much: ______________________________
Other comments: ___________________________
___________________________________________

# Interurban 10

**North/NE Map**
4057 N Mississippi
(503) 284-6669
www.interurbanpdx.com

**Happy Hours**
4:00–6:00pm Mon–Fri; 10:00pm–close Sunday

**Food Deals 3**
$3.00–$5.00
Polenta croquettes, BBQ sandwich, quesadilla, French onion soup, salad, penne, pups & frites, grilled broccolini, and hot oatmeal cookies.

**Drink Specials 3**
$2.00 mini beers; $4.00 jumbo cask draft
$5.00 house wines; $5.00 bubbly cocktails
Plus deals on rotating taster shots of the week

**Atmosphere 3**
This "publican's table" gives us an urban, industrial hideaway with cozy neighborhood charm. From the owner of Prost, originally in partnership with owner of Tasty n' Sons and Toro Bravo. Long, front bar area with a modern speakeasy upstairs and big back patio.

Date visited: __________ **My Rating:** __________
Went with: ____________________
Favorites: ____________________
Not so much: ____________________
Other comments: ____________________

____________________

# Las Primas

8

**North/NE Map**
3808 N Williams, #127
(503) 288-6200
www.lincolnpdx.com

**Happy Hours**
3:00–6:00pm Tues–Sun

**Food Deals 2**
$2.50–$5.00
A couple bucks off select, flavorful, classic sandwiches (pepper-rubbed pork, house-made sausage, or veggie), soup, empanadas, salad.

**Drink Specials 3**
$2.50 Peruvian beer (bottles); $4.00 drafts;
$4.00 house wine; $4.00 sangría
$6.00 pisco sours – choice of six!

**Atmosphere 2**
Simple restaurant with colorful, hand-painted, welcome mural and Peruvian folk art pieces adorning white walls. Patterned after typical Lima-style sandwich shops with open kitchen, counter service, and cement floors.

Date visited: ____________ **My Rating:** ____________
Went with: ______________________________
Favorites: ______________________________
Not so much: ____________________________
Other comments: __________________________
__________________________________________

# Lincoln

10

**North/NE Map**
3808 N Williams, #127
(503) 288-6200
www.lincolnpdx.com

**Happy Hours**
5:30–7:00pm Tues–Fri

**Food Deals 3**
$2.00–$7.00
Americana home cooking with NW culinary bent and big, seasonal, funky-fresh menu: fritters, patty melt, fresh greens, charcuterie or cheese plates, terrines, poutine, olives, fries, onion rings.

**Drink Specials 3**
$3.00 microbrews; $4.00 house wines
$5.00 wells; $6.00 specialty cocktail

**Atmosphere 3**
Located in the northside's HUB building, a strip of chic, renovated loft-style warehouse spaces. Interior is on the more basic side of industrial chic, but warmth is added via dark-red walls, natural woods, friendly staff and votive candles.

Date visited: ____________ **My Rating:** ____________
Went with: ________________________________
Favorites: ________________________________
Not so much: ______________________________
Other comments: ___________________________
___________________________________________

# Lucca

9

**Northeast (off map)**
3449 NE 24th Ave.
(503) 287-7372
www.luccapdx.com

**Happy Hours**
2:30–5:00pm Tues–Fri

**Food Deals 3**
$2.00–$5.00
Eight great plates with dates, crostini with goat cheese and roasted garlic, pate, olives, bread with roasted garlic oil, salami & cheese plate, and salads. Plus wood-fired pizzas ($9.00).

**Drink Specials 3**
$3.00 drafts; $4.00 wines; $4.00 wells
$6.00 cosmos and lemondrops

**Atmosphere 3**
Understated neutrals in wide open room, very relaxing atmosphere with wood-fire oven behind the long bar. Happy Hour here is early, so there will be lots of light coming in the wall-to-wall windows in the front. Cool accent light fixtures. Nice, small group meeting room.

Date visited: ____________ **My Rating:** ____________
Went with: ________________________________________
Favorites: ________________________________________
Not so much: ______________________________________
Other comments: ___________________________________
___________________________________________________

# Mac!&Cheesery 6

**North/NE Map**
3936 N Mississippi
(503) 200-5787
www.macandcheese.biz

**Happy Hours**
3:00–6:00pm Daily
Also during Blazers and Timbers games

**Food Deals 2**
$3.00–$5.00
Smaller versions of usual giant sizes of either the original mac & cheese (served with or without hotdogs–remember that?!) or four-cheese option. Regular menu hosts 17 varieties of mac & cheese!

**Drink Specials 2**
$1.00 off drafts and wine; $3.00 wells

**Atmosphere 2**
Long and light room with upper level and natural wood stairs, bar and booths. Very cute touch with kid's metal lunch boxes adorning the walls. Occasional live music and trivia nights. Note: All mac and cheeses available gluten free!

Date visited: __________ **My Rating:** __________
Went with: ______________________________
Favorites: ______________________________
Not so much: ______________________________
Other comments: ______________________________
______________________________

# Mad Greek Deli 9

**Lloyd Center Map**
1740 E. Burnside; (503) 232-0274
www.madgreekdeli.com

Hillsboro: 18450 NW West Union; (503) 645-1650

**Happy Hours**
4:00–6:00pm Mon–Fri

**Food Deals 3**
$1.00–$5.00
A dozen cheap and tasty options: GREEK fries, souvlaki, Greek salad, olives, spanakopita, tots, hummus and pita, gyros, Greek style pizza.

**Drink Specials 3**
$1.00 off drafts; $4.00 wines
$4.00–$6.00 cocktail of the day

**Atmosphere 2**
Sportsbar-like back area with colorful team scarves strewn overhead, several big-screen TVS, and a lively, open bar. Be sure to "like" their facebook page, as they give away gift certificates like mad! Hillsboro location a bit darker, with counter orders and back bar.

Date visited: ____________ **My Rating:** ____________
Went with: ______________________________
Favorites: ______________________________
Not so much: ____________________________
Other comments: __________________________
__________________________________________

# Mee-Sen Thai

8

**North/NE Map**
3924 N Mississippi Ave
(503) 445-1909
www.meesenpdx.com

**Happy Hours**
3:00–6:00pm and 9:00pm–close Daily
★All night Tuesday

**Food Deals 3**
$3.00–$6.00
Unique Thai tapas! Grilled squid, wings, grilled rib-eye, Thai sausages, pad thai, drunken noodles, salads, noodle bowls, and if you're really brave or really hungry, fried grasshoppers.

**Drink Specials 2**
$1.00 off beer and wine; $2.00 off select cocktails

**Atmosphere 2**
Funky and friendly garage-like space with open doors to a nice stone patio, and built sustainably with materials like old, colorful, barnhouse wood planks – and bicycles!

Date visited: ________ **My Rating:** ________
Went with: ____________________
Favorites: ____________________
Not so much: ____________________
Other comments: ____________________

# Mextiza

10 ★ A Happy Hour favorite!

**North/NE (off map)**
2103 N Killingsworth
(503) 289-3709
www.mextiza.com

**Happy Hours**
5:00–6:00pm Mon–Fri and 9:00–10:00pm Fri-Sat

**Food Deals 3**
$2.00–$5.00
High-quality and delicious small plates brought to us this year by the restaurateur of Autentica (and brand-new Uno Mas in the Ocean Complex at 24th & Glisan). Pork taco/tortilla, salad, jicama, sope, beans, dumplings — and grilled calamari!

**Drink Specials 3**
$1.00 off drafts; $5.00 red or white wine
$5.00 sangria; $5.00 margarita

**Atmosphere 3**
Cozy, long dining room with cement floors, and tiled back bar area in refurbished old auto body shop. Outside and in, it all looks brand-new, and is a greatly-welcomed addtion up north! Large, fenced-in front patio with colorful umbrellas.

Date visited: __________ **My Rating:** __________
Went with: ______________________________
Favorites: ______________________________
Not so much: ______________________________
Other comments: ______________________________
______________________________

# Mint/820

10

Top cover fave 2013!

**North/NE Map**
820 N Russell
(503) 284-5518
www.mintrestaurant.com

**Happy Hours**
4:00–8:00pm Mon–Tues★; 4:00pm–close Wed★
4:00–6:30pm Thurs–Sat; 4:00pm–close Sun★

**Food Deals 2**
$3.50–$9.00
It's all about the sweet potato fries! Limited but delicious, unique menu: lamb burger, calamari, risotto balls, soup, and salad.

**Drink Specials 3**
$2.50 PBR; $5.00 wine; $4.00 well drinks
$6.50 selected cocktails (of "Hip Sips" fame!)

**Atmosphere 3**
A quintessential Happy Hour and cocktail bar. Connected to gorgeous and hip Mint Restaurant (where you can Happy Hour 5-6:30pm); 820 is a trendy, upscale ultra-lounge with nice back deck area to most pleasantly enjoy on a nice day.

Date visited: ____________ **My Rating:** ____________
Went with: ______________________________
Favorites: ______________________________
Not so much: ____________________________
Other comments: __________________________
_________________________________________

# Miss Delta

# 8

**North/NE Map**
3950 N Mississippi Ave.
(503) 287-7629
www.missdeltapdx.net

**Happy Hours**
4:00–6:00pm Daily

**Food Deals 3**
$3.00–$6.50
Huge, exciting Southern menu and it's delicious! Collard greens, red beans & rice, mashed potatoes, mac & cheese, or black-eyed peas. Or try sweet potato fries, hush puppies, corn bread muffin, jambalaya, po'boys, fritters, and lots mo'!

**Drink Specials 2**
$1.00 off drafts, wines and wells

**Atmosphere 2**
Quaint, old-time N'awlins saloon style. Small room with long bar with brick walls, rustic wood floors, antique hanging lamps and for added effect, mason jar candles.

Date visited: ____________ **My Rating:** ____________
Went with: ______________________________
Favorites: ______________________________
Not so much: ______________________________
Other comments: ______________________________
______________________________

# Moloko

8

**North/NE Map**
3967 N Mississippi
(503) 288-6272
www.molokopdx.com

**Happy Hours**
4:00–7:00pm Daily

**Food Deals 2**
$2.00 off sandwiches
Turkey, salami, tuna, grilled cheese or herbed chevre sandwiches. Good prices on other snacks like hummus,chips & salsa, tossed green salad, nut mix, cheese or salami plates.

**Drink Specials 2**
$1.00 off domestics; 50 cents off wells
$5.00 select cocktail; $6.00 Bloody Mary, mimosa

**Atmosphere 3**
A secret Mississippi gem with neon symbols as signage. Ultra-retro, white and mod interior, with 60's seating in both vinyl upholstered and plastic-form lounge chairs. Charming garden gazebo back deck area is heated in the winter. They make their own infusions. Cool fish tanks!

Date visited: __________ **My Rating:** __________
Went with: ______________________________
Favorites: ______________________________
Not so much: ______________________________
Other comments: ______________________________
______________________________

# Ned Ludd

10

**North/NE Map**
3925 NE MLK Blvd. (near Failing)
(503) 288-6900
www.nedluddpdx.com

**Happy Hours**
4:00–6:00pm Mon–Fri

**Food Deals 3** $3.00–$9.00
Ever-changing menu according to monthly or weekly bounty and whims, with an array of earthy delights like greens or vegetable salads, olives, pickles and breads, plus meat and fish smallplates.

**Drink Specials 3**
$3.00–$6.00 selection of beers and ciders
$5.00 red, rose, or white wines or bubbles
$4.00 spirit and pickle jus pairings

**Atmosphere 3**
Ultra-charming, rustic American craft kitchen with decor and graphics perfectly conveying personality. Focal point is a bright pea-green wall with firey brick hearth. Happy Hour restricted to patio or at small bartop only and may be seasonal. Note the address – this place can disappear!

Date visited: ____________ **My Rating:** ____________
Went with: ______________________________
Favorites: ______________________________
Not so much: ____________________________
Other comments: __________________________

__________________________________________

# Newport Seafood Grill

10

**Lloyd Center-ish Map**
1200 NE Broadway; (503) 493-0100
www.newportseafoodgrill.com

0425 SW Montgomery; (503) 227-3474 (p. 45)
9722 SE Washington Street, Mall 205 (255-2722)
9699 SW Washington Square; (503) 620-3474
2865 NW Town Center Loop; Tanasbourne
Newport Bay; (503) 645-2526

**Happy Hours**
3:00–6:00pm Daily

**Food Deals 3** $3.49–$5.99
15 varied menu items including clam chowder, fish & chips, salads, sushi rolls, fish tacos, soup, bay shrimp cocktail, and seasonal items too.

**Drink Specials 3**
Drink specials vary at each location, but good! Usually $3.59 microbrews, wine and wells

**Atmosphere 3**
Popular, big, and bustling bar areas. Upscale restaurant conveniently located near all the malls (Beware: drinking and shopping is dangerous!) Also conveniently nearby movie theaters.

Date visited: ____________ **My Rating:** ____________
Went with: ______________________________
Favorites: ______________________________
Not so much: ____________________________
Other comments: __________________________
__________________________________________

# Noble Rot

9

**Lloyd Center-ish Map**
1111 E Burnside
(503) 233-1999
www.noblerotpdx.com

**Happy Hours**
5:00–6:00pm Mon–Fri

**Food Deals 3**
$6.00–$8.75
Ranges from nibblets to comfort food and changes with the season: olives, onion rings, French fries, cheese plate, exceptional paninos, mac & cheese, hamburger.

**Drink Specials 3**
$3.50 draft beer; $3.50 red or white wine
$5.50 selection of bartender's specialties

**Atmosphere 3**
Stunning wall-to-wall, floor-to-ceiling windows perched high for a wide-open city view; ultra-cool contemporary-retro interior; illuminated circular glass art on ceiling. Rooftop outdoor deck with Happy Hour seating! Sunset Magazine's Best Wine Bar 2009.

Date visited: ____________ **My Rating:** ____________
Went with: ______________________________
Favorites: ______________________________
Not so much: ____________________________
Other comments: __________________________

# Old Town Pizza

8

**North/NE Map**
5201 NE MLK; (503) 200-5988
Old Town: 226 NW Davis; (503) 222-9999
www.oldtownpizza.com

**Happy Hours**
MLK: 3:00-6:00pm and 9:00pm-close Daily
Old Town: 9:00pm-close Daily (late-night only)

**Food Deals 2**
$3.00–$6.00
MLK: Mini-pizzas, Caesar, spinach, or caprese salads, meatball sliders, spaghetti, sandwiches. Old Town: $1.50 cheese or pepperoni pizza slices.

**Drink Specials 2**
$1.00 off house drafts (MLK); they are also a microbrewery now; $2.50 wells (both locations)

**Atmosphere 3**
Old Town Pizza is one of Portland's most unique, historic, and haunted(!) places. The Old Town location is the former lobby of the Merchant Hotel (est. 1880). Word is, ghosts reside in the Shanghai Tunnels below, and maybe at a table or two upstairs! The northside locale extends the vintage charm with period furniture and accessories.

Date visited: ____________ **My Rating:** ____________
Went with: ______________________________
Favorites: ______________________________
Not so much: ____________________________
Other comments: _________________________
_________________________________________

# Paadee

**Lloyd Center-ish Map**
6 SE 28th Ave.
(503) 360-1453
www.paadeepdx.com

10 A Happy Hour favorite

**Happy Hours**
5:00–6:30pm and 9:00-10:00pm Daily

**Food Deals 3**
$2.00–$7.00
Excellent choices and well-made: Grilled squid or pork skewers, tom yum soup with prawns, sausage selections, fish cakes, noodle dishes. Award-winning food at a top PDX restaurant!

**Drink Specials 3**
$3.00 drafts (2nd one for only $2.00 – I like it!)
$5.00 house wines; $6.00 specialty cocktails

**Atmosphere 3**
Cozy industrial-chic, with talented and appropriate interior design choices incorporating subtle Asian stylings. Lots of light, cool bar, curtains, flowers, stained concrete. Long wood tables for groups, smaller 2-4 tops, and sidewalk seating.

Date visited: ____________ **My Rating:** ____________
Went with: ______________________________
Favorites: ______________________________
Not so much: ____________________________
Other comments: _________________________
_________________________________________

# Palace of Industry 7

**Northeast (off map)**
5426 N Gay Ave.
(503) 477-7313
www.palaceofindustrypdx.com

**Happy Hours**
4:00-7:00pm Tues-Fri; ★Noon-6:00pm Sunday
Happy Hour all night for ladies on Tuesdays

**Food Deals 0**
A few big, well-priced sandwiches and salads, but no discounts at Happy Hour.

**Drink Specials 3**
$3.50 beer; $4.00 house wines
$5.00 champagne or sake cocktail creations

**Atmosphere 3**
Unique and very creative space! Part cafe, part coffeeshop, *plus* a thrift/vintage store – and all in a bar. Big kudos on the concept as well as the name! Several lounging areas plus patio.

Date visited: ____________ **My Rating:** ____________
Went with: ______________________________
Favorites: ______________________________
Not so much: ______________________________
Other comments: ______________________________
______________________________

# Pambiche

10

**Lloyd Center-ish Map**
2811 NE Glisan
(503) 233-0511
www.pambiche.com

**Happy Hours**
★2:00–6:00pm Mon–Fri; 10:00pm–mid Fri–Sat

A Happy Hour favori

**Food Deals 3**
$2.00–$5.00
Mmmmpenadas, fried plantains, salads, bean and rice dishes, fried chicken and pork, shredded beef, stew—and don't miss the desserts!

**Drink Specials 3**
$2.50-$3.00 beer
$5.00 house red and white wines
$5.50 red and white sangrias
$5.00-$6.50 select cocktails
$1.00 off espressos, teas, sodas, juices & shakes

**Atmosphere 3**
Fun and colorful Cuban café! Outdoor dining area streetside; bright, cozy and happy inside; vibrant exterior. Captures the Cuban "feel" well.

Date visited: __________ **My Rating:** __________
Went with: ____________________
Favorites: ____________________
Not so much: ____________________
Other comments: ____________________

____________________

# Perry's

9

**North/NE Map**
2401 NE Fremont
(503) 287-3655
www.perrysonfremont.com

**Happy Hours**
4:00–6:00pm Tues–Fri; 12:oopm-6:00 Sat

**Food Deals 3**
$4.00
House or Caesar salad, flatbread w/goat cheese, chicken tacos, sesame Thai chicken, vegetable enchilada, Caesar, mini burger, spaghetti, soup, tostadas, artichoke hearts.

**Drink Specials 3**
$3.00 drafts; $4.00 wines; $5.00 martinis

**Atmosphere 3**
Like a traveler/artist's home; impressive iron work greeting, masks, decorated atrium sky lights, paintings, ethnic and art statues. Cute patio in nice weather, but limited Happy Hour seating there.

Date visited: ____________ **My Rating:** ____________
Went with: ____________________________
Favorites: ____________________________
Not so much: ____________________________
Other comments: ____________________________
____________________________________________

# Petisco

**North/NE Map**
1411 NE Broadway
(503) 360-1048
www.petiscopdx.com

**Happy Hours**
3:00–6:00pm Tues–Sat

**Food Deals 3**
$5.00
Ten superb sandwiches served hot or cold, choice of bread, and can be requested as, or with, salads. Two exceptional prosciutto options, roasted portobello, roast beef with roasted red peppers, ham and brie, or deluxe chicken salad. So good! Great HH concept!

**Drink Specials 2**
$1.00 Miller beers; $4.00 house wines; $3.00 sangrias

**Atmosphere 2**
Cute and casual with European ambiance. Half-sunken basement gives the place added coziness, with a fun patio down below street level. Exposed brick walls, open kitchen and chalkboard menus.

Date visited: ___________ **My Rating:** ___________
Went with: ______________________________
Favorites: ______________________________
Not so much: ____________________________
Other comments: __________________________
__________________________________________

# Petite Provence 8

**Alberta Map**
1824 NE Alberta
(503) 284-6564
www.provence-portland.com

**Happy Hours**
4:00–6:00pm Mon–Fri

**Food Deals 2**
$5.25
Small menu, but it will do the trick: Risotto cake, bruschetta dishes, quiches, and a dessert plate with three mini-desserts!

**Drink Specials 2**
$1.00 off beer, wine and wells

**Atmosphere 3**
Ultra-charming and provincial, gold, white and blue French bistro with dessert counter, arches and inlays, and giant wooden beams. Cute, cute, cuteness!

* Several more locations throughout Portland, but they do not do Happy Hour.

Date visited: ____________ **My Rating:** ____________
Went with: ______________________________
Favorites: ______________________________
Not so much: ______________________________
Other comments: ______________________________
______________________________

# Pour Wine Bar

9

**Lloyd Center-ish Map**
2755 NE Broadway
(503) 288-7687
www.pourwinebar.com

**Happy Hours**
4:30–6:30pm Mon–Sat

A Happy Hour favorit

**Food Deals 2**
$2.00
Very good and insanely inexpensive, but limited: cheese panini, marinated olives, and roasted hazelnuts. Regular menu has some delicious and affordable options too.

**Drink Specials 3**
$3.00 pours of select red and white wines
$5.00 off bottles; $2.00 select beer

**Atmosphere 3**
Striking and sleek 1960s-style Space Odyssey lounge; mod design with cool, white retro chairs and walls; string art mural; silver, candlelight, and real flowers.

Date visited: __________ **My Rating:** __________
Went with: ______________________________
Favorites: ______________________________
Not so much: ______________________________
Other comments: ______________________________
______________________________

# Radio Room

9

**Alberta Map**
1101 NE Alberta St
(503) 287-2346
www.radioroompdx.com

**Happy Hours**
3:00–6:00pm and 11:00pm–2:00am (food) Daily

**Food Deals 3**
$2.00–$5.00
A dozen or so items with many vegetarian, vegan and gluten free options: hummus, wings, beet salad, mahi-mahi tacos, calamari, burgers, grilled cheese, Caesar, edamame, polenta cakes, fries.

**Drink Specials 2**
$3.25 microbrews; $8.00 wine of the week
$3.25 wells

**Atmosphere 3**
All-out sleek and mod interior fitting of big-city style standards; both upper and lower outdoor decks with bright blue umbrellas and big stone firepit; huge bar with open garage doors; cool movie posters; radio room rumored in rear.

Date visited: ____________ **My Rating:** ____________
Went with: ______________________________
Favorites: ______________________________
Not so much: ____________________________
Other comments: __________________________
__________________________________________

# Samurai Blue

9

**Northeast (off map)**
3807 N Mississippi
(503) 284-1020
www.samuraibluepdx.com

**Happy Hours**
★Open/Lunch–6:30pm and 9:00-close Mon-Sat

**Food Deals 3**
$2.00–$6.00
Fresh and delish dishes: edamame, several hand rolls, spring rolls, mussels, gyoza, salads, ceviche, salmon or hamachi kama, and chicken katsu.

**Drink Specials 2**
$1.00 off drafts, sake and sake cocktails

**Atmosphere 3**
Bright orange walls with original and Asian artwork, overhead beams, tsunami wave wall mural and hanging floral room dividers. Black linens and back kitchen open to front rooms.

Date visited: __________ **My Rating:** __________
Went with: ______________________________
Favorites: ______________________________
Not so much: ______________________________
Other comments: ______________________________
______________________________

# Secret Society Lounge

8

**North/NE Map**
116 NE Russell
(503) 493-3600
www.secretsociety.net

A Happy Hour favorite!

**Happy Hours**
5:00–7:00pm / 10:00pm-close Sun–Thurs

**Food Deals 2**
$4.00–$10.00
Small but unique menu that changes seasonally: pickled eggs, salad, house flavored popcorn, mac & cheese, soups, grilled cheese.

**Drink Specials 2**
$1.00 off drafts and wine;
$6.00 cocktails

**Atmosphere 3**
Very cool space! Speakeasy style with candlelit bookcases, prohibition-era paintings, antique light fixtures and floral carpet.

Date visited: __________ **My Rating:** __________
Went with: ______________________________
Favorites: ______________________________
Not so much: ______________________________
Other comments: ______________________________
______________________________

# Slide Inn

9

**Lloyd Center-ish Map**
2348 SE Ankeny
(503) 236-4997
www.slideinnpdx.com

**Happy Hours**
5:30–7:00pm Daily; 9:00pm–close Nightly

**Food Deals 3**
$3.00–$7.00
Big-time gluten-free and veggie options! Also, some heavy aprés ski food. Nibbles like roasted almonds, yam fries, pickled root veggies, paprika chips plus sliders and sausages, spatzle, gnocchi, mac & cheese, chili, or chips w/ vegan sour cream.

**Drink Specials 2**
$3.00 local brews; $4.00 German pints; $5.00 wine

**Atmosphere 3**
Formerly il Piatto. Same owners, different concept. Decor-wise, the revamped interior incorporates Alpine Inn elements with a mid-century modern cocktail swank. Simple charm.

Date visited: ____________ **My Rating:** ____________
Went with: ______________________________________
Favorites: ______________________________________
Not so much: ____________________________________
Other comments: __________________________________
_________________________________________________

# Spints Alehouse

9

**Lloyd Center-ish Map**
401 NE 28th Ave
(503) 847-2534
www.spintspdx.com

**Happy Hours**
4:00–6:00pm and 10:00pm-mid Daily

**Food Deals 2**
$5.00–$7.00 ($3.00 off bar menu)
It's *all* about the "Dirty Pretzel"=YUM!!! (Weekly creative concoctions plopped atop giant pretzels, like banana splits or gyros), daily cheese board, meat smorgasbord, burger, and seasonal specials.

**Drink Specials 3**
$3.00 select drafts; $3.00 bottles
$5.00 wines; $5.00 specialty cocktail

**Atmosphere 3**
A fresh, clean and new alehouse with a homey library feel. Good design with masculine charm brings us this true, quintessential gastropub. FYI – Spints rhymes with mints (a German thing).

Date visited: __________ **My Rating:** __________
Went with: ______________________________
Favorites: ______________________________
Not so much: ______________________________
Other comments: ______________________________
______________________________

# Stanford's

10

**Lloyd Center-ish Map**
Portland
913 Lloyd Center; (503) 335-0811
1440 N. Jantzen Beach Center; (503) 285-2005
Hillsboro
2770 NW 188th Ave.; (503) 645-8000
Lake Oswego
14801 Kruse Oaks Dr.; (503) 620-3541
www.stanfords.com

**Happy Hours**
3:00–6:00pm Daily; 9:00pm–close Daily (10:00pm –close Fri & Sat); Hours vary slightly per location

**Food Deals 3**
$2.50-$7.95
Delicious menu is just a bit different at each restaurant. All are appreciated by *many* a fan.

**Drink Specials 3** (Early HH only)
May vary slightly per location – usually $4.00 microbrews, wine and wells; $12.00 pitchers

**Atmosphere 3**
Classic and popular upscale restaurants with the Happy Hour action at the central bar.

Date visited: __________ **My Rating:** __________
Went with: ____________________
Favorites: ____________________
Not so much: ____________________
Other comments: ____________________

# TaBla

10

**Lloyd Center-ish Map**
200 NE 28th Ave
(503) 238-3777
www.tabla-restaurant.com

A Happy Hour favorite!

**Happy Hours**
5:00–6:00pm Daily

**Food Deals 3**
$2.50–$4.50
One of the Northwest's best offers Happy Hour with a fresh, seasonal menu featuring half-off their bar menu! Steve's cheese or charcuterie plates, crostini, tagliatelle with bolognese, Tabla ravioli, salad, veggies, cod fritters.

**Drink Specials 3**
$3.00 drafts; $6.00 house wines; $12 half carafe
$2.00 off all glass pours; $5.00 wells; $5.00 Negroni

**Atmosphere 3**
Simple, home-style decor with banquette seating, flowers on tables and at windows, plus original art. Not suitable for groups as Happy Hour is at bar only (plus seasonal sidewalk seating).

Date visited: ____________ **My Rating:** ____________
Went with: ______________________________________
Favorites: ______________________________________
Not so much: ____________________________________
Other comments: _________________________________

# Tapalaya

10

**Lloyd Center-ish Map**
28 NE 28th Ave
(503) 232-6652
www.tapalaya.com

A Happy Hour favorite!

**Happy Hours**
4:30–6:00pm Daily
All night Wednesdays if you ride your bike there.

**Food Deals 3**
$2.00–$5.00
Tapas/bites of New Orleans menu just about perfect for getting one of everything to share, like crawfish fritters, mac & cheese, BBQ pork sandwich, and fried okra.

**Drink Specials 3+**
$3.00 drafts; $4.00 red, white, or rosé wine
$2.00 martinis and $3.00 hurricanes (YES!)
$5.00 signature cocktail specials

**Atmosphere 3**
Laissez les bon temps rouler! Not wild, but fun; more cozy and cute; neighborhoody and nice. Live music Thursdays – check calendar.

Date visited: ____________ **My Rating:** ____________
Went with: ______________________________
Favorites: ______________________________
Not so much: ____________________________
Other comments: __________________________

# Tasty n Sons

8

**North/NE Map**
3808 N Williams
(503) 621-1400
www.tastynsons.com

**Happy Hours**
2:30–5:00pm Daily

**Food Deals 3**
$1.00–$7.00
12 small plates like bacon-wrapped dates, burger, hush puppies, fries, and egg dishes. They're famous for burgers and brunch anytime. Menu changes often, based on the season and the kitchen crew's inspiration! Owners of Toro Bravo.

**Drink Specials 2**
$5.00 wine; $7.00 tasty cocktail specials

**Atmosphere 3**
Industrial loft-style interior with stained concrete floors, red cinder block walls and roll-up, garage door windows. Sit in the front bar area for nice summer breezes, or side/back area along the open kitchen with butcher's block chef's bar for a view of the cooking! Alert: it's quite loud here.

Date visited: ___________ **My Rating:** ___________
Went with: ______________________________
Favorites: ______________________________
Not so much: ____________________________
Other comments: __________________________

# Tin Shed

9

**Alberta Map**
1438 NE Alberta
(503) 288-6966
www.tinshedgardencafe.com

**Happy Hours**
3:00–6:00pm and 9:00–10:00pm Mon–Sat;
3:00–close Sundays★

**Food Deals 3**
$3.00–$6.00
Limited, but fresh and oh-so-tasty! Special mac & cheese of the day, sliders, potato cakes, quesadilla, salads, and nachos.

**Drink Specials 3**
$3.00 microbrews; $4.00 wine
$5.00 specialty drinks

**Atmosphere 2**
Rustic corrugated tin walls; colorful & bright elsewhere. Loud interior; big and wonderful outdoor garden café with fireplace. Family- and dog-friendly in the sunny summertime. Cute!

Date visited: ____________ **My Rating:** ____________
Went with: ______________________________
Favorites: ______________________________
Not so much: ______________________________
Other comments: ______________________________

# Trébol

10

**NE/Mississippi Map**
4835 N Albina Ave
(503) 517-9347
www.trebolpdx.com

**Happy Hours**
5:00-6:30pm and 9:00pm–close Daily

**Food Deals 3**
$2.00–$6.00
Authentic and interesting Mexican dishes with soup to nuts, enchiladas, tacos, pork sandwich, quesadilla, flautas (all fancier than they sound).

**Drink Specials 2**
$2.00 beers; $5.00 wines and sangrias
$6.00 specialty margaritas; $5.00 mimosas
Note: There are 100+ tequilas here!

**Atmosphere 3**
Perfect balance of modern and traditional style with rustic, wood tables, exposed rafters and vents, gold and orange walls with framed prints, huge, illuminated bar and cool curtain dividers.

Date visited: ____________ **My Rating:** ____________
Went with: ____________
Favorites: ____________
Not so much: ____________
Other comments: ____________

# Uchu Sushi

9

**NE/Mississippi Map**
3940 N Mississippi
(503) 281-8248
www.uchusushi.com

**Happy Hours**
2:00-6:00pm Daily; 12:00pm-close Mon–Wed★
9:00pm–close Thur–Sat

**Food Deals 3**
$4.00–$5.00
Wow! Delightful and very extensive menu offers 14 small plates and 14 sushi rolls! Baked mussels, egg rolls, wings, poppers, gyoza, calamari, yakitori, several salads, and the full array of classic sushi rolls. A few dinner bowls served as well.

**Drink Specials 3**
$3.00 beers (7 styles); $4.00 wines
$1.00 off sake; $4.00-$6.00 cocktails

**Atmosphere 2**
Officially known as Uchu Sushi & Fried Chicken. Casual, Portland-style, industrial chic. Cement floors, long front bar, wood tables and roll top garage doors/window. Iconic, ironic, giant fish tanks!

Date visited: ____________ **My Rating:** ____________
Went with: ________________________________
Favorites: ________________________________
Not so much: ______________________________
Other comments: ___________________________

# Yakuza

**7**

**North/NE Map**
5411 NE 30th Ave
(503) 450-0893
www.yakuzalounge.com

**Happy Hours**
5:00–6:00pm Wed, Thur, and Sun; plus
10:00-11:00pm Fri-Sat

**Food Deals 3**
$4.00–$8.00
A touch pricey for HH, but the quality is there! Cute little menu that changes periodically, with things like kale salad, veggie or fish hand roll, katsu, or that incredible burger they are famous for.

**Drink Specials 0**
No drink specials

**Atmosphere 3**
This Japanese pub is yet another masterpiece created by Micah Camden of Beast and DOC fame, all in the same neighborhood. Interior has simple wooden bench seating with hanging draperies to softly separate spaces. Beautiful, colorful murals adorn walls. Wonderful patio!

Date visited: ____________ **My Rating:** ____________
Went with: ______________________________
Favorites: ______________________________
Not so much: ______________________________
Other comments: ______________________________

## Alberta Street Pub

**Alberta Map** 1036 NE Alberta; (503) 284-7665
www.myspace.com/albertastreetpub

**Happy Hours** 5:00–7:45pm Mon–Fri; 10pm–mid Wed

**Food Deals 3** $3.00 Basic but big: turkey sandwich, Guinness beef stew, salad, nachos, BLT, veggie melt.

**Drink Specials 3** $1.00 PBRs; $2.50 micros
$2.75 wells; $2.75 selected wine

**Atmosphere 2** Warm and inviting, dark Irish pub. High-walled booths enable private conversation.

## Alibi Tiki Lounge

**North/NE Map** 4024 N Interstate; (503) 287-5335

**Happy Hours** 3:00–7:00pm Daily

**Food Deals 3** $1.95–$4.95
Big Happy Hour menu featuring bar fare with island touches: quesadilla, hot wings, soup, burger, pork sandwich, tater tots, potato skins, shoyu chicken, pepperjack mac & cheese, and more.

**Drink Specials 1** $2.00 PBR and Coors; $3.50 wells

**Atmosphere 3** Top marks for over-the-top tacky Tiki; bizarrely dark & divey; a unique Portland treasure!

## Alleyway Café

**Alberta Map** 2415 NE Alberta St.; (503) 287-7760

**Happy Hours** 3:00–7:00pm Daily

**Food Deals 3** $2.00–$5.00 Fresh taste in a long list of little nibbles with big discounts: sliders, grilled cheese, sweet potato fries, tacos, chips & salsa, Caesar, onion rings. Many vegan options also!

**Drink Specials 3** $1.50 Rainers; $3.00 micros
$4.00 mimosas, Bloody Marys or mojitos; $2.50 wells!

**Atmosphere 2** Low-key and ultra-casual neighborhood café with artsy, rotating gallery wares.

## Ate-Oh-Ate www.ate-oh-ate.com

**Lloyd Center-ish Map** 2452 E Burnside; (503) 445-6101

**Happy Hours** 4:00-6:00pm Daily

**Food Deals 2** $2.00-$5.00 Hard-to-find authentic Hawaiian food! Enjoy nibbles like kalua pig or chicken sliders, wings, poke, fried rice, or Spam tempura!

**Drink Specials 1** $1.00 off drafts; $10.00 bucket o' beer $5.00 mai-tais. Full bar with unusual beer choices.

**Atmosphere 2** Very casual... cafeteria? Quite stark and Hawaiian theme isn't pushed much in decor. Counter service only, but brought to us by same owners of Simpatica and Laurelhurst Market. Hawaii area code 808.

## Bar Bar (at Mississippi Studios)

**North/NE Map** 3943 N Mississippi; (503) 288-3895 www.mississippistudios.com

**Happy Hours**
4:00-7:00pm Mon–Thurs; Noon-6:00pm Fri-Sun

**Food Deals 0** Limited menu at Happy Hour prices at all times: $5.00 burgers or salads.

**Drink Specials 2** $3.00 drafts; $5.00 Margarita deals $1.00 off house cocktails

**Atmosphere 2** Formerly Mississippi Station. Renovated and removed all the old station charm, but understated and nice enough. Great back patio! Concerts next door.

## Beech Street Parlor

**North/NE Map** 412 NE Beech; (503) 946-8184 www.beechstreetparlor.com

**Happy Hours** 5:00-7:00pm Mon-Sat

**Food Deals 1** $1.00 off bar menu that will have your hunger covered: salads, ham & cheese, tart, hot dog.

**Drink Specials 2** $1.00 off drafts/wine; $3.50 wells

**Atmosphere 3** Vintage style! It's like an older, vampy, sister to the Liberty Ale House. Similar in tone to a speak-easy, but with welcoming front porch, and several rooms upstairs with parlor couches. Cute!

## Bella Faccia Pizzeria

**Alberta Map** 2934 NE Alberta St.; (503) 282-0600
www.bellafacciapizzeria.com

**Happy Hours** 4:00–6:00pm Mon–Fri; 3–5pm Sat–Sun

**Food Deals 2** $2.25-$3.00 pizza slices. Huge salads could feed up to 4 people $8.00–$9.00

**Drink Specials 1** $1.00 off pints

**Atmosphere 2** Very casual pizza place with coffee-house vibe; pleasant back patio and sidewalk seating.

## Branch Whiskey Bar

**Alberta Map** 2926 NE Alberta; (503) 206-6266
www.branchwhiskeybar.com

**Happy Hours** 5:00–7:00pm Daily (Fri-Sat food only)

**Food Deals 2** $2.00 off unique but very limited menu with items like pork rillette, grilled romaine salad, veggie pasta, red potatoes, or duck fat fries.

**Drink Specials 3** $3.00 drafts; $5.00 wines; $4.00 wells

**Atmosphere 2** Get your whiskey on or branch out to scotch or rye at this small and cozy, brick-walled bar, that's really more of a restaurant, ambiance-wise.

## Bye & Bye www.thebyeandbye.com

**Alberta Map** 1011 NE Alberta; (503) 281-0537

**Happy Hours** 4:00–7:00pm Daily

**Food Deals 2** $1.00 off dinner entrees; $2.00 chips and salsa and $4.00 edamame. Vegans *love* this place!

**Drink Specials 2** $1.00 off selects drafts and wells
$6.00 mason jar specialties

**Atmosphere 2** Part diner-like, part hipster bar. Patio seating in back; more outdoor seating next to parking lot.

## Cha Cha Cha www.chaportland.com

**On each of the three map pages in this section**
2635 NE Broadway; (503) 288-1045
4727 NE Fremont; (503) 595-9131
3808 N Williams; (503) 281-1655

**Happy Hours** 3:00–6:00pm Daily

**Food Deals 3** $4.00 Nice array of homemade Mexican: tostadas, fish tacos, quesadillas, burritos, salads.

**Drink Specials 2** $3.00 beer; $5.00 Margaritas

**Atmosphere 2** Part of the Cha Cha Cha family taken up a notch to the nicer side in the three Northside eateries. Menus vary slightly per location.

## Clyde's Prime Rib www.clydesprimerib.com

**Southeast (off map)** 5474 NE Sandy; (503) 281-9200

**Happy Hours** 4:00–6:00pm Mon-Fri (bar only)

**Food Deals 3** $2.50–$6.00 Prime rib is rarely found period, so at Happy Hour, medium rare at $6.50 is a fantastic find worth traveling for! Plus sauteéd shrooms, mac & cheese, burgers, wings, rings, skins, and more.

**Drink Specials 1** $4.00 nightly, rotating, cocktail

**Atmosphere 2** Ultra-old-school in a very authentic way. Red-vinyl, semi-circle booths – and a big parking lot. Way-retro dining room for dinner only.

## County Cork

**North/NE Map**1329 NE Fremont; (503) 284-4805
www.countycorkpublichouse.com

**Happy Hours** 3:00–6:00pm Mon–Fri

**Food Deals 3** $2.00–$6.00 Good and big real meals: fish and chips, Guinness stew, bangers & mash, shepherd's pie with side salads, turkey wrap, burgers.

**Drink Specials 2** $1.00 off drafts ($3.95 most pints—Imperials); 25 notable beers on a beautiful tap lineup

**Atmosphere 2** Big, fun and colorful Irish pub with hand-painted tables, pub decor, bench seating, windows that open to the street, and sidewalk seating.

## Crow Bar www.crowbarpdx.com

**North/NE Map** 3954 N Mississippi;(503) 280-7099

**Happy Hours** 3:00–8:00pm Daily (drinks)

**Food Deals 0** $3.00–$4.00 Very limited, but unique options; but no discounts.

**Drink Specials 2** $3.00 drafts; $1.50 PBR; $3.00 wells

**Atmosphere 2** Dark basic bar with good tunes; low-key crowd of neighborhood hipsters plus random drop-ins.

## Cruz Room www.cruzroom.com

**NE/North Map** 2338 NE Alberta; (503) 208-3483

**Happy Hours** 4:30–6:30pm Daily (from 4pm Fri-Sat)

**Food Deals 3** $2.00 Tiny tapas taco experiments made with creativity and flavor! Asian style (lemon-grass chicken, coconut milk, spicy peanut-butter slaw); American (potato, bacon and avocado); or Mexican (black bean with roasted corn and jalapeno salsa).

**Drink Specials 2** $3.00 drafts; $4.00 house drinks

**Atmosphere 2** Long, narrow room is divided into two halves; red bar top and floors. Nice side patio with artist mural.

## del Inti

**Alberta Map** 2315 NE Alberta; (503) 288-8191
www.delinti.com

**Happy Hours** 4:00–7:00pm Tues–Sat; 9:00–10:00pm Fri-Sat

**Food Deals 1** $1.00 off bar menu food items. Choose from three ceviches, skewers, wontons, empanada of the day, fried green tomatoes, soup, causas, lomos. Good enough food, but only $1.00 off.

**Drink Specials 1** $3.00 beer; $6.00 wine; $5.00 well

**Atmosphere 2** Bright blue building with wrought iron fence and big front patio. Colorful and well-designed Peruvian interior makes it a stand-out on Alberta. Happy Hour confined to bar and enjoyable fire pits.

## Freehouse

**NE (off map)** 1325 NE Fremont; (503) 946-8161

**Happy Hours** 4:00–5:30pm Daily

**Food Deals 1** $2.00 off entire food menu

**Drink Specials 2** $1.00 off drafts, wells, cocktails

**Atmosphere 2** By definition, a British pub that is owned independently of the breweries that supply it. By neighborhood crowd translation, it rocks! Patio. New owners since February 2012.

## Good Neighbor Pizzeria

**NE (off map)** 800 NE Dekum St.; (503) 285-7400
www.goodneighborpizzeria.com

**Happy Hours** 4:00-6:00pm and 10:00pm-mid Daily

**Food Deals 2** $2.00–$5.00 Italian mini-eats: garlic knots and knots with mozz, salads, pizza, roasted veggie sandwich, roasted potatoes, calzones.

**Drink Specials 2** $3.50 drafts or bottles of beer
$5.00 wines; $3.00 well drinks

**Atmosphere 2** Friendly, neighborhood pizza joint with brewery vibe, good beer, 'za and ice cream treats.

## Hilt www.thehiltbar.com

**Alberta Map** 1934 NE Alberta St; (971) 255-1793

**Happy Hours** 4:00-7:00pm Daily

**Food Deals 2** $3.00–$5.00 Half-off many appetizers which are kind of bar-ish and kinda Mediterranean: lamb gyros, beet salad, veggie burger, cheese fries.

**Drink Specials 2** $1.00 off taps & wells

**Atmosphere 2** Not decorated crazily to the hilt, and actually quite non-descript, but a comfortable neighborhood hangout on Alberta with big, outdoor patio.

## Jade Lounge www.jadeloungepdx.com

**Lloyd Center Map** 2342 SE Ankeny; (503) 236-4998

**Happy Hours** 5:30–6:30pm Daily

**Food Deals 2** $3.00–$5.00 Edamame, egg rolls, seafood or veggie salad rolls, veggie tempura, satay.

**Drink Specials 2** $1.00 off drafts & wine; $4.00 wells; $1.00 PBR and $2.00 microbrews all Sunday★

**Atmosphere 2** Asian lounge with jade lanterns hung from high ceilings and low coffee table seating.

## Liberty Glass

**North/NE Map** 938 N Cook; (503) 517-9931

**Happy Hours** 3:00–6:00pm Daily

**Food Deals 2** $3.00-$8.00 Nice menu with a crowd-pleasing array of eats. Cozy, pubby items like trisket nachos, mac & cheese, beets, salad, soups, nibbles.

**Drink Specials 1** $1.00 off taps and wells

**Atmosphere 2** Cute pink house, manned up with antlers and woods. Peaceful, 1776 Colonial pub vibe.

## Pause

**Northeast (off map)** 5101 N Interstate; (971) 230-0705

**Happy Hours** 4:00–6:00pm Daily

**Food Deals 0** Sadly, no discounts at Happy Hour.

**Drink Specials 2** $1.00 off drinks

**Atmosphere 2** Casual and just a bit retro. Two open room halves with red walls, cement floors. Patio.

## Por Que No www. porquenotacos.com

**Northeast Map** 3524 N Mississippi; (503) 467-4149
**Southeast Map** 4635 SE Hawthorne; (503) 954-3138

**Happy Hours** 3:00–6:00pm Daily; Tues 3:00pm–close

**Food Deals 1** $.50 cents off tacos; $1.00 off chips and guacamole or salsa. Tasty, simple, authentic Mexican.

**Drink Specials 2** $.50 cents off drafts; $1.00 off sangria and rum drinks; $1.50 off margaritas

**Atmosphere 2** A true taqueria vibe, complete with loud music, warm colors, and noisy kitchen clatter. Active sidewalk seating with Happy Hour available.

## Red Fox www.redfoxpdx.com

**Northeast Map** 5128 North Albina; (503) 282-2934

**Happy Hours** 3:00–7:00pm Daily (drinks only)

**Drink Specials** $1.00 off wells

Casual place w/microbrewery tone. Affordable bar food stepped up a notch and much is organic. Nice patio.

## Rontoms www.rontoms.net

**Lloyd Center Map** 600 E Burnside; (503) 236-4536

**Happy Hours** 4:30–6:30pm Mon–Sat

**Food Deals 2** $4.50 Several seasonal selections like grilled cheese with soup, beet salad, chicken skewers, fondue, pumpkin soup, or wild mushroom risotto.

**Drink Specials 1** $1.00 off wells

**Atmosphere 2** Big, open room a la 1970s; giant party patio with ping pong; fireplace; lounge chair groupings.

## Sidecar 11 www.sidecarpdx.wordpress.com

**North/NE Map** 3955 N Mississippi; (503) 208-3798

**Happy Hours** 4:00–7:00pm and 9:00pm-close (food) Daily ★All day Sunday; Closed Mondays

**Food Deals 2** $4.50 Small bar menu of seasonal appetizers yet with a good range of options about half-off. Choose from a couple flatbreads, chicken or steak skewers, tapenade plate, olives, and nuts.

**Drink Specials 2** $1.00 off beer, wine and cocktails

**Atmosphere 2** Tiny, somewhat hard-to-find place, plus handcrafted, classic cocktails gives Sidecar 11 a certain speak-easy appeal at night. By day, too bright.

## Spirit of '77 www.spiritof77bar.com

**North/NE Map** 500 NE MLK Jr Blvd; (503) 232-9977

**Happy Hours** 4:00–6:00pm Mon–Fri

**Food Deals 2** $3.00–$6.00 Olives, spiced corn nuts, hotdog, or burger, plus other chalkboard specials.

**Drink Specials 2** $4.00 select draft; $5.00 wines or bubbles ; $6.00 martini, manhattan, or old-fashioned

**Atmosphere 3** Big and fun sports bar! Open, warehouse space with exposed wooden beams with scores of hanging lights. A giant lightbulb-filled "Spirit of 77" sign illuminates the bar. Lots of long, thin and high community tables aimed at a *giant* projection screen.

## Tavin's www.tavinspub.com

**North/NE Map** 102 NE Russell; (503) 719-4890

**Happy Hours** 3:00–7:00pm Daily

**Food Deals 2** $1.00-$4.50 Good food here, but more needs to be added to Happy Hour menu: nachos (chicken or beef), chips & salsa, wings, fries, tacos.

**Drink Specials 2** $3.50 drafts; $3.00 wells

**Atmosphere 2** Formerly Afrique, now a very comfortable neighborhood sports pub. Cushioned seats (yay!), high ceilings with lofted seating area, and a traditional, classic bar. Five high-def big-screen TVs.

## Thai Noon (My Thai Lounge)

**Alberta Map** 2635 NE Alberta St.; (503) 282-2021
www.thainoon.com

**Happy Hours** 4:30–6:30pm Daily

**Food Deals 2** $2.75–$7.00 Thai basics like egg rolls, wontons, satay, fried rice, pad thai, padkeemow.

**Drink Specials 2** $3.00 beers; $2.00 PBRs;
$4.50 cocktails; $3.00 well drinks

**Atmosphere 1** Super casual, somewhat spartan lounge next to the Thai Noon restaurant.

## Windows

**Lloyd Center Map** 1021 NE Grand (Top Floor Red Lion); (503) 235-2100

**Happy Hours** 4:00–7:00pm Daily

**Food Deals 2** $2.00–$5.00 Good but small menu of bar food: sushi rolls, Caesar salad, spinach dip, soup, shrimp tempura, beef satay, wings.

**Drink Specials 2** $1.00 off select beer and wells
$5.00 house wines; Trail Blazer specials

**Atmosphere 3** Skyline and river views, sunsets, and outdoor deck – all very near Convention Center and Rose Garden Arena in the Red Lion Hotel. Who knew?! Kinda hotel-y inside, but nice out on the patio in the summer!

## Zilla Saké (Sushi)

**Alberta Map** 1806 NE Alberta; 503-288-8372
www.zillasakehouse.com

**Happy Hours** 5:00–7:00pm Mon–Fri

**Food Deals 2** $1.00–$5.00 California rolls, miso soup, edamame, salad, and spicy squid jerky.

**Drink Specials 3** $4.00 Sapporo beer; $4.00 wine
$2.50 wells; $4.00 specialty cocktail
$6.00–$15.00 Six choices of hot and cold sakes

**Atmosphere 2** Cool and artsy zen. Huge sake menu. Dramatic, large-scale art and big screen TV.

# SE/Central East Side

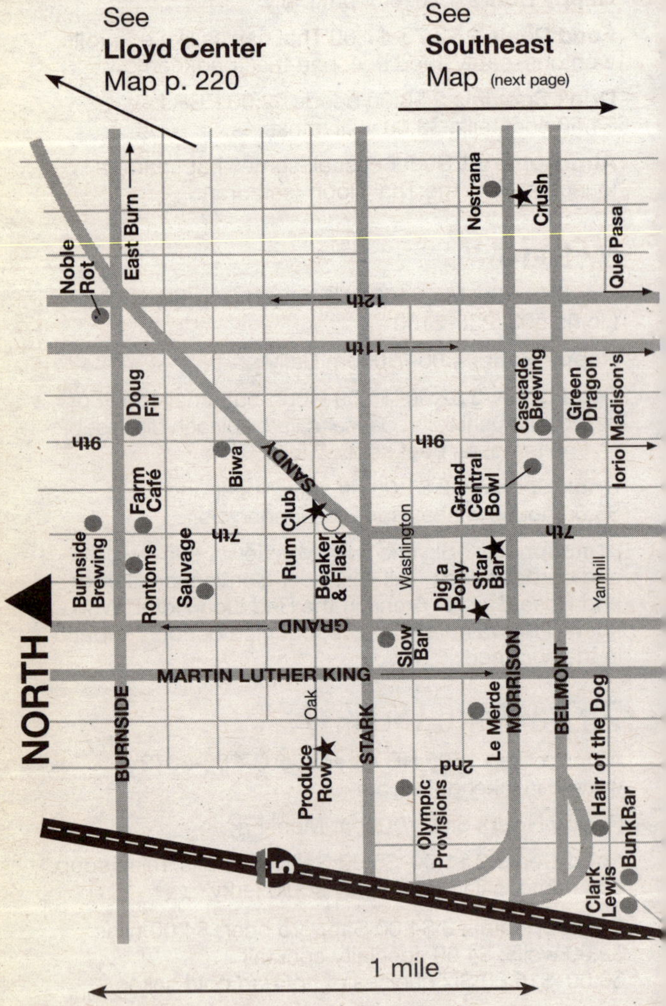

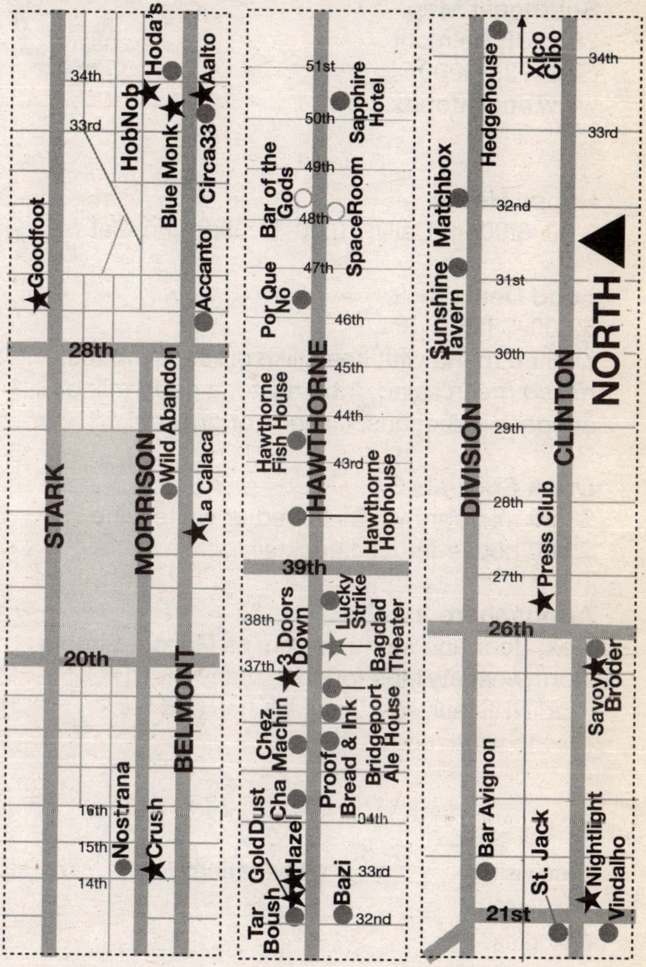
Hoda's
34th
HobNob
Aalto
33rd
Blue Monk
Circa33
Goodfoot
Accanto
28th
Wild Abandon
STARK
MORRISON
La Calaca
BELMONT
20th
Nostrana
Crush
16th
15th
14th
51st
Sapphire Hotel
50th
Bar of the Gods
49th
48th
SpaceRoom
Por Que No
47th
46th
45th
Hawthorne Fish House
HAWTHORNE
44th
43rd
Hawthorne Hophouse
39th
Lucky Strike
38th
3 Doors Down
Bagdad Theater
37th
Chez Machin
Bridgeport Ale House
Proof
Bread & Ink
GoldDust
Hazel
Tar Boush
Bazi
33rd
32nd
Hedgehouse
Xico
Cibo
34th
33rd
Matchbox
32nd
Sunshine Tavern
31st
30th
NORTH
DIVISION
CLINTON
29th
28th
Press Club
27th
26th
Savoy
Broder
Bar Avignon
St. Jack
Nightlight
Vindalho
21st

# Accanto

9

**Southeast Map**
2838 SE Belmont
(503) 235-4900
www.accantopdx.com

**Happy Hours**
5:00–6:00pm Daily; 10:00-11:00pm Fri–Sat

**Food Deals 3**
$2.00–$8.00
Limited menu with items like olives, almonds, mixed green salad, fritto misto, a good mix of antipasti selections, lasagna or gnocchi.

**Drink Specials 3**
$3.50 microbrews; $5.00 red or white wine
$5.00 house-infused cocktail

**Atmosphere 2**
Next door and same owners as Genoa. Simple Northwest stylings found in many SE PDX foodie restaurants. Open kitchen and back private wine room.

Date visited: ____________ **My Rating:** ____________
Went with: ______________________________________
Favorites: ______________________________________
Not so much: ____________________________________
Other comments: _________________________________
_________________________________________________

# Bar Avignon

9

**Southeast Map**
2138 SE Division
(503) 517-0808
www.baravignon.com

**Happy Hours**
5:00–6:00pm Mon–Fri

**Food Deals 3**
$3.00–$6.00
Ultra-fresh and gourmet menu of 10 or so fancy items like mussels, salads, smoked salmon, mussels, baguettes, marinated olives, daily charcuterie/cheese. Oysters on the half-shell $1.50.

**Drink Specials 3**
$4.00–$4.50 drafts (nice choices); $5.00 wines
$5.50 wells; $5.00 select cocktail

**Atmosphere 2**
Small, industrial-fresh restaurant with big bar and small, back table room surrounded by wine. Lots of light by day makes it coffee-shop-like, but by night it's more romantic, but not Frenchy like the name might imply.

Date visited: ____________ **My Rating:** ____________
Went with: ______________________________
Favorites: ______________________________
Not so much: ____________________________
Other comments: __________________________
__________________________________________

# Biwa

7

**Central Eastside Map**
215 SE 9th Avenue
(503) 239-8830
www.biwarestaurant.com

**Happy Hours**
5:00–6:30pm and 9:00-10:00pm Daily

**Food Deals 2**
$1.00–$4.00
Incredible skewers only $2 each! Pork belly, chicken breast, hanger steak and garlic. Also, go-withs onigiri (rice balls) and miso soup. Different late-night options: just ramen or udon.

**Drink Specials 2**
$3.00 Sapporo drafts; $5.00 house wines
$5.00 sake and well drinks

**Atmosphere 2**
Spartan NW foodie-style space in half-basement. Must sit at counter facing open kitchen to get Happy Hour pricing. Discounts are only $1.00 off regular prices, so might as well get a table to enjoy more of an array of other Japanese tapas, and enjoy more comfortable surroundings.

Date visited: ____________ **My Rating:** ____________
Went with: ____________________________
Favorites: ____________________________
Not so much: ____________________________
Other comments: ____________________________
____________________________________________

# Bread & Ink 10

**Southeast Map**
3610 SE Hawthorne
(503) 239-4756
www.breadandinkcafe.com

**Happy Hours**
3:30–6:30pm Daily

**Food Deals 3**
$4.00–$6.00
Focus on locally-sourced ingredients and fresh, seasonal menu with about 15 items: grilled asparagus with herbed chévre, curried chicken, gnocchi verde, salads, grilled shrimp, hummus plate, BBQ pork, black bean cakes, and soup.

**Drink Specials 3+**
$2.50 microbrews; $5.00–6.50 cocktails
$4.50 red or white wine ($12.00 select bottles)

**Atmosphere 3**
More than 25 years strong and they finally started a Happy Hour – and it's a good one! A long-time favorite of writer types both because of the name and the mellow and pleasant scene. Open breakfast through late dinner.

Date visited: __________ **My Rating:** __________
Went with: ____________________
Favorites: ____________________
Not so much: ____________________
Other comments: ____________________
____________________

# Broder

8

**Southeast Map**
2508 SE Clinton
(503) 736-3333
www.broderpdx.com

**Happy Hours**
5:00–6:00pm Wed–Sat

**Food Deals 3**
$4.00–$10.00
Enjoy surf or turf boards, Swedish meatballs, traditional lefse, and aebleskiver. Salad, soup, or potato pancake sides. Legendary for weekend brunches with two-hour waits (but try it at night instead with the all-day breakfast menu)!

**Drink Specials 2**
$1.50 off draft beer; $1.00 off cocktails

**Atmosphere 2**
One of southeast's finest started a Happy Hour! A sweet but sleek Swedish breakfast cafe that turns into a classically cool European-style bar at night. Interesting overhead branch lighting, dark woods, yellow bar stools, blue checker napkins.

Date visited: __________ **My Rating:** __________
Went with: ______________________________
Favorites: ______________________________
Not so much: ______________________________
Other comments: ______________________________
______________________________

# Café Castagna 10

**Hawthorne (off map)**
1758 SE Hawthorne
(503) 231-9959
www.castagnarestaurant.com

**Happy Hours**
5:00-6:00pm and 9:00pm–close Mon–Sat

**Food Deals 2**
$4.00–$6.00
YES! They've added an early Happy Hour! Menu changes often, but hosts items like arancini, spicy grilled pork skewers, oysters, meatballs, butter lettuce salad, salmon rillettes, chickpea fritters, and their famously delicious burger!

**Drink Specials 3**
$3.00 drafts; $5.00 wines and wells
$5.00 specialty cocktails

**Atmosphere 3**
Contemporary simplicity with sleek lines, natural colors within a neutral color palette, and big front windows, which give this half of the restaurant more of a café feel.

Date visited: __________ **My Rating:** __________
Went with: ______________________________
Favorites: ______________________________
Not so much: ______________________________
Other comments: ______________________________
______________________________________________

# Cibo

6

**Southeast Map**
3593 SE Division
(503) 719-5377

**Happy Hours**
5:00–6:30pm / 10:00pm–close Daily

**Food Deals 1**
$5.00 Wood-fired cheese pizza or wings. Food is good enough, but I know they have it in them to do a better Happy Hour. Keep your eyes peeled.

**Drink Specials 2**
$1.00 off beer & wells; $2.00 off wine

**Atmosphere 2**
Pronounced CHEE-bo. A new, neighborhood bar from the owner of Basta's, but the casual bar vibe is a disconnect from the fancy food served. Tables and booths line the slatted wood walls, surrounding the giant central bar/kitchen that the whole place revolves around.

Date visited: ____________ **My Rating:** ____________
Went with: ________________________________________
Favorites: ________________________________________
Not so much: ______________________________________
Other comments: ___________________________________
___________________________________________________

# Circa 33

8 ★

**Southeast Map**
3348 SE Belmont Ave
(503) 477-7682
www.circa33bar.com

**Happy Hours**
4:00–6:00pm Daily; ★All night Monday

**Food Deals 2**
$3.00–$6.50
Bar menu with slight twists on basics and seasonal variations: burger, reuben rolls, fries, house chips, grilled asparagus, calamari, salad, sautéed Swiss chard, or mac & cheese.

**Drink Specials 3**
$3.50 Pilsner; $5.00 house wine
$4.00 wells; $5.00 planter's punch

**Atmosphere 3**
Around about the 33rd block, so you'll always remember where it is, and also relates to 1933, the year Prohibition was repealed. It's true to theme and concept, and exudes a genuine character. Best at night! Alleyway patio too.

Date visited: ____________ **My Rating:** ____________
Went with: ______________________________
Favorites: ______________________________
Not so much: ______________________________
Other comments: ______________________________
______________________________

# Clarklewis

10

**Central Eastside Map**
1001 SE Water Ave.
(503) 235-2294
www.clarklewispdx.com

**Happy Hours**
4:30–6:30pm Mon–Sat

**Food Deals 3**
$1.00–$6.00
Menu changes often, with about 12 or so choice nibbles like baby greens, spaghetti, cauliflower arancini, soup, meatballs, clams, or a burger.

**Drink Specials 3**
$3.00 draft; $5.00 house wine
$5.00 martini or gimlet

**Atmosphere 3**
Sophisticated renovation of old loading dock with northwest and industrial-chic stylings; full, long wall of streetscape gridded windows (open or candlelit), big wooden tables for groups and tucked-away two-tops. A perfect date place!

Date visited: ____________ **My Rating:** ____________
Went with: ________________________________
Favorites: ________________________________
Not so much: ______________________________
Other comments: ___________________________
___________________________________________

# Farm Café

10

**Central East Side Map**
10 SE 7th Ave
(503) 736-3276
www.thefarmcafe.com

A Happy Hour favorite!

**Happy Hours**
5:00–6:00pm Mon–Fri

**Food Deals 3**
$2.00–$6.00
Short but sweet menu – fresh goodies change with the seasons, and even daily: hummus plate, hot wings, mountain-o-fries, crostini, salads, soup.

**Drink Specials 2**
$1.00 off draft beer; $5.00 red and white wines
$5.00 choice cocktails

**Atmosphere 3+**
High-level cuteness alert! Located in a renovated, old Victorian home dripping with charm. Romantic and intimate with several meandering, cozy dining rooms. Big seasonal patio and back bar.

Date visited: __________ **My Rating:** __________
Went with: ______________________________
Favorites: ______________________________
Not so much: ______________________________
Other comments: ______________________________
______________________________

# Grand Central Bowl

8

**Central Eastside Map**
839 SE Morrison
(503) 236-BOWL (2695)
www.thegrandcentralbowl.com

**Happy Hours**
3:00–6:00pm Mon–Fri;
10:00pm–close Sun–Thurs (food only)

**Food Deals 2**
$2.95–$5.95
Almost 20 bar basics like sliders, fries, nachos, artichoke dip, onion rings, lettuce wraps, hummus, cheese sticks, spicy tuna rolls and pizzas.

**Drink Specials 2**
$2.75 domestics; $3.75 select drafts; $2.50 wells

**Atmosphere 3**
A flashy, fancy-smancy bowling mecca! It's a party place in a giant space with several bars, lounges, game rooms and plenty of hi-def, big-screen TVs.

Date visited: ____________ **My Rating:** ____________
Went with: ______________________________
Favorites: ______________________________
Not so much: ______________________________
Other comments: ______________________________
______________________________

# Hazel Room

10

**Hawthorne Map**
3279 SE Hawthorne
(503) 756-7125
www.thehazelroom.com

**Happy Hours**
4:00–7:00pm Tues–Sat (for now, they *close* at 7)

**Food Deals 3**
$2.00–$3.00
Super fresh and delicious! Several small plates with a menu that changes weekly with items like a dolma plate or pulled pork slider, and salad specialties like a beet, quinoa or chicken salad.

**Drink Specials 3**
$2.50 beers; $4.00 wines; $4.00–$5.00 wells

**Atmosphere 3**
Charming and homey tea house with wood floors and thick moldings, copper-tiled walls and large chalkboard menu, friendly service, and just cuteness all around! Outdoor seating on tiered front porch. Named in honor of Katie's Great Grandmother who ran a tea house/ speakeasy during prohibition.

Date visited: ____________ **My Rating:** ____________
Went with: ______________________________
Favorites: ______________________________
Not so much: ______________________________
Other comments: ______________________________
______________________________

# Hokusei Sushi

9

**Southeast Map**
4246 SE Belmont
(971) 279-2161
www.hokuseisushi.com

**Happy Hours**
5:00-6:00pm Daily; ★All night Monday

**Food Deals 3**
$2.00–$6.00
Exceptional sushi here, and a big menu, but prices are all over the board, and (relatively) not much of it discounted for Happy Hour. Eight menu items with funny names like wakame salad, edamame, tatsuta age, harumaki, gyu tan yaki.

**Drink Specials 2**
$1.00 off drafts and sake (half-off small hot sake)
$5.00 Happy Hour cocktail

**Atmosphere 3**
Serene, simple, and stark space. Contemporary design with clean lines, natural woods, open-air garage door wall, and cement floors. Super-long group table, pretty artwork, and sushi bar seating.

Date visited: ____________ **My Rating:** ____________
Went with: ______________________________
Favorites: ______________________________
Not so much: ______________________________
Other comments: ______________________________
______________________________

# La Calaca Comelona

10

**Southeast Map**
2304 SE Belmont
(503) 239-9675
www.lacalacacomelona.com

**Happy Hours**
4:00-6:00pm and 8:00pm-close Mon–Sat

**Food Deals 3**
$2.00–$6.50
Authentic, truly delicious Mexican food! Pork and pineapple tacos (plus other varieties); grilled cactus, spicy potatoes, mini quesadillas, taquitos—and grilled grasshoppers!

**Drink Specials 3**
50 cents off beer; $5.00 wines; $3.50 wells
$4.00 Margaritas and other bartender specials

**Atmosphere 3+**
Take a Mexican vacation to this Day-of-the-Dead-inspired taverna named "The Hungry Skeleton." Bright colorful walls, Mexican-style folk art at every glimpse and turn, and you can sit anywhere in the whole loco restaurant early on, but late-night, Happy Hour is at the bar only. Enchanting patio out back, but for dinner only.

Date visited: ____________ **My Rating:** ____________
Went with: ______________________________
Favorites: ______________________________
Not so much: ______________________________
Other comments: ______________________________
______________________________

# Lucky Strike

9

**Southeast Map**
3862 SE Hawthorne
(503) 206-8292
www.luckystrikepdx.com

**Happy Hours**
4:00-6:00pm Daily

**Food Deals 3**
$4.00–$7.50
About a dozen or so eats including pot stickers, spring rolls, spicy Sichuan (Szechuan) noodles, kung pao chicken, Guinness pork ribs, dumplings, stir-fried beans with beef and baby bok choy.

**Drink Specials 3**
$3.00 beer; $4.00 red and wine wines
$4.00 top-shelf well drinks; $5.00 daily cocktail

**Atmosphere 2**
A funky space that matches the Hawthorne area vibe, with a giant wall mural of a tattoo-art dragon dominating the scene. Lots of small tables and nice outdoor patio available at Happy Hour.

Date visited: ____________ **My Rating:** ____________
Went with: ______________________________
Favorites: ______________________________
Not so much: ______________________________
Other comments: ______________________________
______________________________________________

# Mi Mero Mole 8

**Southeast Map**
5026 SE Division
(503) 232-8226
www.mmmtacospdx.com

**Happy Hours**
4:00-5:30pm Tues–Fri

**Food Deals 3**
$2.00–$5.00
Mexican "street food" specialists! Everything, including moles, salsas, and rice and beans, is made from scratch. Happy Hour menu offers a delicious line-up which changes, but gooood.

**Drink Specials 1**
No beer or wine deals; $6.50 select cocktails
$4.00–$6.00 delicioso margaritas

**Atmosphere 2**
A lively taqueria where you walk in and immediately order at the typically crowded counter which is open to the active and delicious-smelling kitchen. Restaurant seating is in the adjoining, very bright and colorful room, dominated by a hand-painted, giant mural. Very casual.

Date visited: __________ **My Rating:** __________
Went with: ____________________
Favorites: ____________________
Not so much: ____________________
Other comments: ____________________
____________________

# Nostrana

9

**Southeast Map**
1401 SE Morrison St
(503) 234-2427
www.nostrana.com

**Happy Hours**
9:00pm–close Daily (Nightly)

**Food Deals 3**
$3.00–$6.00
It's all about the wood-fired pizza! Get marinara or margherita style (add arugula, prosciutto or anchovies). Also salad, mac & cheese, spiced nuts, roasted olives and cheeses.

**Drink Specials 3**
$4.00 seasonal ale or pils; $5.00 house wines
$3.00 fresh lemonade; $5.00 select cocktails

**Atmosphere 3**
Giant, hanger-like space in a mini strip mall with an overhead, complex grid of wood ceiling beams. Interior still manages to feel friendly and intimate with candles, suspended framed art, and a long, communal bar with giant, towering shelves.

Date visited: ____________ **My Rating:** ____________
Went with: ______________________________
Favorites: ______________________________
Not so much: ______________________________
Other comments: ______________________________
______________________________

# The Observatory 9

**Southeast (Off Map)**
8115 SE Stark
(503) 445-6284
www.theobservatorypdx.com

**Happy Hours**
3:00–6:00pm Daily; 10:00pm–close Sun–Thur

**Food Deals 3**
$2.00–$5.00
Extra points for being a foodie place, but limited choices at HH. Seasonal: salad, soup, smoked whitefish spread, ginger sake mussels, paté.

**Drink Specials 3**
$1.00 domestics (cans); $3.00 microbrews
$5.00 house wines; $3.00 wells; $5.00 cocktail

**Atmosphere 2**
Not too lounge-y, and it's probably more of a restaurant, but their signature cocktails are quite impressive! Big L-shaped bar dominates this upscale diner beneath a high-strung globe-light constellation.

Date visited: __________ **My Rating:** __________
Went with: ______________________________
Favorites: ______________________________
Not so much: ______________________________
Other comments: ______________________________
______________________________

# Olympic Provisions

8

**Central Eastside Map**
107 SE Washington; (503) 954-3663
1632 NW Thurman; (503) 894-8136
www.olympicprovisions.com

**Happy Hours**
3:00–6:00pm Daily

**Food Deals 2**
$4.00–$7.00
Appertif hour offers sandwiches, a couple of veggie items, and some dessert plates. Not that big of a price break from regular menu, but if you love sausages, you've found your heaven!

**Drink Specials 2**
$5.00 Several unique apértifs and soda mixers, beer, plus red or white house wine options

**Atmosphere 3**
Both interiors are similar and follow a trendy NW-gritty-cute look. Cool, industrial spaces with painted white brick walls, lots of cement, old woods, and metal. A funky, illuminated "meat" sign dominates the eastside location. Their new outpost is the old Carlyle. Meet up, or meat-to-go.

Date visited: ____________ **My Rating:** ____________
Went with: ____________________________________
Favorites: ____________________________________
Not so much: __________________________________
Other comments: ________________________________
______________________________________________

# Otto

# 8

**Southeast (Off map)**
1852 SE Hawthorne
(503) 517-7770
www.ottopdx.com

**Happy Hours**
4:00-6:00pm Tues-Sat

**Food Deals 2**
20% off entire menu
Specializing in global comfort food. Select from their menu of about 20 unique items like boneless braised beef shortribs, pan seared sturgeon, crispy chicken with kimchee, or spinach salad with shrimp with fun appetizers too.

**Drink Specials 2**
$1.00 off drinks

**Atmosphere 3**
Down the road a piece from the Hawthorne strip, but worth seeking out. Nice, modern-but-cozy space in the former Sel Gris and Fin spot. Long, zig-zag, stand alone bartop, carrot-colored walls, and giant, mounted antler trophies.

Date visited: __________ **My Rating:** __________
Went with: ____________________
Favorites: ____________________
Not so much: ____________________
Other comments: ____________________
________________________________________

# Press Club

10

**Southeast Map**
2621 SE Clinton
(503) 233-5656
www.pressclubpdx.com

**Happy Hours**
3:00–7:00pm Mon–Fri; ★All night Monday

A Happy Hour favorite

**Food Deals 3**
$3.00–$7.00
Fresh salads and soup, crepes or sandwiches (named after famous authors).

**Drink Specials 3**
$1.00 off beer and wine (i.e. $2.50 imports!)
$6.00 cocktails; plus nightly specials and coffee
Plus $5.00 Bloody Marys all day Sunday

**Atmosphere 3**
If the ever-so-treasured Powell's Bookstore was a small neighborhood bar, it would be The Press Club. There's a sweet, laid-back vibe here that works well if you are a fan of coffee houses, bookstores, Paris, or hipster concert venues.

Date visited: ____________ **My Rating:** ____________
Went with: ______________________________
Favorites: ______________________________
Not so much: ______________________________
Other comments: ______________________________
______________________________

# Proof

9

**Hawthorne Map**
3564 SE Hawthorne
(503) 236-6001

**Happy Hours**
3:00-6:00pm Daily

**Food Deals 2**
$3.00–$7.00
Same munchies menu as the late night bites with pulled pork or bison sliders, sweet potato fries, chips & salsa, mac & cheese, olives & bread, salad, cheese plate, or fried green beans.

**Drink Specials 3**
$2.75 drafts; $4.00 wines; $3.50 well drinks
$2.75 pints all day Tuesday

**Atmosphere 3**
Cool cocktail bar side of connected coffeeshop, the Cup & Saucer. A special “love-at-first-sight” kind of place with rotating gallery art adorning deep red walls. Simple, cozy, and nice.

Date visited: __________ **My Rating:** __________
Went with: ____________________
Favorites: ____________________
Not so much: ____________________
Other comments: ____________________

____________________

# Rum Club

9

**Central Eastside**
720 SE Sandy Blvd.
(503) 467-2469
www.rumclubpdx.com

**Happy Hours**
4:00-7:00pm Mon–Sat; ★All day Sunday

**Food Deals 2**
$4.00–$5.00
Four to five items in about the four to five price range. Classic cocktail nibbles that change weekly with unique things like pickled eggs for a buck, lil' smokies, BBQ ribs, focaccia or skewers.

**Drink Specials 3**
$6.00 cocktails (choice of only four, but they are so good they score top marks!)

**Atmosphere 3**
Simple but cool, retro style lounge. Small place with big horseshoe bar and barely-tropical wall paper. Cocktail and regular tables, but sit at the bartop where you can watch the masters at work! Next door to also-wonderful Beaker & Flask.

Date visited: ____________ **My Rating:** ____________
Went with: ______________________________
Favorites: ______________________________
Not so much: ____________________________
Other comments: _________________________
__________________________________________

# Sapphire Hotel 10

A Happy Hour favorite!

**Southeast Map**
5008 SE Hawthorne
(503) 232-6333
www.thesapphirehotel.com

**Happy Hours**
4:00pm–6:00pm Daily
10:00pm-close Sun–Thurs

**Food Deals 3**
$3.00–$6.00
Meze platters, soup, several salads, artichoke dip, tandoori spiced chicken, salmon corncakes.

**Drink Specials 3**
$2.00 PBRs; $5.00 selected wine
$4.00 well drinks; $5.0-$6.00 cocktail specials

**Atmosphere 3**
Mysteriously sexy and intriguing; trés swanky! Intimate creative lounge decor. Ex-brothel. Outdoor sidewalk seating.

Date visited: __________ **My Rating:** __________
Went with: ____________________
Favorites: ____________________
Not so much: ____________________
Other comments: ____________________

____________________

# Sauvage

8

**Southeast Map**
537 SE Ash
(503) 807-5565
www.sauvagepdx.com

**Happy Hours**
4:00-6:00pm and 10:00–11:00pm Tues–Fri

**Food Deals 2**
$2.00–$6.00
Unique eats to complement NW wine palates. Seasonal changes with items like 1/2 dozen oysters (pair with cava), wings, market salad, deviled quail eggs, or cheese and pickles.

**Drink Specials 2**
$5.00 nightly wine special (Full menu has about 50 wines by the glass)

**Atmosphere 3**
Tucked away in a renovated, old industrial building, the loft interior is intimate and cozy, with an urban edge. Brick walls, white tiles, curtains to soften, and hanging lights made of beer/wine carboys. Next door to owner's own *Fausse Piste* Winery (Yay! Another boutique urban winery conveniently located near downtown Portland).

Date visited: ____________ **My Rating:** ____________
Went with: ______________________________
Favorites: ______________________________
Not so much: ______________________________
Other comments: ______________________________

______________________________

# St. Jack

9

**Southeast Map**
2039 SE Clinton
(503) 360-1281
www.stjackpdx.com

**Happy Hours**
4:00-5:00pm Daily

**Food Deals 3**
$3.00–$9.00
Classic French bistro hor d'oeuvres: charcuterie plate sampler, mussels, pommes frites, olives, gruyére burger, roasted beet salad; or if you're brave, try the fried tripe!

**Drink Specials 2**
$4.00 select draft beers; $5.00-$7.00 wines
$7.00 choice of two cocktails

**Atmosphere 3**
Rustic, white, and open bistro space with front pâtisserie/bar area and two romantic restaurant rooms in back. Bright by day with sidewalk café seating, and characteristically candlelit by night. Named the Oregonian's Rising Star 2011!

Date visited: __________ **My Rating:** __________
Went with: ____________________
Favorites: ____________________
Not so much: ____________________
Other comments: ____________________

____________________

# Sunshine Tavern 9

**Southeast Map**
3111 SE Division
(503) 688-1750
www.sunshinepdx.com

**Happy Hours**
5:00-6:00pm and 10:00-11:00pm Daily

**Food Deals 3**
$2.00–$6.00
Comfort/bar food with a NW-gourmet twist: poutine, romaine salad, crackling/pork rinds, crispy oysters, ham & swiss panini, corn dog, candied hazelnuts.

**Drink Specials 3**
$4.00 draft beer; $5.00 house wines
$5.00 slushy margarita
$5.00 bartender's choice cocktail

**Atmosphere 3**
Rain or shine, the sky-high windows let in lots of light, and the wood walls and booths warm the place up. After the sun sets, it takes on a totally different, more intimate glow, perfect for indulging those late-night munchie cravings.

Date visited: ____________ **My Rating:** ____________
Went with: ______________________________
Favorites: ______________________________
Not so much: ______________________________
Other comments: ______________________________
______________________________

# TarBoush

9

**Southeast Map**
3257 SE Hawthorne
(503) 235-3277
www.tarboushbistro.com

**Happy Hours**
★ 2:00pm–6:00pm Daily

**Food Deals 3**
$4.00–$6.50 (plus $7.50–$12.00 platters)
Unique, mostly vegetarian, Lebanese appetizers with several full-size meat dishes too: tabbouli, hummus, baba ghannouj, fava and garbanzo beans, soups, salad, cheeses, and stuffed pitas.

**Drink Specials 2**
$1.00 off beer, wine and wells

**Atmosphere 3**
An absolutely gorgeous and giant Victorian home on Hawthorne houses this funky and lively Lebanese restaurant. Nice summer patio area — and hookahs too!

Date visited: ____________ **My Rating:** ____________
Went with: ______________________________
Favorites: ______________________________
Not so much: ____________________________
Other comments: __________________________
__________________________________________

# Three Doors Down

9

**Southeast Map**
1429 SE 37th Ave
(503) 236-6886
www.3doorsdowncafe.com

**Happy Hours**
★5:30–9:00pm Tues–Thur; 4:00–9:00pm Sun

**Food Deals 3**
$2.50–$10.00
Changing 15-item menu of delicious, Italian-focused specials like fettucine, tortiglione, spicy prawns, zuppa de mare, sausage & peppers, eggplant, daily lasagna, arancini, mac & cheese.

**Drink Specials 2**
$5.00 house wines; $6.00 manhattans / martinis (Beware $6.00 beers *not* included in Happy Hour, but you can get a Rolling Rock for $2.50)

**Atmosphere 3**
Just off Hawthorne, three doors down on 37th. The Happy Hour bar side is just off the cuter and quieter restaurant side, but has a similar, romantically social, wine bar vibe. Enjoy it all night!

Date visited: ____________ **My Rating:** ____________
Went with: ______________________________
Favorites: ______________________________
Not so much: ____________________________
Other comments: __________________________
__________________________________________

# Vie de Bohème

9

**Southeast Map**
1530 SE 7th Ave.
(503) 360-1233
www.viedebohemepdx.com

**Happy Hours**
4:00–7:00pm Tues–Fri

**Food Deals 3**
$1.95–$5.25
Smallplate menu with about a dozen items made for sitting and sipping: nuts, olives, or chips; baguettes with olive oil, brie or chèvre, ham or paté; pork sliders; hummus, or cheese & salami plate.

**Drink Specials 2**
$3.00 bottles; $4.00 drafts; $1.00 off wine, wells, and apéritifs (Recently added taps and full bar)

**Atmosphere 3**
An urban winery tucked inside a well-appointed warehouse space. Central dance floor and Oriental rug stage (big live music venue). Main level seating with a second elevated tier, plus a cozy back wine tasting/library room. The *perfect* place for parties!

Date visited: ___________ **My Rating:** ___________
Went with: ______________________________________
Favorites: ______________________________________
Not so much: ____________________________________
Other comments: _________________________________
_________________________________________________

# Vindalho

9

**Southeast Map**
2038 SE Clinton
(503) 467-4550
www.vindalho.com

**Happy Hours**
5:00–6:00pm Tues–Sun

**Food Deals 2**
$5.00
Five choices that rotate somewhat based on seasonal ingredients plus an array of condiments and naan. Items like kabobs, mussels, wings, fritters or samosas.

**Drink Specials 3**
$3.50 draft beer; $5.00 wine; $4.00 wells
$7.00 specialty cocktails

**Atmosphere 3**
Very cool and contemporary architecture defies convention and expected southeast hash house decor, and bears few signs of old, traditional India. Sadly, Happy Hour is confined to the bar.

Date visited: __________ **My Rating:** __________
Went with: ______________________________
Favorites: ______________________________
Not so much: ____________________________
Other comments: __________________________
__________________________________________

# Wild Abandon



**Southeast Map**
2411 SE Belmont
(503) 232-4458
www.wildabandonrestaurant.com

**Happy Hours**
4:30–6:30pm Mon, Wed–Fri

A Happy Hour favorite!

**Food Deals 3**
$1.00-$7.00
Choose from about 15 gourmet specialties including shrimp or chicken with peppers over polenta, extra-delicious portobello sandwich(!), soup, burger, several salads, mac & cheese, BBQ pork sandwich, goat cheese torta, or fries.

**Drink Specials 3**
$2.00–$3.00 beer; $5.00 wine; $5.00 well drinks
$5.00–$6.00 array of cocktail specialties

**Atmosphere 3**
A funky little "Love Shack" as viewed from the street; things change inside with cozy, dimly-lit dining. Colorful, glass hanging lamps and a mish mash of framed prints add to the garage-sale-chic, retro look. Wonderful garden patio in back!

Date visited: ____________ **My Rating:** ____________
Went with: ______________________________
Favorites: ______________________________
Not so much: ______________________________
Other comments: ______________________________
______________________________

## 4-4-2 Soccer Bar www.442soccerbar.com

**SE (off map)** 1738 SE Hawthorne; (503) 238-3693

**Happy Hours** 3:00–7:00pm Mon–Fri

**Food Deals 1** $2.00–$6.00 Four choices: spicy or regular sausage sandwiches, hotdogs, Mediterranean plate.

**Drink Specials 2** $2.00 PBR; $1.00 off drafts; $3.00 wells

**Atmosphere 2** Well-loved soccer bar! Cozy and fun place with hanging soccer jerseys and memorabilia.

## Aalto Lounge www.aaltolounge.com

**Southeast Map** 3356 SE Belmont (503) 235-6041

**Happy Hours** 4:00–7:00pm Daily★

**Food Deals 2** $2.00 Simple. Grilled cheese sandwiches with tomato soup or pretzel w/cheese,

**Drink Specials 1** $2.00 select house cocktails or draft.

**Atmosphere 2** Compelling and retro-y with artsy vibe, subtle funkiness, loungy ambience. Back patio.

## Blitz Ladd www.blitzbarpdx.net

**Southeast (off map)** 2239 SE 11th Ave; (503) 236-3592

**Happy Hours** 3–6pm Mon-Fri; 9pm-close (food) Daily (10:00pm-close Fri-Sat)

**Food Deals 2** $3.00–$5.00 Similar bar food menu as other Blitzes

**Drink Specials 3** $3.50 drafts, wine, and wells

**Atmosphere 2** Huge room with several seating areas. Plenty of hi-def TVs (including 15 52" screens, plus a giant 12 ft. projection screen). Plenty of tables and couches too. Pool, shuffleboard and ping pong.

## Blue Monk

**Southeast Map** 3341 SE Belmont; (503) 595-0575
www.thebluemonk.com

**Happy Hours** 5:00–7:00pm Daily

**Food Deals 2** $5.50 for nice variety: shrimp tacos, seared ahi carpaccio, bruschetta plate, coconut polenta, meatball and sausage subs.

**Drink Specials 3** $3.00 for drafts; $3.00 wells $5.50 house wine; $4.50 specialty cocktails

**Atmosphere 2** Happy Hour downstairs where blue theme continues with pool and cool tunes.

## Cha Cha Cha

**Southeast Map** 3433 SE Hawthorne; (503) 236-1100

**Happy Hours** 3:00–6:00pm Daily

**Food Deals 2** $4.00–$6.00 Array of Mexican basics: tostadas, fish tacos, quesadillas, tacos, soup, salads.

**Drink Specials 2** $3.00 beer: $5.00 sangrias and Margaritas

**Atmosphere 2** Part of the Cha Cha Cha family as represented with characteristic, southeast style. Very casual with a nice, covered patio just off the street.

## Chez Machin Creperie

**Southeast Map** 3553 SE Hawthorne; (503) 736-9381
www.chezmachincreperie.com

**Happy Hours** 4:00–6:00pm Mon–Fri

**Food Deals 0** No discounts

**Drink Specials 2** $1.50 off all beer; $2.00 off wines

**Atmosphere 3** Trés cute!!! Dripping with charm like a good creperie should be, with a patio too. Great crepes. Good crowd and low prices, so no need for food deals.

## The Conquistador

**Southeast Map** 2045 SE Belmont; (503) 232-3227

**Happy Hours** 3:00–7:00pm Daily

**Food Deals 1** Cheap food, but no discounts

**Drink Specials 2** $3.00 micros; 3.25 wells

**Atmosphere 3** I love the vibe here! It was formerly The Globe. It's still not a fancy place, but they opened up the upstairs with a living room lounge right out of the 60s and the whole place has vinyl curved booths, conquistador paintings, and artifacts everywhere. It's definitely a bar, but they put lots of effort into theme.

## Crush www.crushbar.com

**Southeast Map** 1412 SE Morrison; (503) 235-8150

**Happy Hours** 4:00–7:00pm Tues–Sun
★All day Tuesdays

**Food Deals 3** $2.75–$5.75 Good-size menu of Happy Hour food: yams w/curry sauce (vegans love it), baba ganoush, quesadillas, and flat nachos.

**Drink Specials 3** $3.25 microbrews; $4.50 house wines $3.00–$3.50 wells; $4.50 cocktails

**Atmosphere 2** Open, artsy lounge with stunning bottle chandelier; a favorite neighborhood hangout.

## Delta Café

**SE (Not on Map)** 4607 SE Woodstock; (503) 771-3101
www.deltacafebar.com

**Happy Hours** 4:00–6:00pm/11:00pm-1:00am Mon–Thur
★All night Tuesday includes $5.00 specialty cocktails

**Food Deals 3** $1.00–$3.00 Hush puppies, sweet potato fries, corn bread, fritters, mac & cheese.

**Drink Specials 2** $2.50 drafts or wells (woo hoo!)

**Atmosphere 2** They've decked themselves out with very colorful SE PDX-meets-Delta style! Loud, garish and fun with graffiti and folk art everywhere.

## Dig a Pony www.digaponyportland.com

**Central Eastside** 736 SE Grand Ave.; (971) 279-4409

**Happy Hours** 4:00–7:00pm Daily

**Food Deals 2** $3.00 Small menu of unique bar eats: fried plantains, Cubano sandwich, arugula and pear salad, fries, nuts, churro dessert.

**Drink Specials 2** $3.00 choice of drafts; $3.00 wells

**Atmosphere 3** Dig the atmosphere. Cool space! Brick walls, big windows, and book nooks, in a giant, rustic-loft style room. Appropriately, there's a very large, horseshoe-shaped bar in the middle. A popular crowd scene, can be loud, and very dark.

## Doug Fir www.dougfirlounge.com

**Central Eastside** 830 E Burnside; (503) 231-9663

**Happy Hours** 3:00–6:00pm Daily

**Food Deals 2** $2.00–$5.00 Lots of hearty comfort food: burgers, mashers and gravy, croque monsieur, tomato soup, salads, bread pudding, cheese fries.

**Drink Specials 3** $3.00 drafts, wine, wells

**Atmosphere 3** Twin Peaks meets the Sinatra 50s in classy-kitsch, Northwest lodge theme; couch pits for groups; outdoor patio seating. Order at the bar. Great place to see bands downstairs!

## Eastburn www.theeastburn.com

**Central Eastside** 1800 E Burnside; (503) 236-2876

**Happy Hour** 4:00-6:00pm Daily

**Food Deals 2** $5.00 Five for five seasonal and fresh menu items: autumn may bring spaetzle, spinach and pear salad, BLTs, elk sliders or red pepper fritters.

**Drink Specials 2** Rotating nightly specials like $2.00 drafts all night on Tuesdays

**Atmosphere 2** Very casual local place that's more of a bar with one exception – excellent food. There's a true bar in the basement, and great patio with swings!

## Gold Dust Meridian

**Southeast Map** 3267 SE Hawthorne; (503) 239-1143
www.golddustmeridian.com

**Happy Hours** ★2:00–8:00pm Daily

**Food Deals 2** $4.00–$6.00 Menu follows period style and includes deviled eggs, grilled cheese trio (served with soup and salad), fritters, salami plate, mac & cheese.

**Drink Specials 1** .50 cents off pints & wells; $1.00 off wine

**Atmosphere 3** Marathon Happy Hour joint with a dark interior that is steeped deep in authentic retro charm and is at once swanky, chill, and ultra-cool.

## Goodfoot

**Central Eastside** 2845 SE Stark; (503) 239-9292
www.thegoodfoot.com

**Happy Hours** 5:00–9:00pm Daily

**Food Deals 2** $5.00 Select menu items with semi-healthy pub food. Menu items under $7.00 at all times.

**Drink Specials** 2 $3.50 organic drafts; $2.00 PBRs $3.00 Burnette's gin drinks

**Atmosphere 2** Big, open space showcases local artist rotating galleries and four red felt pool tables.

## Hawthorne Fish House

**Southeast Map** 4343 SE Hawthorne; (503) 548-4434
www.corbettfishhouse.com

**Happy Hours** 3:00–6:00pm Daily ('til 5:30pm Fri-Sat)

**Food Deals 2** $3.95 Wow! Gluten-free fish & chips! Plus fish tacos, tuna melt or catfish sliders, clam or chicken strips, Caesar salad, and shrimp cocktail.

**Drink Specials 2** $4.00 imperial pints, wine and wells

**Atmosphere 2** Kinda cute, kinda kitsch-fishy. Café-like atmosphere with salmon-pink walls adorned with lots of colorful seafood life.

## Hobnob Grille

**Southeast Map** 3350 SE Morrison; (503) 445-3665
www.hobnobgrille.com

**Happy Hours** 4:00-7:00pm Daily; mid-2:30am Fri-Sat

**Food Deals 2** $2.00–$6.00 Bar food taken up a notch: Sesame chicken plate, angus and pulled pork sliders, creole calamari, soup, salad, rib trio w/mashed potatoes.

**Drink Specials 2** $1.00 Rainer; $4.00 wine
$3.00 cocktail of the day; plus nightly speicals

**Atmosphere 2** Very basic interior, almost diner-like in style. Neutrals, big bar, ping pong. Friendly staff, and a great place for groups of all sizes.

## Iorio www.ioriorestaurant.com

**Southeast Map** 912 SE Hawthorne; (503) 445-4716

**Happy Hours** 5:00–6:00pm Wed–Fri

**Food Deals 2** $7.00–$8.00 Big servings, but only four choices: pulled pork sandwich, risotto, pasta, burger.

**Drink Specials 0** Sadly, no drink specials

**Atmosphere 3** Big on red in big, open room with long, central family table and window seats. Low light, dark wood floors, and original paintings depicting country life in bright colors and ornate gold frames.

## Iron Horse www.portlandironhorse.com

**SE (off map)** 6034 SE Milwaukie; (503) 232-1826

**Happy Hours** 3:00–6:00pm Tues–Sun

**Food Deals 2** $3.00–$5.00 Delicious Mexican food: nachos, salad, bean dip, tacos, poppers, taco salad.

**Drink Specials 2** $2.50 domestics; $3.50 microbrews
$3.00 wells; $4.95 margarita

**Atmosphere 2** Colorful neighborhood hangout. Choice of bar, restaurant, or sidewalk seating. Family friendly.

## Jam on Hawthorne

**Southeast (off map)** 2239 SE Hawthorne;
(503) 234-4790 www.jamonhawthorne.com

**Happy Hours** 3:00–6:00pm Tues–Sat

**Food Deals 3** $2.00–$6.00 Burgers (regular or vegan), spinach salad, fries, hummus, brussel sprouts, soup, potato skins, meatballs, and a brownie sundae!

**Drink Specials 2** $1.00 PBR; $4.00 wells
$8.00 bartender's choice cocktail

**Atmosphere 2** Jam on Hawthorne (aka "Big Jam"), is in the space where "Imbibe" used to be, taken over and redone to expand upon "Little Jam." Seems like a breakfast place that's a bar, or a bar that's a breakfast place. They ripped out the walls, and now it's quite plain and open, with cement floors and not a lot of character.

## Landmark Saloon

**SE (off map)** 4847 SE Division; (503) 894-8132
www.thelandmarksaloon.com

**Happy Hours** 4:00–7:00pm Mon–Fri

**Food Deals 0** No deals on food

**Drink Specials 2** $1.00 or so off drinks

**Atmosphere 2** Casual, borderline dive-y, and locally loved, neighborhood saloon. Yes – truly a saloon, country tunes and all. Big oudoor patio with "corn hole."

## Le Merde www.montageportland.com

**Central East Side** 301 SE Morrison; (503) 234-1324

**Happy Hours** 5:00–6:00pm Daily

**Food Deals 2** $3.00–$4.00 Basics from Montage next door: macaronis, gumbo, rice & beans, fritters or maybe even gator bites!

**Drink Specials 3** $3.00 draft beers, wine and wells
$1.00 off specialty cocktails

**Atmosphere 1** Dark and different from adjacent restaurant, Montage (which is kinda cute), Le Merde is the lounge side (which is kinda grungy, but cool).

# Madison's www.madisonsgrill.com

**SE (off map)** 1109 SE Madison; (503) 230-2471

**Happy Hours**
★3:00–8:00pm Sun–Fri and 3:00–10:00pm Sat
$2.50 Tuesdays = 16 taps w/ microbrew deal all night

**Food Deals 2** $2.25–$5.25 Hummus, quesadilla, wings, mound of nachos, onion rings, salads, sliders, fish or shrimp tacos, dips, and BBQ chicken skewers.

**Drink Specials 2** Beers are 75 cents off
$2.75 well drinks; $4.00 select house wines

**Atmosphere 2** Friendly, casual hang-out place; brass and fern family style; outdoor wood deck. Free pool!

# Matchbox Lounge

**Southeast Map** 3203 SE Division; (503) 234-7844
www.matchboxlounge.com

**Happy Hours** 4:00–6:00pm Daily; ★All Night Sunday

**Food Deals 2** $3.00–$5.00 It's all about the burgers (meat or veggie, plus $1.00 add-ons for something more interesting), salad, nut mixes, or olives.

**Drink Specials 3** $2.00 PBR; $3.50 micros; $3.00 wells
$5.00 wines; $5.00 cocktails

**Atmosphere 2** Borderline divebar to me, but *so* many people claim it as a favorite! Small space with red walls and rotating original art. Sidewalk scene.

# Muddy Rudder

**Southeast (Off Map)** 8195 SE 7th Ave; (503) 233-4410
www.muddyrudderpdx.com

**Happy Hours** 4:00–6:00pm Daily

**Food Deals 2** $5.00 Pizza, soup and salad, soup and half sandwich, or bruschetta.

**Drink Specials 3** $3.00 drafts; $4.25 wine; $3.75 wells

**Atmosphere 2** Nice, nautical, neighborhood pub. Cozy, converted home was a true labor of love. Great place to see live music, and excellent side patio!

# Nightlight Lounge

**Southeast Map** 2100 SE Clinton; (503) 731-6500
www.nightlightlounge.net

**Happy Hours** ★2:00–7:00pm Daily (3-7pm Sat–Sun)
11:00pm–1:00am Sun–Thurs

**Food Deals 2** $3.00–$5.00 Soup, salad, grilled cheese, Caesar salad, quesadilla, mac & cheese, nachos.

**Drink Specials 2** $3.50 microbrews; $1.50 PBRs; $.50 off well drinks; $1.00 off wine

**Atmosphere 2** Artsy, casual, and comfortable, yet trendy; outdoor dining on nice back deck.

# Por Que No

**Southeast Map** 4635 SE Hawthorne; (503) 954-3138

**Happy Hours** 3:00–6:00pm Daily; Tues 3:00pm–close

**Food Deals 1** $.50 cents off tacos; $1.00 off chips & guac or salsa. Cheap menu at all times!

**Drink Specials 2** $2.75 bottled beer; $3.75 drafts $5.00 and $7.50 margaritas; $6.50 Mexican specialty cocktails; $5.00 sangrias

**Atmosphere 2** A true taqueria vibe, complete with loud music, warm colors, and noisy kitchen ramblings.

# Produce Row Café

**Central Eastside Map** 204 SE Oak St.; (503) 232-8355
www.producerowcafe.com

**Happy Hours** 4:00-7:00pm and 11:00pm–2:00am (food) Daily ; No late-night HH on Sunday

**Food Deals 2** $4.00–$5.00 Small menu with food that goes well with beer: pita pizza, pork sliders, corn-dogs, potato skins, nachos and frito pie.

**Drink Specials 2** $1.00 off pints, wine, and wells

**Atmosphere 3** Turn-of-the-century beer hall charm mixed with urban Portland vibe. Gorgeous, mahogany front bar with beer selections written on giant mirror. Tin ceilings, wooden beams, tables, and floors.

## Que Pasa Cantina

**SE (not on Map)** 1408 SE 12th Ave.; (503) 230-9212
www.quepasacantinapdx.com

**Happy Hours** 5:00–6:00pm Mon–Wed;
4:00–6.00pm Thur–Fri; 3:00–6:00pm Sat

**Food Deals 2** $5.00 Simple range of the usual but popular, Mexican eats.

**Drink Specials 2** $2.00 PBRs / Tecates; $3.00 drafts $3.00 sangria; $4.00 wells; $5.00 Margaritas

**Atmosphere 2** Formerly Aqui Mexican. Can't always judge a book by its cover – it's shockingly cute inside! Authentic Mexican taqueria that's quite cozy.

## Savoy Tavern www.savoypdx.com

**SE Map** 2500 SE Clinton; (503) 808-9999

**Happy Hours** 4:00–6:00pm &10:00pm–close Daily

**Food Deals 2** $3.00–$8.00 Nostalgic Americana menu with their famous fried cheese curds, burgers, salad, wings, fries, smoked trout, deviled eggs, mac & cheese.

**Drink Specials 3** $4.00 beer; $4.00 wine; $3.50 wells; $5.00 cocktails – plus nightly specials

**Atmosphere 2** The bar has character! Kitschy 1950s lodge look by day, but cute & romantic candlelit at night.

## Slow Bar www.slowbar.net

**Central East Side** 533 SE Grand; (503) 230-7767

**Happy Hours** 3–6pm Mon–Fri; mid–close Sun–Thurs

**Food Deals 2** $2.00–$5.50 Pizzetta, green salad, mixed nuts, fries, cevicho, Southern fry, olives. Just get the burger!

**Drink Specials 2** $1.00 off all drinks

**Atmosphere 2** Dark and smoky, popular, laid-back hipster scene; all black; group seating at window.

## Star Bar www.star-bar-rocks.com

**Southeast Map** 639 SE Morrison; (503) 232-5553

**Happy Hours** ★4:00–8:00pm Daily

**Food Deals 3** $2.00 There's true dedication to really fresh, seasonal food here! Stellar sliders, edamame, hummus, fries, giant salads and tasty focaccias.

**Drink Specials 2** $1.50 PBR; $3.00 micros
$5.00 house wines; $3.00 wells

**Atmosphere 3** The old Maiden shines on with more of a no-frills, dive bar tone and velvet paintings. Best at night with candlelight and lounge couches.

## Vintage Cocktail Lounge

**SE (not on map)** 7907 SE Stark; (503) 262-0696
www.vintagepdx.com

**Happy Hours** 5:00-7:00pm and 11:00pm–close Daily

**Food Deals 0** Sadly, no food discounts

**Drink Specials 2** $1.00 off drafts, wine, cocktails
Note: Some of the city's best classic cocktails and house creations here!

**Atmosphere 2** Part wine bar in style (formerly Cru) and part old-school cocktail lounge with lots of red in walls, lighting and everywhere. Casual and welcoming.

## Xico www.xicopdx.com

**Southeast** 3715 SE Division; (503) 548-6343

**Happy Hours** 5:00–6:00pm Mon–Fri

**Food Deals 1** $2.00-$5.00 Three items for now: Totopos con chile (tasty loaded chips), Sonoran hot dog (about as good as a dog could be and with bacon), plus popsicles.

**Drink Specials 2** $3.00 Negra Modelo or Pacifico; $6.00 Margarita $4.00 mezcals for not much money

**Atmosphere 2** Nice new place to keep your eye on for future improvement with mini-menu Happy Hour served in the small bar area only. Elsewhere, there's a pleasant garden and cool, minimalist-mod decor.

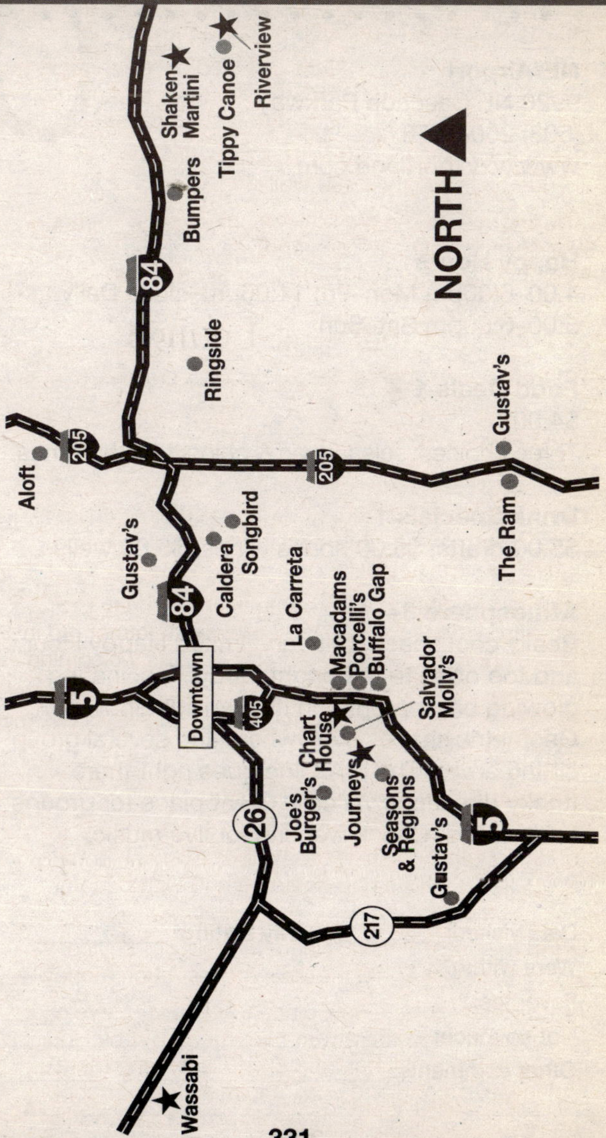
Shaken Martini
Tippy Canoe
Riverview
Bumpers
84
NORTH
Ringside
Gustav's
Aloft
205
205
Songbird
Caldera
Gustav's
84
The Ram
La Carreta
Macadams
Porcelli's
Buffalo Gap
Salvador Molly's
Downtown
5
405
Chart House
Joe's Burger's
Journeys
Seasons & Regions
26
5
Gustav's
217
Wassabi

# Aloft Wxyz Bar

6

**NE/Airport**
9920 NE Cascade Parkway
(503) 200-5678
www.wxyzportland.com

**Happy Hours**
4:00–6:00pm Mon–Fri; 11:00pm–close Daily
5:00–6:00pm Sat–Sun

**Food Deals 1**
$4.00
Three choices: salsa, guac & chips, tots, hummus.

**Drink Specials 1**
$5.00 drafts; $5.00 house wines; $5.00 wells

**Atmosphere 3+**
Really cool space, but very limited Happy Hour and too open to the bright lobby. Fascinating glowing bar top puts on its own lightshow. Geometric shapes everywhere and several group sitting areas. The MAX line goes right there (tricky directions via car). Great place for groups and parties. Check website for live music.

Date visited: ____________ **My Rating:** ____________
Went with: ______________________________
Favorites: ______________________________
Not so much: ______________________________
Other comments: ______________________________
______________________________

# Buffalo Gap

7

**Southwest/Macadam**
6835 SW Macadam
(503) 244-7111
www.thebuffalogap.com

**Happy Hours**
4:00–6:00pm & 10:00pm–mid Daily
★1:00pm–mid Sunday

**Food Deals 3**
$2.95–$3.95
Ten of the best basic bar food standards like build-your-own tacos, pita pizzas, nachos, BBQ pork sliders, quesadillas, and chips.

**Drink Specials 1**
Nightly specials that vary; many revolving around NFL, Trail Blazers and college games.

**Atmosphere 2**
Reminiscent of a small-town tourist pub in dining area; meandering rooms with some down-home touches; TVs/sports.

Date visited: ____________ **My Rating:** ____________
Went with: ______________________________
Favorites: ______________________________
Not so much: ____________________________
Other comments: _________________________
_________________________________________

# Bumpers

9

**Far Northeast near Edgefield's**
21935 NW Halsey; Fairview
(503) 618-1855
www.bumpersgrill.com

**Happy Hours**
3:00–6:00pm & 9:00pm–close Daily
★All day Sunday

**Food Deals 3**
$2.95–$4.95
Big menu with several offerings at each price point: Onion rings, soup, Caesar, fries, calamari, potato skins, BBQ chicken quesadilla, buffalo wings, french dip, prawn cigars, BBQ ribs.

**Drink Specials 3**
$1.00 off draft beers; $4.00 wine; $3.00 wells
$3.00 Margaritas; plus occasional nightly specials

**Atmosphere 3**
It's in a small strip mall, but it's a nice fine-dining restaurant. Impressive and giant, 18-foot-long(!), 900-gallon aquarium defining the bar. Two long rows of bar stools, but only four four-tops, so get there early. Reservations for groups. Patio seating.

Date visited: ____________ **My Rating:** ____________
Went with: ______________________________
Favorites: ______________________________
Not so much: ____________________________
Other comments: __________________________

# Caldera Public House

8

**Southeast/Mt. Tabor**
6031 SE Stark
(503) 233-8242
www.calderapublichouse.com

**Happy Hours**
5:00–6:00pm & 9:00pm–close Daily

**Food Deals 2**
$3.00–$9.00
Short list of bar menu items like fries, tots, garlic bread, hummus plate, calamari, coconut shrimp.

**Drink Specials 2**
$1.00 off pints, wine, wells and cocktails
$2.00 off pitchers

**Atmosphere 3**
Kinda hidden over in the far east, but this little Montavilla neighborhood is continuing to sprout some new favorites. Inside a turn-of-the-century, two-story drugstore, Caldera reminds me both of my old Chicago taverns and some in Ireland. It has character! And a great back deck too.

Date visited: ____________ **My Rating:** ____________
Went with: ______________________________
Favorites: ______________________________
Not so much: ______________________________
Other comments: ______________________________
______________________________________________

# Chart House

10

**Near OHSU**
5700 SW Terwilliger Blvd
(503) 246-6963
www.chart-house.com

**Happy Hours**
4:00–7:00pm Daily

A Happy Hour favorite!

**Food Deals 3**
$4.00–$6.00
Three options at $4.00, $5.00 or $6.00 each: bruschetta, artichoke hearts, firecracker shrimp, hummus, prime rib sliders, tacos and calamari.

**Drink Specials 3**
$4.00 drafts; $5.00 selection of red or white wines
$5.00 wells; $6.00 cocktails; $6.00 martinis

**Atmosphere 3**
Wow! Definitely one of the best views in the city, especially on a clear day when you can see Mt. Hood and Mt. Adams through the floor-to-ceiling, wall-to-wall windows. Happy Hour is downstairs in the lounge. Cozy fireplace for winter warmth. Free valet parking.

Date visited: ____________ **My Rating:** ____________
Went with: ____________________________________________
Favorites: ____________________________________________
Not so much: __________________________________________
Other comments: _______________________________________
_______________________________________________________

# Gustav's

7

**Several Locations:**
5035 NE Sandy Blvd. (503) 288-5503
12605 SE 97th Ave. (503) 653-1391
10350 SW Greenburg Rd, Tigard (503) 639-4544
1705 SE 164th Ave, Vancouver (360) 883-0222
www.gustavs.net

**Happy Hours**
3:00–6:00pm and 9:00pm–close Daily

**Food Deals 3**
$1.99–$5.99
A large array of German specialties and other hardy, old stand-bys: reuben or shepard's pie, fish & chips, burgers, schnitzel strips, chicken skewers, swiss fondue, sliders, potato pancakes.

**Drink Specials 0**
Only the Vancouver location offers drink specials (see page 393).

**Atmosphere 3**
With some imagination and a couple beers from the strong and authentic European tap line-ups, you too, can be transported to a genuine Bavarian bierstube. Gold star for pushing the concept.

Date visited: __________ **My Rating:** __________
Went with: ______________________________
Favorites: ______________________________
Not so much: ______________________________
Other comments: ______________________________

# Joe's Burgers

9

**Multnomah Villiage**
4439 SW Beaverton-Hillsdale Hwy.
(503) 892-6686
www.joesburgers.com

Downtown: 625 SW 4th Ave.; 503-248-5637
PSU: 540 SW College; (503) 432-8022
Bridgeport: 7409 SW Bridgeport; (503) 598-1111

**Happy Hours** (Downtown drinks only; PSU tbd)
3:00–6:00pm and 9:00pm–close Mon–Fri
Saturday same hours but 11:00am start
★All day Sunday

**Food Deals 2**
$2.00–$4.00
Great burgers, but not on HH menu :-( About a dozen cheap bar bites like tacos, chili cheese fries, salads, pizza, mac & cheese bites, chips.

**Drink Specials 3**
$3.00 drafts; $4.00 wine; $5.00 special cocktails

**Atmosphere 3**
The old Jopa. Happy Hour is on the patio out back, or in the bar only (basically a nondescript, simple room). Overall, outstanding burger joints!

Date visited: __________ **My Rating:** __________
Went with: ____________________
Favorites: ____________________
Not so much: ____________________
Other comments: ____________________

# Journeys

9

**Multnomah Villiage**
7771 SW Capitol Hwy.
(503) 245-4573
www.journeyspdx.com

**Happy Hours**
4:00–7:00pm Mon–Sat

**Food Deals 3**
$5.00–$6.50
Some fresh alternatives too, but they are most famous for their grilled cheese bites (four styles), cheddar and apple plate, hummus, black bean hummus, salad with chicken, soup & salad, artichoke & jalapeno dip, and a charcuterie plate.

**Drink Specials 2**
$3.50 select beer; $5.00 red or white wines

**Atmosphere 3**
This is a generous three points, but people *love* it here like it was their own home! It's actually in a cute house – on a tiny hill – with a wonderful outdoor front patio. They have many regulars who are very passionate about this place for its friendliness, games, and wine and beer selections.

Date visited: ____________ **My Rating:** ____________
Went with: ____________
Favorites: ____________
Not so much: ____________
Other comments: ____________

____________

# La Carretta

9

**Southeast near Sellwood**
4534 SE McLoughlin Blvd
(503) 236-8089

**Happy Hours**
3:00–6:00pm Mon–Fri; 9:00pm–mid Sun–Mon

**Food Deals 3**
$1.00–$2.00
Less than a dollar each for some decent Mexican food, albeit a bit on the Americanized, greasy side. Less than a dollar each for many items. Small chalkboard menu: taco, enchilada, salad, bean dip, soup or fries. Free chips and salsa!

**Drink Specials 3**
$1.45 domestics; $1.99 wells and margaritas! There's also a cocktail special of the day.

**Atmosphere 3**
Strikingly bright and colorful exterior! Very festive and traditional Mexican restaurant with tiled table tops, stucco walls, arches, hand-painted murals, a peek at the river, and a drunken parrot.

Date visited: ____________ **My Rating:** ____________
Went with: ________________________________________
Favorites: ________________________________________
Not so much: ______________________________________
Other comments: ___________________________________
___________________________________________________

# Macadams

9

**Southwest/Macadam**
5833 SW Macadam
(503) 246-6227
www.macadamsbarandgrill.com

**Happy Hours**
3:00–6:00pm and 10:00pm–mid Daily
★All night Sunday (3:00–close)

**Food Deals 3**
$2.50–$5.00
Big bar menu includes pulled pork sliders, cheeseburger, or chicken strips with fries; brat, jalapeno-artichoke dip, Buffalo wrap, Caesar, mac & cheese, tacos, bean dip, calamari.

**Drink Specials 3**
$4.00 drafts; $4.00 wines; $3.50 wells

**Atmosphere 3**
Lofted lodge effect with traditional manly-man tans and browns. Plenty of TVs for watching your favorite games. Outdoor patio area. Family friendly in restaurant until 8:00pm.

Date visited: __________ **My Rating:** __________
Went with: ______________________________
Favorites: ______________________________
Not so much: ______________________________
Other comments: ______________________________
______________________________

# Osaka-ya

6

**North/NE Map**
7007 SW MacAdam Ave.
(503) 293-1066

**Happy Hours**
3:00–6:30pm Mon–Fri
★Noon–6:30pm Sat–Sun

**Food Deals 3**
$1.50–$4.50
Ten sushi rolls plus ten appetizers! California, Oregon, albacore, tuna and salmon, spicy tuna or salmon, eel and avocado, avocado-cucumber, or all vegetable. Plus, salads, edamame, veggie tempura, gyoza, chicken skewers and soups. *And* chicken or salmon rice bowls.

**Drink Specials 0**
Sadly, no drink deals

**Atmosphere 2** Driving up, you'll see this white, authentic Japanese house, and inside, the restaurant is pretty nice too. Happy Hour is in the very basic bar though, so lacks the personality going on elsewhere here. Unbeatable food deals though, and at lunchtime on weekends!

Date visited: ____________ **My Rating:** ____________
Went with: ______________________________
Favorites: ______________________________
Not so much: ____________________________
Other comments: _________________________
_________________________________________

# Porcelli's

9

**North/NE Map**
6500 SW Virginia Ave.
(503) 245-2260
www.porcellisristorante.com

**Happy Hours**
3:00–6:00pm Daily; ★All night Tuesday ('til 9:00pm)

**Food Deals 3**
$2.00–$5.00
No way! An 8" pizza with four toppings for only $4.00! Plus, all kinds of other good stuff (and cheap too): spaghetti, pastrami sub, steamed clams, antipasto plate, bruschetta, salads, soup.

**Drink Specials 3+**
$3.00 drafts; $1.00 off wines (and all drinks, really)
$2.50 wells; $3.50 several styles of cocktails

**Atmosphere 2**
Porcelli's Ristorante & Bar opened in 2009 and is located in the old Porcelli Grocery on the corner. There's a big open space when you first walk in, a long open kitchen, and the bar area is in the back, so it has a rather awkward layout. Caught between fancy and casual, it's nice for the area, and has that Italian romance vibe going after dark.

Date visited: __________ **My Rating:** __________
Went with: ____________________
Favorites: ____________________
Not so much: ____________________
Other comments: ____________________

# Ringside Glendoveer 9

**Glendoveer**
14021 NE Glisan
(503) 255-0750
www.ringsidesteakhouse.com

**Happy Hours**
3:00–6:00 pm and 8:30pm–close Daily

**Food Deals 3**
$2.25-4.95
15 menu items: steak bites (YUM!), calamari, wings, prime rib dip, crab cake, ground steak burger, chili poppers, garlic bread, Caesar salad, oysters on the half shell, steamed clams.

**Drink Specials 3**
$5.00 microbrew draft beers, red or white wine, select well drinks, margaritas or Manhattan

**Atmosphere 2**
Less dramatic, but bigger and more open than downtown location with dark, wood paneling and wall-to-wall windows. Views of on-site golf course. Great outdoor patio! Big, open fireplace.

Date visited: ____________ **My Rating:** ____________
Went with: ______________________________
Favorites: ______________________________
Not so much: ____________________________
Other comments: __________________________
__________________________________________

# Salvador Molly's

**Hillsdale (NW of Multnomah Village)**
1523 SW Sunset Blvd.
(503) 293-1790
www.salvadormollys.com

9

**Happy Hours**
4:00–6:00pm (and last hour open) Daily

A Happy Hour favorite!

**Food Deals 3**
$2.50
YUM!! Unique nibbles from around the globe – and only two bucks! Revolving menu hosts BBQ pork sliders, Caesar salad, Thai tofu salad, chicken tacos buffalo cheese fries, or a roasted veggie quinoa salad. Bold flavors!

**Drink Specials 2**
$2.00 PBR tallboys; $3.00 cocktail of the day

**Atmosphere 3**
International fun and flair! Bold vibrant colors in both food and decor. Entire walls and table tops are covered in worldly memorabilia. Happy Hour in bar side only or outside on the deck.

Date visited: ____________ **My Rating:** ____________
Went with: ______________________________
Favorites: ______________________________
Not so much: ______________________________
Other comments: ______________________________
______________________________

# Seasons & Regions 6

**Just North of Multnomah Village**
6660 SW Capitol Hwy
(503) 244-6400
www.seasonsandregions.com

**Happy Hours**
3:00-5:30pm Daily; 8:30-9:30pm Mon-Sat
8:00-9:00pm Sun

**Food Deals 3**
$2.95
Seasonal menu (but of course) changes monthly with sizeable portions of items like mac & cheese, hummus platter, bean burritos, spinach salad, pasta, sandwiches or wraps, tostada, hummus, or key lime pie (yum)! Many gluten-free and vegetarian options on regular menu.

**Drink Specials 0**
Sadly, no drink specials

**Atmosphere 2**
Sweet café inside, nice tented patio outside. Has more of a breakfast/lunch bistro vibe with buttercream walls and well-worn wooden booths.

Date visited: __________ **My Rating:** __________
Went with: ______________________________
Favorites: ______________________________
Not so much: ____________________________
Other comments: __________________________

# Shaken Martini Lounge



**Downtown Troutdale**
101 W Historic Columbia River Hwy.
(503) 512-7485

**Happy Hours**
4:00–7:00pm Mon–Fri

**Food Deals 0**
$4.00–$6.00
Actually, there's no discount at Happy Hour per se, but it's still priced for it with absolutely *delicious* grilled sandwiches, salads, soups and flatbreads.

**Drink Specials 3**
$2.00 off any cocktail on the menu (spend some time reading the creative and informative menu)

**Atmosphere 3**
The neighborhood is ecstatic about this place, and it's a great place to know about even if you don't live nearby. Cool martini bar with a James Bond themed menu – and killer cocktails! Same owner and similar gig as the Shaken Martini formerly on Fremont in Portland. I love it!

Date visited: ____________ **My Rating:** ____________
Went with: ______________________________________
Favorites: ______________________________________
Not so much: ____________________________________
Other comments: _________________________________
__________________________________________________

# Songbird

9

**Southeast Map**
6839 SE Belmont
(503) 477-6735
www.songbirdpdx.com

**Happy Hours**
3:00-5:30pm Tues–Sat

**Food Deals 3**
$4.00–$7.00
Fresh, seasonal, and tasty treats like roasted beets or cauliflower, salad, fries, lamb meatballs, burgers or grilled portobello mushroom sandwich.

**Drink Specials 3**
$3.00 drafts (rotating local taps); $5.00 wine
$3.00 wells; $5.00 cocktail-of-the-day

**Atmosphere 3**
A sweet little neighborhood eatery. Cuteness! Pretty, new patterned woods throughout, blue cushioned seats, red barstools, and other white accents. Sidewalk dining. And put a bird in it – ask for a signature songbird latte!

Date visited: __________ **My Rating:** __________
Went with: ______________________________
Favorites: ______________________________
Not so much: ______________________________
Other comments: ______________________________
______________________________

# Wassabi

10

**Hillsboro (Near Tanasbourne)**
1861 NW 188th Ave
(503) 747-2354
www.wassabipdx.com

**Happy Hours**
3:00–7:00pm Daily; 10:00pm–close Mon–Sat

**Food Deals 3**
$1.00–$5.00
More than 20 delicious Pan-Asian delights! All the basics plus lots more: springrolls, calamari, rolls (California, spicy tuna, shrimp, salmon), nachos, coconut shrimp, veggie tempura, wings, sliders.

**Drink Specials 3**
$3.00 domestics; $4.00 micros; $5.00 wines
$4.00 sake; $4.00 wells; $5.00 martinis

**Atmosphere 3**
Three great spots for Happy Hour! Relax out on the giant wrap-around patio, in the Ginger Room Lounge, a contemporary sports bar, or in the beautiful and serene, fine-dining restaurant. The number one place to go in Hillsboro by far.

Date visited: ____________ **My Rating:** ____________
Went with: ______________________________
Favorites: ______________________________
Not so much: ____________________________
Other comments: _________________________
_________________________________________

# Cool Dive Bars

**These are some fun places that are more casual than those in rest of book, but have style all their own. Ultra-cheap grub and drinks, and some of the best "dive bars" in town!**

## Ash Street Saloon

**Old Town Map**
225 SW Ash St; (503) 226-0430
www.ashstreetsaloon.com
4:00–8:00pm Daily  $2.00–$3.00 menu items
$1.25 PBRs; $2.75 micros & wells
Good sidewalk seating.

## Bar of the Gods

**Hawthorne Map**
4801 SE Hawthorne; (503) 232-2037
4:00–8:00pm Mon–Fri
$1.50 PBRs; $2.50 wells; 50 cents off menu items
Great back patio.

## Beulahland

**Lloyd Center-ish Map**
118 NE 28th Ave.; (503) 235-2794
4:00–7:00pm Daily $1.00 off menu items
$3.50 pints & $3.00 wells and select cocktails
Funky decked-out walls.

## Captain Ankeny's

**Old Town Map**
50 SW 3rd Ave; (503) 223-1375
4:00–7:00pm Daily  Rotating daily specials
$3.00 micros/imports; $3.00 wells
Good tap lineup.

## Florida Room

**North/NE Map**
435 N. Killingsworth St. ; (503) 287-5658
3:00–7:00pm Daily $2.75 snacks
$.50 off cheap wells and taps
Budget beach decor. Known for weekend Bloody Marys.

## Gypsy

**Old Town Map**
625 NW 21st Ave.; (503) 796-1859
4:00–8:00pm Tues–Fri $2.95–$4.95 big bar menu!
$3.50 micros; $2.00 domestics and wells
The Velvet Lounge in bar side is a bit more swanky.

## Kelly's Olympian

**Old Town Map**
426 SW Washington; (503) 228-3669
4:00–7:00pm Mon–Fri $2.00–$4.00 menu
$3.00 well & micros
Motorcycles and garage stuff everywhere. Since 1902.

## LaurelThirst Pub

**Old Town Map**
2958 NE Glisan; (503) 232-1504
Before 5:00pm Mon–Fri $3.75 micros; $2.00 PBR
6:00–8:00pm Free live music
Sidewalk seating.

## Lotus Room

**Downtown (East) Map**
932 SW Third Ave; (503) 227-6185
3:00–7:00pm / 9:00pm–close Daily $2.95–$4.95 apps
$3.00 wells & $3.50 drafts
Huge bar and cool back card room; sidewalk seating.

## Low Brow Lounge

**Old Town Map**
1036 NW Hoyt; (503) 226-0200
5:00–7:00pm Daily
$1.00 off drafts and wells $5.00 burgers, sandwiches
A famous favorite!

## Matador

**Old Town Map**
1967 W Burnside St; (503) 222-5822
Noon–7:00pm Daily
$2.00 PBRs; $3.00 wells
Bull-fighting-themed dive bar. Really.

## Space Room

**Southeast Map** 4800 SE Hawthorne; (503) 235-8303
www.spaceroomlounge.com
11:00am–7:00pm Daily $2.50 wells $2.25 micros
Blacklight UFO theme.

## Tiger Bar

**Old Town Map** 317 NW Broadway; (503) 467-4111
www.tigerbarpdx.com
5:00–8:00pm Tues–Fri
$3.00–$5.00 Bar eats (good burgers)
$2.25 domestics; $3.00–$3.50 wells
Dark bar with black and brick walls; tiger elements.

## Virginia Cafe

**Downtown (West) Map**
820 SW 10th Ave.; (503) 227-8617
virginiacafepdx.com
4:00–7:00pm Mon–Fri $2.25–$7.00 eats
$1.00 off drafts and wells
It's transplanted, "new" home retains just a bit of the old, nostalgic charm. More of a café-y dive.

(Cedar Hills Mall Area)

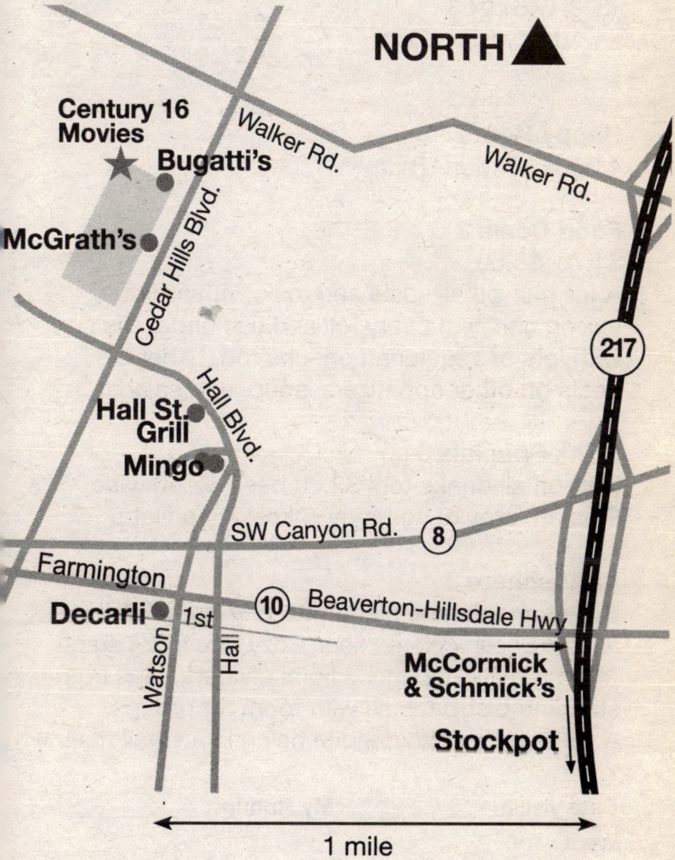

# Banya

10

**Beaverton Map**
8166 SW Hall Blvd.
(503) 646-6753
www.banyasushi.com

**Happy Hours**
4:00–6:00 Mon–Thur

**Food Deals 3**
$1.75–$5.50
A full half-off all sushi and maki with about a million choices! Every roll and fish under the sun with lots of vegetarian options too. Other big deals on other appetizers, soup, and salads.

**Drink Specials 3**
Half-off all drinks too! $2.00 beer; $2.50 wine
Plus an array of so many sakes; Try a flight!

**Atmosphere 3**
Sweet and serene place with pea-green walls and an ocean colored floor. Cozy little four-person "rooms" with Japanese floral dividers, plus free-standing bistro tables with room for groups.
A pleasant respite despite being in a small mall.

Date visited: __________ **My Rating:** __________
Went with: ____________________
Favorites: ____________________
Not so much: ____________________
Other comments: ____________________
____________________

# Big Al's

9

**Beaverton (off map)**
14950 SW Barrows Rd.; (503) 748-6118
**Vancouver** 16615 SE 18th; (360) 944-6118
www.ilovebigals.com

**Happy Hours**
3:00–6:00pm Mon–Fri;
Daily late-night 9:00–close (10:00-close Fri–Sat)

**Food Deals 3**
$2.00–$5.00
Long and cheap list of bar menu items: tostadas, corndogs, Southwest wraps, cheeseburger, fries, potato skins, wings, quesadilla, soup, and dessert.

**Drink Specials 3**
$3.00 domestics; $3.50 micros; $3.00 wells
Plus select pitcher specials

**Atmosphere 3**
Bright lights, loud noises, lots of excitement, and kids everywhere. That being said, they *do* have tons of bowling (glowing and not), pool, and dozens of TVs, so it's fun for adults too. The three, side-by-side, mega-huge movie screens are pretty dang cool to watch sports on!

Date visited: ___________ **My Rating:** ___________
Went with: ______________________________
Favorites: ______________________________
Not so much: ____________________________
Other comments: _________________________
_________________________________________

# B.J. Willy's

8

**Beaverton (off map)** (near Cinetopia)
12345 SW Horizon Blvd; (503) 747-7319
**West Linn Map**
1717 Willamette Falls Dr; (503) 656-4410
22000 Willamette Dr; (503) 650-6020
www.bjwillys.com

**Happy Hours**
3:00–6:00pm Daily; 9:30pm–close Sun–Thurs

**Food Deals 2**
$2.99–$5.99
Giant bar menus that vary slightly per location: chips, fries, tots, rings, wings, sliders, pizzettas, hummus, mac & cheese, wings, penne, clams.

**Drink Specials 3**
$1.00 off drafts and well drinks; $4.50 wines
$4.00 margaritas, cosmos and lemon drops

**Atmosphere 2**
A collection of locally-owned, casual but nice, hang-out pubs catering to sports nuts, families and late-nighters. Wood-fired pizza specialists. Locations all somewhat similar in style and spirit.

Date visited: ____________ **My Rating:** ____________
Went with: ______________________________
Favorites: ______________________________
Not so much: ______________________________
Other comments: ______________________________
______________________________

# Bugatti's

**10**

**Beaverton Map**
2905 SW Cedar Hills Blvd; (503) 626-1400
**Hillsboro Map** (Tanasbourne)
2364 NW Amber Brook; (503) 352-5252
**West Linn Map** (opens 4:30pm, no drink deals)
18740 Willamette, West Linn; (503) 636-9555
**Oregon City** (off map areas)
334 Warner Milne; (503) 722-8222
www.bugattisrestaurants.com

**Happy Hours**
3:00–6:00pm and 8:00pm–close Daily
All Day Sunday★

**Food Deals 3**
$3.00–$7.00
Menus vary, but all offer about a dozen items like prawns, salads, pizzas, pastas, calamari, soup.

**Drink Specials 3**
$4.00 drafts; $4.50 wine; $3.50 well cocktails

**Atmosphere 3**
Basic bar areas compared to the somewhat fancier attached restaurants. All quite nice though and more modern than old Italian in style.

Date visited: ____________ **My Rating:** ____________
Went with: ______________________________
Favorites: ______________________________
Not so much: ______________________________
Other comments: ______________________________

# Decarli

10 ★

**Beaverton Map**
4545 SW Watson Avenue
(503) 641-3223
www.decarlirestaurant.com

**Happy Hours**
4:30–6:00pm and 9:00pm–close Tues–Sat
★All night Sunday (5:00–9:00pm)

**Food Deals 3**
$2.00–$7.00
Big menu and one of the best in the area: fries, almonds, olives, bruschetta, meatballs, salads, several paninis, rib sandwich, pizzettas, burger.

**Drink Specials 3**
$3.50 draft beer; $2.00 off wine;
$6.00 specialty cocktail

**Atmosphere 3**
Warm and welcoming with exposed red brick walls and an open kitchen. A neighborhood gem at home in the suburbs, that really seems more like a friendly, local New York hangout. Get here early for HH or you might be left out!

Date visited: __________ **My Rating:** __________
Went with: ____________________
Favorites: ____________________
Not so much: ____________________
Other comments: ____________________

# Fireside Grill

6

**Beaverton Map**
8136 SW Hall Blvd.
(503) 747-4661
www.thefiresidegrillpdx.com

**Happy Hours**
4:00–6:00pm and 10:00pm–mid Daily

**Food Deals 2**
$3.00–$5.00
Nice array of bar food: Gorgonzola chips, mini chef salad, Scotch egg, wings, waffle-fried chicken, hummus, salad, mac & cheese.

**Drink Specials 1**
No drink deals early; 15% off all drinks late

**Atmosphere 2**
Formerly a McMenamin's place in a small mall, now an upscale sports bar of sorts. It's all about the patio here, as the fire is outside in the middle of a giant stone table. Great deck! Inside, it's quite simple, with light wood, ski-lodge paneling, glass doors to the deck, a long bar, and TVs. No minors.

Date visited: ____________ **My Rating:** ____________
Went with: ____________________________________________
Favorites: ____________________________________________
Not so much: __________________________________________
Other comments: _______________________________________
_____________________________________________________

# Hall Street Grill

10 ★

**Beaverton Map**
3775 SW Hall
(503) 641-6161
www.hallstreetgrill.com

**Happy Hours**
3:00–6:30pm and 9:00pm–close Mon–Sat
★All night Sunday (3:00–10:00pm)

**Food Deals 3**
$3.00–$13.00
High-end restaurant = yummy Happy Hour eats! Coconut prawns, burgers, hummus, fries, soup, calamari, meat & cheese platter, famous Caesar, pork belly, reuben bites, empanadas, poutine.

**Drink Specials 3**
$3.00–4.00 beer; $1.00 off wine; $20.00 bottles
$4.00 wells; $5.00 cocktails

**Atmosphere 3**
Big and bustling Happy Hour scene inside what is arguably the nicest place in Beaverton. Pacific Northwest stylings with lots of wood. Fun patio out back too. Love it!

Date visited: ______ **My Rating:** ______
Went with: ______
Favorites: ______
Not so much: ______
Other comments: ______

# McGrath's

**Beaverton Map**
3211 SW Cedar Hills Blvd.; (503) 646-1881
Milwaukee (off map)
11050 SE Oak; (503) 653-8070
Vancouver (off map)
12501 SE Second Circle; (360) 514-9555
www.mcgrathsfishhouse.com

**Happy Hours**
3:00–6:00pm Daily (3:00–5:00pm Friday)
Late Happy Half-Hour 9:00–9:30pm Mon–Thurs

**Food Deals 3**
$2.00–$5.00
Unique spins on more than 20 bar menu items like salmon BLT, seared ahi, crab & artichoke dip, prawn or chicken kabobs, oysters, crab cakes.

**Drink Specials 3**
$3.25–$4.25 drafts; $5.00 wine
$3.50 wells; $4.50 select cocktails

**Atmosphere 3**
Casually-quaint waterfront fish house decor, with nautical knick-knacks covering pretty much every inch of space in their cavernous rooms.

Date visited: ____________ **My Rating:** ____________
Went with: ______________________________
Favorites: ______________________________
Not so much: ______________________________
Other comments: ______________________________
______________________________

# Mingo

9

**Beaverton Map**
12600 SW Crescent (The Round)
(503) 646-6464
www.mingowest.com

**Happy Hours**
2:30–6:00pm Tues-Fri; 5:00–6:00pm Sun–Mon

**Food Deals 3**
$5.00–$7.00
Somewhat small-ish but delish menu with veggie skewers, pizzas, burgers, penne pasta, grilled eggplant, raviolis, Caesar salad.

**Drink Specials 3**
$4.00 beer; $4.00 red or white wine
$5.00 wells; $6.00 daily cocktail

**Atmosphere 3**
Pea green walls, over-sized paper sculptures and lanterns, and window-doors that open to an inviting piazza with an outdoor Happy Hour bar. Same owners as Serratto and Mingo in NW PDX.

Date visited: ____________ **My Rating:** ____________
Went with: ______________________________
Favorites: ______________________________
Not so much: ______________________________
Other comments: ______________________________
______________________________

# Stockpot Broiler 8

**Beaverton** (Not on Map)
8200 SW Scholls Ferry Rd.
(503) 643-5451
www.stockpot.ypguides.net

**Happy Hours**
4:00–6:00pm and 9:00pm–close Daily
★All night Monday (3:00–close)

**Food Deals 3**
$2.50–$4.50
Extensive menu of big, cheap servings includes platter of giant onion rings, bruschetta, salad, beef satay, nachos, burgers, mac & cheese, Caesar, beef tips, meatballs, fish tacos, soup.

**Drink Specials 2**
$3.50 microbrews; $3.75 wells

**Atmosphere 2**
A dark lounge even by day with black tables and chairs, bar rails, walls, bricks and fireplace. Golf course views from wonderful seasonal patio. Reminiscent of early 1980s decor with music often reflecting that.

Date visited: __________ **My Rating:** __________
Went with: ______________________________
Favorites: ______________________________
Not so much: ______________________________
Other comments: ______________________________
______________________________

# Vinotopia

8

**Beaverton**
12345 SW Horizon Blvd
(503) 597-6900
www.cinetopia.com

**Happy Hours**
3:00–6:00pm and 8:00pm–close Daily

**Food Deals 3**
$5.00–$6.00
A dozen bar-style selections: house or spinach salads, wings, fries, artisan pizza, quesadilla, fish & chips, hummus, nachos, pulled pork sliders.

**Drink Specials 2**
$4.00–5.00 drafts; $5.00 red or white wine

**Atmosphere 2**
Inside the all-new, highly anticipated, Cinetopia Theater. Smallish, elevated bar area with lots of nearby windows. Restricted seating at Happy Hour prohibits patio partaking if you want the HH deals. Author's note: Seeing cutting egde, high-action, and 3-D movies at the Cinetopia Theaters is totally worth the drive (there's another one in Vancouver and a BREWtopia too!).

Date visited: ____________ **My Rating:** ____________
Went with: ______________________________
Favorites: ______________________________
Not so much: ____________________________
Other comments: __________________________
__________________________________________

# Bistro 153

**Beaverton** (Off Map)
3203 SW 153rd Drive; (503) 626-8282; bistro153.net

**Happy Hours** 2:00–7:00pm and 9pm–close Mon-Fri
★All Day Saturday and Sunday

**Food Deals 2** $3.00–$4.00 Big menu of 20+ items two bucks off: Three sliders (beef, lamb, chicken), burger, pot stickers, quesadilla, fries, rings.

**Drink Specials 2** $3.75 micros; $3.50 wine or wells

**Atmosphere 2** Bistro-bar located within an office complex, so there's an active after-work scene. Two long bartops, carpeted, outdoor seating on patio.

# B.J.'s Brewhouse www.bjsrestaurants.com

7390 NE Cornell, Hillsboro; (503) 615-2300

**Happy Hour** 3:00–7:00pm Mon–Fri and
10:00–11:00pm Sun–Thur

**Food Deals 2** $2.00 off appetizers (17 items)
Huge lineup of pretty much *all* the bar basics with 1/2 price personal pizzas too.

**Drink Specials 2** $1.00 off pints and wells

**Atmosphere 3** New brewpub! National chain, so decor matches high-energy and fun casual standards.

# McCormick & Schmick's

**Beaverton Map** www.mccormickandschmicks.com
9945 SW Beaverton-Hillsdale Hwy; (503) 643-1322

**Happy Hours** 3:00–6:00pm Mon–Sat; 4–6:00pm Sun
9:00–10:45pm Nightly

**Food Deals 3** $1.95–$4.95 Over a dozen menu items at four price tiers: cheeseburger with fries, fish tacos, quesadilla, clam strips, hummus, pizza, ahi, spring rolls.

**Drink Specials 1** Rotating nightly specials

**Atmosphere 3** A very popular Happy Hour with fun dining and drinking in upscale warehouse-style bar.

## Monteaux's Public House

**Beaverton** (Off Map) www.monteauxs.com
16165 SW Regatta Lane; (503) 439-9942

**Happy Hours** 3:00–6:00pm / 8:00pm–close Mon-Sat (9:00pm–close Fridays)

**Food Deals 2** $3.50–$5.00 Half-off appetizer menu of basic bar eats like quesadillas, nachos, hummus or "oomph" it with 20% off anything on dinner menu.

**Drink Specials 3** $3.00 beer, wine or wells

**Atmosphere 2** Turn-of-the-century charm mixed with modern-day neighborhood pub appeal, as depicted in their hand-painted mural.

## Old Chicago

**Beaverton** (Off Map) www.oldchicago.com
17960 NW Evergreen Pkwy; (503) 533-4650

**Happy Hours** 3:00–6:00pm and 9:00pm–mid Daily
Fri–Sat later HH starts at 9:30pm

**Food Deals 2** $3.00–$5.00 Big bar menu with nachos, salads, artichoke dip, pizza, wings.

**Drink Specials 2** $1.00 off all drinks

**Atmosphere 2** Sure it's a chain, but with 101 beers as a theme/tour, Chicago in the name, and 15 TVs.

## Outback Steakhouse

**Beaverton** (Off Map) www.outback.com
11146 SW Barnes; (503) 643-8007

**Happy Hours** 4:00–6:00pm Daily

**Food Deals 2** $3.50–$5.00 Meaty bar menu with items like cheeseburgers, prime rib sandwich, cheese fries, shrooms, quesadillas, soup & salad, Caesar.

**Drink Specials 3** $2.50-$3.00 beer; $3.50 wine
$3.50 margaritas; $2.50-$4.50 cocktail specials

**Atmosphere 2** Follows casually-fun, Outback-style.

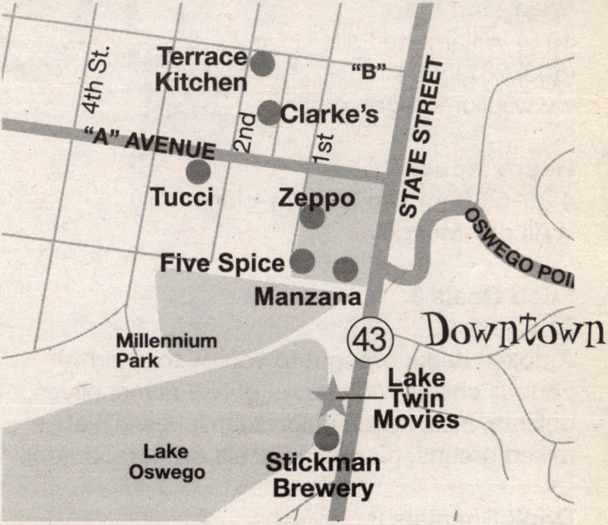
Terrace Kitchen
"B"
4th St.
Clarke's
2nd
1st
"A" AVENUE
STATE STREET
Tucci
Zeppo
OSWEGO POI
Five Spice
Manzana
43
Downtown
Millennium Park
Lake Twin Movies
Lake Oswego
Stickman Brewery

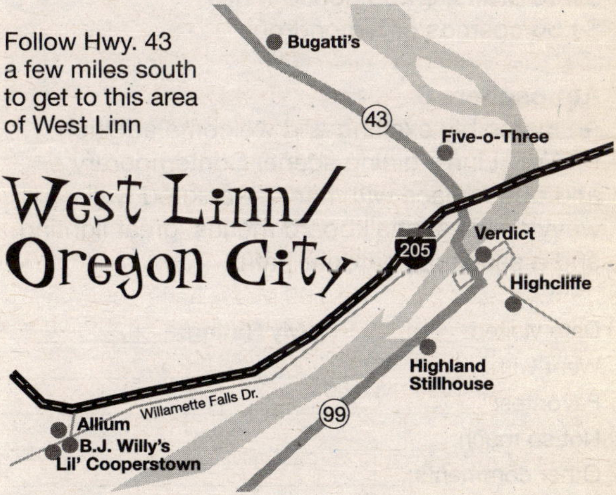
Follow Hwy. 43 a few miles south to get to this area of West Linn
Bugatti's
43
Five-o-Three
West Linn/ Oregon City
205
Verdict
Highcliffe
Highland Stillhouse
Willamette Falls Dr.
99
Allium
B.J. Willy's
Lil' Cooperstown

# Allium

**10** ★

**West Linn Map**
1914 Willamette Falls Drive
(503) 387-5604
www.alliumoregon.com

**Happy Hours**
4:30–6:30pm and 8:30pm–close Daily
★All day Monday

**Food Deals 3**
$1.50–$8.00
A dozen items brought to you by top, former Fenouil chefs! Wide range of NW faves: olives, polenta, fries, french onion soup, cheese plate, mixed greens, pizzas, mussels, oysters, burger.

**Drink Specials 3**
$4.00 drafts; $4.50 house wines
$4.50 cosmos or lemondrops

**Atmosphere 3**
An incredibly exciting and welcome addition to West Linn's dining scene! Contemporary and open space with harvest-colored walls, wavy ceilings, chalkboard menus, great lighting, and a seasonal, outdoor patio.

Date visited: ____________ **My Rating:** ____________
Went with: ______________________________
Favorites: ______________________________
Not so much: ______________________________
Other comments: ______________________________
______________________________________________

# Clarke's

8

**Lake Oswego Map**
455 2nd St.
(503) 636-2667
www.clarkesrestaurant.net

**Happy Hours**
4:30–6:00pm Mon–Sat

**Food Deals 3**
$1.00–$5.00
Half-off bar extra-delicious grub menu: burger with fries, artisan cheese plate, truffled fries, quiche w/soup, salad, duck rolls, shepards pie.

**Drink Specials 2**
No corkage fee on Monday (added point for thinking of this concept!); 25% off wine bottles Wednesday.

**Atmosphere 2**
Tiny, but cozy & comfortable modern, bistrostyle bar area. Neutral tones with wine and bar as focal points. Outside summer patio seating.

Date visited: __________ **My Rating:** __________
Went with: ______________________________
Favorites: ______________________________
Not so much: ______________________________
Other comments: ______________________________
______________________________

# Five-o-Three 10

**West Linn Map (South)**
21900 Willamette Dr.; West Linn
(503) 607-0960
www.restaurant503.com

**Happy Hours**
3:00–6:00pm Mon–Fri; ★Monday until 9:00pm
4:00pm–6:00pm Sat; 9:00–10:00pm Fri–Sat

**Food Deals 3**
$3.00–$6.00
All kinds of goodies! Soup, salad, 503 burger, hummus, veggie tempura, olives, curry chicken sandwich, quiche of the day, skewers, calamari, salmon cakes, and mussels.

**Drink Specials 3**
$3.50 drafts; $5.00 house wines; $5.00 wells
$5.00 lemon drops or cosmos

**Atmosphere 3**
Warm tones with artistic flair looks coolest at night! Big and welcoming front bar, but you are welcome to sit anywhere in the restaurant at Happy Hour. Pleasant and peaceful patio too.

Date visited: ____________ **My Rating:** ____________
Went with: ______________________________
Favorites: ______________________________
Not so much: ____________________________
Other comments: __________________________
__________________________________________

# Highcliffe

10

**West Linn Map (South)**
602 7th Street, Oregon City
(503) 212-2008
www.thehighcliffe.com

**Happy Hours**
2:00–6:30pm Mon–Fri; 4:00pm–6:30pm Sat–Sun
★All day Monday

**Food Deals 3**
$3.00–$6.00
New menu brings things a little closer to typical bar food: fries, tots, wings, rings, nachos, salads, mac & cheese, quesadilla, burgers, pork sliders.

**Drink Specials 3**
$2.00–$3.50 drafts; $4.00 house wines
$4.50 wells; $4.00 daily cocktail

**Atmosphere 3**
Housed inside a gorgeous, 1920s former Odd Fellows Club mansion. Upscale, mellow and very pleasant with buttercream walls, tin ceiling, and a 40-foot long bartop. It's tricky traveling (get good directions), but worth a trip – take a joyride down south and hang out a while!

Date visited: ____________ **My Rating:** ____________
Went with: ________________________________
Favorites: ________________________________
Not so much: ______________________________
Other comments: ___________________________

# Jefe

9

**Lake Oswego Map**
16360 Boones Ferry Rd
(503) 635-1900
www.jefemex.com

**Happy Hours**
2:00–6:00pm and 8:30pm–close Daily

**Food Deals 3**
$4.95–$6.95
About half-off 12 items, with some extras exclusive to their Hora Feliz: chicken, beef or fish tacos, quesadilla, calamari, chimichuri shaved steak, ceviche, salad, soup, skewers, or beans & rice.

**Drink Specials 2**
$4.00 drafts; $5.50 house wines
$6.00 sangria, margarita, Moscow mule

**Atmosphere 3**
Beautifully-designed space with a big central bar, roll-up garage-style doors leading to a pleasant outdoor patio, and *Architectural Digest*-worthy touches featuring slate and stone, iron and wood. Memorable and fascinating wall of suspended wine bottles, flasks built right into stonework, and an open circular fireplace table.

Date visited: __________ **My Rating:** __________
Went with: ____________________
Favorites: ____________________
Not so much: ____________________
Other comments: ____________________

____________________

# Terrace Kitchen

10

**Lake Oswego Map**
485 2nd St.
(503) 699-1136
www.terracekitchen.com

**Happy Hours**
5:00–6:00pm Tues–Fri

**Food Deals 3**
$5.00
Superior quality in Happy Hour food, artfully prepared and presented. As examples, items like hand-made tortilla chips (beautiful) served with handmade guacamole and salsa, soup of the day, salads, or BBQ beef sandwichettes.

**Drink Specials 3**
$3.00 drafts; $5.00 wines; $5.00 well cocktails

**Atmosphere 3**
Located in the building that formerly housed Amadeus Restaurant, remodel still retains historic look, though with a toned down and minimalist interior. Head for the outside terrace!

Date visited: __________ **My Rating:** __________
Went with: ______________________________
Favorites: ______________________________
Not so much: ______________________________
Other comments: ______________________________
______________________________

# Tucci

**Lake Oswego Map**
220 "A" Ave.
(503) 697-3383
www.tucci.biz

**Happy Hours**
4:00–6:00pm Daily

**Food Deals 3**
$5.00
Choose from more than a dozen Italian "bites": Caesar, risotto fritters, crab bruschetta, Tuscan beef skewers, pasta of the day, steamed mussels, artichoke dip, calamari, ravioli, and pizzas.

**Drink Specials 3**
$5.00 draft beer; $5.00 red or white wine
$6.00 house cocktails

**Atmosphere 3**
A very well-decorated, modernized old Italian-style restaurant. Warm, golden tones, gorgeous tile and iron work, rich dark woods and comfy, upholstered seating.

Date visited: __________ **My Rating:** __________
Went with: ______________________________
Favorites: ______________________________
Not so much: ____________________________
Other comments: _________________________
_________________________________________

# Zeppo

9

**Lake Oswego Map**
345 First St. Ste 105
503) 675-2726
www.zepporestaurant.com

**Happy Hours**
2:00–6:00pm and 8:30pm–close Daily

**Food Deals 3**
$4.95
Mixed-quality Italian eats like Margherita pizza, Caesar and caprese salads, bruschetta, risotto cakes w/red pepper, penne chicken & mushrooms, fettuccini, linguini, chicken skewers.

**Drink Specials 3**
$3.50 bottles; $4.00 drafts
$5.50 house wines; $6.00 sangria or cocktails

**Atmosphere 3**
Creative cutlery and kitchenware decor. Warm and friendly place with central bar, coppertopped tables and painted concrete floor. Cool Leaning Tower of Pizza wall art.

Date visited: __________ **My Rating:** __________
Went with: ______________________________
Favorites: ______________________________
Not so much: ______________________________
Other comments: ______________________________
______________________________________________

## Highland Stillhouse

**Oregon City Map**
201 S. 2nd Street
(503) 723-6789
www.highlandstillhouse.com

See Brewvana Section, page 58.

## Stickmen Brewery & Skewery

**Lake Oswego Map**
40 N State; Lake Oswego; (503) 344-4449
www.stickmenbeer.com

See Brewvana Section, page 54.

## The Verdict

**Oregon City Map**
110 8th St.; (503) 305-8429
www.verdictbarandgrill.com

**Happy Hours** 3:00–6:00pm Daily
8:00–9:00pm Sun–Thurs; 9:00–10:00pm Fri–Sat

**Food Deals 2** $3.95–$5.95 Pass the bar food: grilled shrimp, pork shanks, seared ahi tuna, wontons, cheeseburger, quesadilla, Cajun totos, hummus.

**Drink Specials 3** $3.50 drafts; $1.00 off wine & wells
Occasional other specials at a whim :-)

**Atmosphere 3** Follow the river to the Big V, pursue the patio, and don't bother with any plea-bargaining, because with their "Abatement Period", they cut a deal with everyone. So sit back and relax – they've got you surrounded with guilty pleasures.

# Tigard

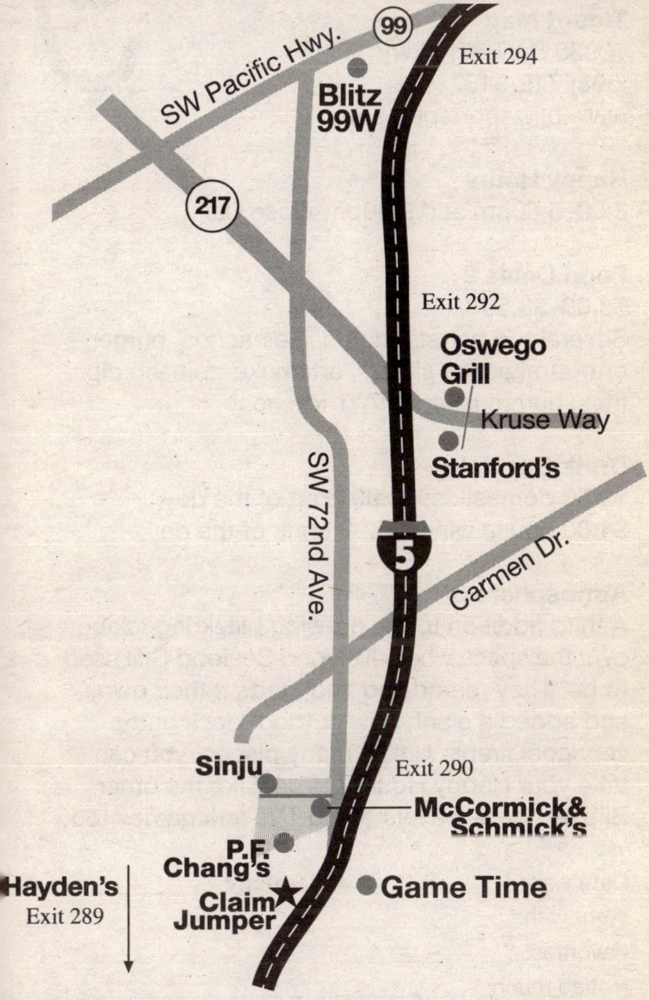

99
SW Pacific Hwy.
Exit 294
Blitz 99W
217
Exit 292
Oswego Grill
Kruse Way
Stanford's
SW 72nd Ave.
5
Carmen Dr.
Sinju
Exit 290
McCormick& Schmick's
P.F. Chang's
Hayden's
Exit 289
Claim Jumper
Game Time

# Blitz 99W

9

**Tigard Map**
10935 Sw 68th Pkwy.
(503) 719-5157
www.blitzsportspub.com

**Happy Hours**
3:00–6:00pm and 9:00pm-close Daily

**Food Deals 2**
$3.00–$5.50
Several top bar standards like nachos, burger or brat/sausage sliders, artichoke-spinach dip, fries, hummus, and YAY! Totchos!

**Drink Specials 3**
$2.50 domestics; $3.00 draft of the day
$4.00 house wine; $5.00 drink of the day

**Atmosphere 3**
A third addition to the growing blitzkrieg taking over the space where Newport Seafood Grill used to be. They remodeled and made it their own, and added a giant, new outdoor deck and a very cool firepit. Unlike many places, you can take your Happy Hour outside! Like the other Blitzes, there are *lots* of big TVs and games too.

Date visited: ___________ **My Rating:** ___________
Went with: ______________________________________
Favorites: ______________________________________
Not so much: ____________________________________
Other comments: __________________________________
_________________________________________________

# Claim Jumper 10

**Tigard Map**
18000 SW Lower Boones Ferry
(503) 670-1975
Clackamas Town Center
9085 SE Sunnyside; (503) 654-3700
www.claimjumper.com

**Happy Hours**
3:00–7:00pm Mon–Fri

**Food Deals 3**
$2.00–$7.00
Big portions of tasty bar favorites including three kinds of mini-pizzas, Irish nachos, wings, bottomless chips & salsa, burgers, Caesar, tacos (chicken, fish or pork), and calamari.

**Drink Specials 3**
$3.00–$4.00 drafts; $5.00 wines (6 choices)
$4.00 specialty drinks (7 choices)

**Atmosphere 3**
Inside and out it's rocks and big wooden timbers, open air and ironworks. Experience the northwest frontier from the comfort of your barstool.

Date visited: ____________ **My Rating:** ____________
Went with: ____________
Favorites: ____________
Not so much: ____________
Other comments: ____________

# Oswego Grill

8

**Tigard Map (Lake Oswego)**
7 Centerpointe Dr.
(503) 352-4750
www.theoswegogrill.com

**Happy Hours**
3:00–6:00pm and 9:00pm–close Daily

**Food Deals 3**
$1.95–3.95
A little bit of everything with 18 items including linguini, fish, tacos, artichoke dip, Caesar, soup, turkey cobb salad, flatbreads, Caribbean sweet potatoes, quesadillas – and creme brulee!

**Drink Specials 1**
$1.00 off drafts

**Atmosphere 3**
It's the old Chili's off I-5, and almost a kind of new Stanford's in appearance, but not. Restaurant side is quite nice and traditional, but bar area for Happy Hour is a bit cramped and ordinary. Nice patio in the summer.

Date visited: __________ **My Rating:** __________
Went with: ______________________________
Favorites: ______________________________
Not so much: ______________________________
Other comments: ______________________________
______________________________________________

# Game Time

6

**Tigard Map (Lake Oswego)**
17880 SW McEwan Rd.
(503) 726-GAME (4263)
www.game-time.com

**Happy Hours**
3:00–6:00pm and 8:00pm–close Mon–Thur

**Food Deals 2**
$2.00
Limited bar menu, but cheap deals! Nachos, Caesar or Greek salad, pizzas, hummus, or mini corndogs.

**Drink Specials 0**
Sadly, no drink specials

**Atmosphere 3**
It's a high-concept family entertainment complex with arcades and bowling, so if that's up your alley, you'll love it. Tons of hi-def TVs, but may be hard to hear above loud music and rowdy kids during daytime. Fun party rooms and two bars.

Date visited: __________ **My Rating:** __________
Went with: ______________________________
Favorites: ______________________________
Not so much: ____________________________
Other comments: __________________________
_________________________________________

# Sinju

**10** A Happy Hour favorite

**Tigard Map (Bridgeport)**
7339 SW Bridgeport Rd
(503) 352-3815
www.sinjurestaurant.com

**Happy Hours**
3:00–6:00pm and 9:00pm–close Daily

**Food Deals 3+**
$1.00–$6.00
Wow! New menu brings 12 varieties of sushi rolls and 12 types of nigiri! *Plus,* there's another 10 delicious snacks like miso soup, edamame, gyozas, wings, BBQ platter, shrimp, and ahi tower.

**Drink Specials 3**
$3.00 beer; $6.00 wine; $6.00 sake
$4.00 wells; $7.00 specialty drinks

**Atmosphere 3**
Red! Fiery! I love it! This is the perfect place to come after a movie at Bridgeport. Great group room with red cast and open fireplace. Painted ceilings, wood-slat panels and grids bar it up.

Date visited: __________ **My Rating:** __________
Went with: ____________________
Favorites: ____________________
Not so much: ____________________
Other comments: ____________________

# Thirsty Lion Pub

8

**Washington Square Mall (off map)**
10205 SW Washington Square Rd.
(503) 352-4030
www.thirstylionpub.com

**Happy Hours**
3:00–6:00pm and 10:00pm-close Mon–Fri

**Food Deals 2**
$2.95–$4.95
Nice pub food menu with items like scotch eggs, fries, Caesar, edamame, potato cakes, Reuben or burger sliders, wood-fired pizzas, nachos, calamari, and beer fondue with soft pretzels.

**Drink Specials 2**
$2.50 domestics; $3.50 craft pints; $3.25 wells

**Atmosphere 3**
The second version of a big, new national chain perhaps? Follows established format of the original in Old Town Portland. Same neighborhood English Pub theme, being even more new, yuppie and huge. Food, spirits, ales, live music, and sports on several TVs. A hugely-welcomed addition to the area!

Date visited: __________ **My Rating:** __________
Went with: ______________________________
Favorites: ______________________________
Not so much: ______________________________
Other comments: ______________________________
______________________________

## Cheesecake Factory (off the map/at the mall)

9309 Washington Square Rd; (503) 620-1100
www.thecheesecakefactory.com

Happy Hours: 4:00-6:00pm Mon-Fri
$4.00 beer, $5.00 wine, $5.00 specialty cocktails and $5.00 wells; Loads of appetizer options $4.95-$6.95
Crazy and vibrant interior design!

## Chevy's Fresh Mex (Tigard Map)

14991 Bangy Rd., Lake Oswego (503) 620-7700
12520 SE 93rd Ave., Clackamas (503) 654-1333
1951 NW 185th Avenue, Hillsboro (503) 690-4524
4315 NE Thurston Way, Vancouver (360) 256-6922
www.chevys.com

Happy Hours: 2:00-7:00pm Daily; 9:00pm–close
$3.99 deals on full array of Mexican apps and drinks.

## McCormick & Schmick's (Bridgeport Village)

17015 SW 72nd Ave.; (503) 684-5490
www.mccormickandschmicks.com

Happy Hours: 3:00–6:00pm and 9:00pm–close Daily
Rotating daily drink specials. Food $2.95–$5.95
See full review on page 75.

## P.F. Changs (Bridgeport Village)

7463 SW Bridgeport; (503) 430-3020
www.pfchangs.com

Happy Hours: 3:00–6:00pm Mon–Fri
Deals on drinks, dim sum, and street fare.
See full review on page 186.

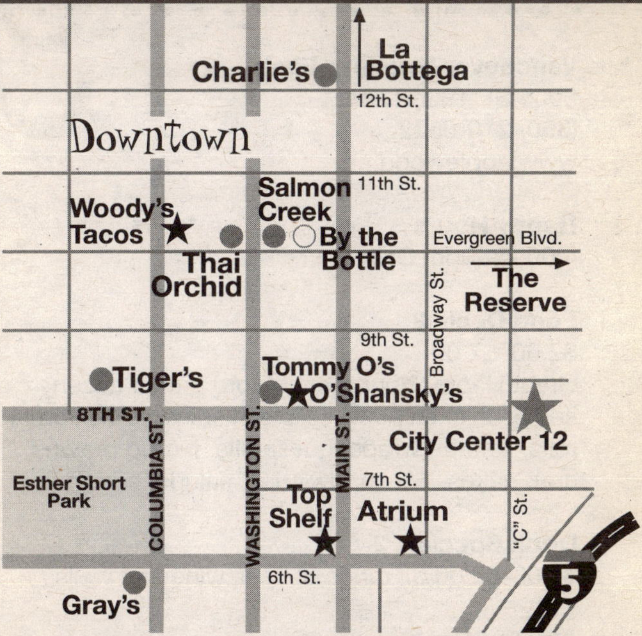


See **"Waterfront"** for Vancouver riverside places.

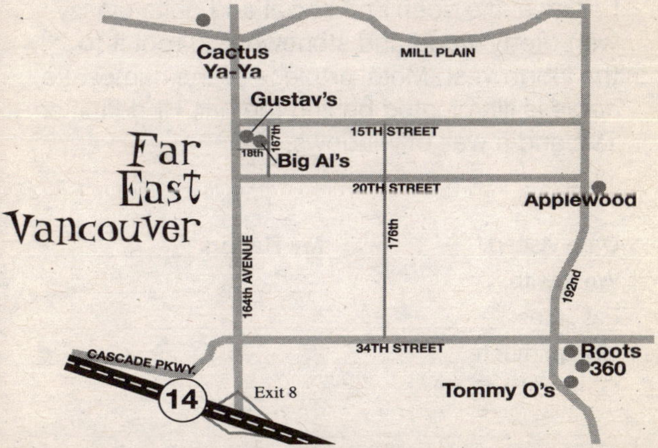

# Applewood

9

**Vancouver Map (Far East)**
2005 SE 192nd Ave.
(360) 210-5522
www.applewood.net

**Happy Hours**
4:00–6:00pm Daily

**Food Deals 3**
$2.00–$7.00
Great Happy Hour menu! More than a dozen items: chicken pinwheels with spinach, California rolls, salmon wraps, quesadilla, jumbo prawns, crab cakes, 1/2 sandwiches, salads, hummus.

**Drink Specials 2**
$1.00–$2.00 off range of beer, wine and wells

**Atmosphere 3**
A bit of an odd layout, but nice enough in the bar area. It's open and social and quite classy, with pretty wood and stonework to root it to the Northwest. Metal artpiece of the namesake *apple* is illuminated behind the bar. Hi-definition TVs and a wall of windows.

Date visited: ____________ **My Rating:** ____________
Went with: ____________
Favorites: ____________
Not so much: ____________
Other comments: ____________

# Black Angus

8

**Vancouver Map (Downtown)**
415 East 13th Street
(360) 695-1506
www.blackangus.com

**Happy Hours**
4:00–7:00pm Mon–Fri

**Food Deals 2**
$3.50, $4.50 and $5.50
Several big bullseye bar eats at each price point: quesadillas, loaded potato skins, garlic bread, grilled artichoke, wings and rings, and more. Minus a point for no steak bites or burger deals.

**Drink Specials 2**
$3.50 beer (bottles and drafts)
$3.50-$5.50 variety of select wines (great idea!)
$3.50 wells; $4.50 margaritas and martinis
Needs some quality NW beer & wine selections.

**Atmosphere 3**
Heavy western theme follows the founder's (Seattle's Stuart Anderson) corporate-cowboy style. Dark and windowless with rough wood panel walls covered with framed cowboy pics.

Date visited: __________ **My Rating:** __________
Went with: ______________________________
Favorites: ______________________________
Not so much: ____________________________
Other comments: __________________________

# Brewtopia

8

**Vancouver (off map)**
8700 NE Vancouver Mall Dr.
(360) 448-4100
www.cinetopia.com

**Happy Hours**
3:00–6:00pm Daily / 8:00–close Daily

**Food Deals 3**
$4.99–$5.99
About 10 beer go-withs like pork sliders, Caesar, fries, wings, hummus, mac & cheese, fish tacos, nachos, cup of chili, or chicken quesadilla.

**Drink Specials 1**
$1.00 off drafts

**Atmosphere 3**
You can sample brews from dozens of local and international breweries ($1.90–$2.40 for tasters, with pints $6.50–$7.00). Contemporary and sleek design similar in style to the other Cinetopias, with a couple of small parlor rooms, a 21+ Living Room theater, and two XL grand theaters.

Date visited: ____________ **My Rating:** ____________
Went with: ______________________________
Favorites: ______________________________
Not so much: ____________________________
Other comments: _________________________

# Charlie's Bistro

10

**Vancouver Map (Downtown)**
1220 Main Street
(360) 693-9998
www.charliesbistro.com

**Happy Hours**
3:00–6:00pm Daily / 9:00–11:00pm Fri-Sat

**Food Deals 3**
$2.00–$6.00
A dozen well-rounded options including olives, shrimp, buffalo wings, flat bread, spring green salad, BBQ pork slider, cheddar-bacon burger.

**Drink Specials 3**
$1.00 off drafts, wine and wells
$5.00 cocktail of the day

**Atmosphere 3**
Cozy and warm upscale bar area with big stone fireplace and hi-def TV. Long, wooden bar with black & white, historical photos of the founding father/character, Charlie, with family and friends.

Date visited: __________ **My Rating:** __________
Went with: ______________________________
Favorites: ______________________________
Not so much: ______________________________
Other comments: ______________________________

# Ginger Pop

9

**Vancouver Map (Downtown)**
2520 Columbia House Boulevard
(360) 699-7273
www.gingerpopthai.com

**Happy Hours**
3:00–6:00pm Daily; 8:30pm–close Fri–Sat

**Food Deals 3+**
$1.00–$3.50
About a dozen fresh and delish Thai treats: shrimp chips, crispy noodles, salad or egg rolls, grilled pork, prawns, or chicken, lettuce wraps, Thai or yum salads, chicken wings and soups. And at this price, you can order a *lot!*

**Drink Specials 3**
$3.00 drafts; $3.00 wines; $5.00 cocktails

**Atmosphere 2**
Very diner-like in look and feel, but a little all over the place with decor ideas. The main walls are painted a neon green, so the place is cheerful and bright, and original art mixed with some very cool lighting jazzes things up too. Patio and roll-up doors, but it's right next to the parking lot.

Date visited: ____________ **My Rating:** ____________
Went with: ______________________________
Favorites: ______________________________
Not so much: ____________________________
Other comments: __________________________
__________________________________________

# Grant House

9

**Vancouver Map (off map)**
1101 Officer's Row
(360) 906-1101
www.thegranthouse.us

**Happy Hours**
4:00–6:00pm Tues–Fri

A Happy Hour favorite!

**Food Deals 3**
$4.00
Enjoy high-end restaurant quality food and ambiance: Pot stickers, chicken quesadilla, calamari, seasonal mixed green salad, slider burgers, short ribs, hummus plate, flat bread.

**Drink Specials 2**
$4.00 drafts; $5.00 wines

**Atmosphere 3**
Inside the grounds of historic Fort Vancouver. Charming, turn-of-the-century estate (Ulysses S. Grant lived here in the 1850s). Gorgeous patio or wrap-around porch allows Happy Hour patrons to sit outside and savor. Worth a trip!

Date visited: ____________ **My Rating:** ____________
Went with: ______________________________
Favorites: ______________________________
Not so much: ______________________________
Other comments: ______________________________
______________________________

# Gray's at the Park 9

**Vancouver Map (Downtown)**
301 W 6th St
(360) 828-4343
www.graysatthepark.com

**Happy Hours**
★2:00–6:00pm Daily

**Food Deals 2**
$5.00–$14.00
Pricey, but top restaurant quality, with a lot of options in starters, small plates, and salads: grilled sirloin brochettes, crabcake, burger, sliders, butternut squash ravioli, ahi tuna, fries, mac & cheese, prawns and pizza.

**Drink Specials 3**
$4.00 drafts; $5.00 select house wines
$5.00 wells and daily cocktails; $6.00 martinis

**Atmosphere 3**
Well, the Hilton's are just fancy! A gorgeous, sleek hotel lobby with contemporary style on through to the high-class, retro-mod lounge with fireplace. Across from the south side of Esther Shore Park.

Date visited: __________ **My Rating:** __________
Went with: ____________________
Favorites: ____________________
Not so much: ____________________
Other comments: ____________________

# Gustav's

**Vancouver Map**
1705 SE 164th Ave.
(360) 883-0222
www.gustavs.net
See page 337 for other locations.

**Happy Hours**
3:00–6:00pm and 9:00pm–close Daily

**Food Deals 3**
$1.99–$5.99
More than 20 items on the Happy Hour menu, with mostly German specialties and other hardy, old stand-bys: reuben or shepard's pie, fish & chips, burgers, schnitzel strips, chicken skewers, swiss fondue, sliders, potato pancakes.

**Drink Specials 3**
$4.00 select drafts; $5.00 house wines
$4.00–$5.00 margaritas, mojitos, other cocktails

**Atmosphere 3**
With some imagination and a couple beers from the strong and authentic European tap line-ups, you too, can be transported to a genuine Bavarian bierstube. Gold star for pushing the concept.

Date visited: ____________ **My Rating:** ____________
Went with: ______________________________
Favorites: ______________________________
Not so much: ____________________________
Other comments: __________________________

# Hudson's

## 10

**Vancouver (off map)**
7801 NE Greenwood Drive
360-816-6100
www.hudsonsbarandgrill.com

**Happy Hours**
4:00–6:00pm Daily

**Food Deals 3**
$5.00
Wow! More than a dozen items that change up just a bit depending on the time of year. They have it all, and for less: cheddar burger, roasted brussel sprouts, salmon BLTs, fish & chips, chips, mac & cheese, beef carpaccio, calamari, Caesar, olives, hummus, lamb meatballs, and more!

**Drink Specials 3**
$3.00 drafts; $5.00 house wines
$5.00 cocktail specials

**Atmosphere 3**
Very NW-woodsy, earthy, and rustic, both inside and out, located in the Heathman Lodge. I'd say Hudson's is probably Vancouver's best Happy Hour, but it's already often way too crowded.

Date visited: __________ **My Rating:** __________
Went with: ______________________________
Favorites: ______________________________
Not so much: ______________________________
Other comments: ______________________________
______________________________

# Lapellah

**10** ★

**Vancouver (off map)**
2520 Columbia House Blvd.
(360) 828-7911
www.lapellah.com

**Happy Hours**
3:30-6:00pm Daily plus 9:00–11:00pm Fri-Sat

**Food Deals 3**
$1.00–$6.00
All kinds of delicious and unique options with seasonal variations: mussels, prawns, burger, mac & cheese, calamari, flat bread, salads, wings, olives, fries, and bacon-wrapped jalapenos.

**Drink Specials 3**
$3.50 drafts; $4.00 select wines
$4.00 wells and $5.00 specialty cocktails

**Atmosphere 3**
Northwest-style, natural and woody interior is much like that of their other upscale restaurant, Roots. Central and long group table dominates surrounding upolstered booths. Cool lighting.

Date visited: ____________ **My Rating:** ____________
Went with: ______________________________
Favorites: ______________________________
Not so much: ______________________________
Other comments: ______________________________
______________________________

# Roots

9

**Vancouver Map (Far East )**
19215 SE 34th St.; Camas
(360) 260-3001
www.rootsrestaurantandbar.com

**Happy Hours**
3:00–6:00pm Daily
9:00–11:00pm Fri–Sat

**Food Deals 3**
$3.00–$8.50
Fresh from the Northwest with about 20 items! Cheese plate, penne pasta, onion tart, calamari, soups, mussels, fish & chips, spicy wings, fries, burger, and several salad alternatives.

**Drink Specials 2**
$3.75 draft beer; $6.00 red and white wines
$4.75 well drinks; $5.95 select cocktails

**Atmosphere 3**
Understated and dimly-lit bar in the Riverstone Marketplace. Pacific Northwest style inside and out. Neutral tones and lots of wood and slate.

Date visited: ___________ **My Rating:** ___________
Went with: ___________
Favorites: ___________
Not so much: ___________
Other comments: ___________

# Thai Orchid 10

**Vancouver (Downtown)**
1004 Washington
(360) 695-7786
www.thaiorchidvancouver.com

**Happy Hour**
3:00–6:00pm / 9:00pm–close Mon–Fri

**Food Deals 3**
$2.75–$4.50
Over a dozen mostly Thai apps: Pot stickers, calamari, coconut prawns, tom yum or tom kha soup, orange chicken, BBQ pork salad, veggie and shrimp tempura over rice, Thai salad.

**Drink Specials 3**
$3.00 drafts; $4.00 wine
$3.50 wells; $4.50 cocktails of the month

**Atmosphere 3**
Nice place! It's quite a fine-dining experience. Be greeted by a lovely Thai hostess, either a real one, or the front & center, life-size statue one. Happy Hour is anywhere in this upscale restaurant. Lots of windows, cafe curtains, brick walls.

Date visited: ____________ **My Rating:** ____________
Went with: ____________________________________
Favorites: ____________________________________
Not so much: __________________________________
Other comments: ________________________________
_______________________________________________

# Tommy O's

**Vancouver Maps (Two locations)**
801 Washington St.; (360) 694-5107
4101 Se 192nd Ave; (360) 892-2484
www.tommyosaloha.com

**Happy Hours**
3:00–6:00pm Daily; 9:00–11:00pm Fri–Sat
★All day Sunday

**Food Deals 3**
$3.00-$5.00
A dozen or so tropically-themed eats like skewers, nachos, beef ribs, fries, coconut shrimp, salad, burgers, calamari, quesadilla, and spring rolls.

**Drink Specials 3**
$1.00 off drafts; $3.50 red and white wine
$4.50 specialty cocktails like mai-tais

**Atmosphere 3**
Tommy Bahama refinement in this upscale Hawaiian lounge next door to Tommy's restaurant. Wicker lounge chairs, huge bar, natural tones, bamboo, and surfboards. Live music weekends downtown. East side bar is quite small and doesn't have quite as much of the full-on Hawaiian feel.

Date visited: __________ **My Rating:** __________
Went with: ____________________
Favorites: ____________________
Not so much: ____________________
Other comments: ____________________

# Vinotopia

8

**Vancouver Map (off map)**
11700 Se 7th St.; (360) 213-2800
www.cinetopiatheaters.com

**Happy Hours**
3:00–6:00pm and 8:00pm–close Daily

**Food Deals 3**
$4.00–$5.00
About a dozen pre-show attractions: pizza, coconut shrimp, nachos, hummus, fish tacos, grilled shrimp, pork sliders, fries, fish & chips.

**Drink Specials 3**
$3.50 domestics; $4.50 microbrews
$4.99 wine (steward's choice)
No deals, but *room* of wall-to-wall wine to taste!

**Atmosphere 3**
Inside Cinetopia movie theater. Happy Hour seating currently at the bartop and nearby tables only, but within sight is the big and open restaurant with stunning fireplace area and occasional piano player. Serene outdoor garden patio.

Date visited: ____________ **My Rating:** ____________
Went with: ____________
Favorites: ____________
Not so much: ____________
Other comments: ____________

## 360° Pizzeria www.360pizzeria.com

**Vancouver (East)** 3425 SE 192nd; (360) 260-3605

**Happy Hours** 4:00–6:00pm Daily

**Food Deals 2** $1.00–$3.00 off regular menu prices: Pizza slices; small plates like bruschetta, grilled pesto prawns or meatballs; many pastas and salads.

**Drink Specials 3** $3.50 beer; $5.00 wine; $5.50 cosmo

**Atmosphere 2** Right across the parking lot from sister restaurant, Roots. Colorful and cool with patio.

## Atrium Lounge

**Downtown Map** 606 Broadway; (360) 980-8370
www.atriumlounge.com

**Happy Hours** 4:00–7:00pm Thur–Sat

**Food Deals 2** $2.00 off all short list of appetizers: wings, hummus, dip, fries, tots, pot stickers, mozz stix.

**Drink Specials 2** $1.00 off beer, wine and wells
Rotating nightly bartender's choice concoction

**Atmosphere 2** Cool old pool hall and a big space with a stage for live music on weekends. Very woody (wood floors, wood tables, wood girders). Antique-style bar with wood ice chest and brick wall.

## Cactus Ya-Ya

**Vancouver (East)**
15704 SE Mill Plain Blvd; (360) 944-9292

**Happy Hours** 3:00–6:00pm and 9:00pm–close Daily

**Food Deals 3** $3.95–$5.25 Super-delicious, infamous ya-ya rolls (chicken, salmon or steak), nachos, fish taco, burger, quesadilla, skewers and salads.

**Drink Specials 1** Rotating special of the day

**Atmosphere 2** A happenin' and very popular area restaurant. Bar side thus gets packed, being somewhat small – locals just love it! Outdoor patio for overflow and fun. Artsy Mexicali touches with some cool ironworks, paintings, and sculptures.

## La Bottega Cafe www.labottegafoods.com

**Downtown Map** 1905 Main St; (360) 571-5010

**Happy Hours** 3:00-6:00pm Daily

**Food Deals 2** $4.00–$6.00 Small menu with nice little nibbles: veggie plate, antipasti, olives, crostini and bruschetta, baked polenta.

**Drink Specials 2** $1.00 off beer; $5.00 house wine

**Atmosphere 2** I vaguely remember a bodega being a grocery store in Spanish. Add in lots of wine bottles for sale and you have bottega! Cute little cafe/store/wine bar.

## Shanahan's www.shanahanspubvancouver.com

**Downtown Map** 209 W McLoughlin; (360) 735-1440

**Happy Hours** 3:00-8:00pm Daily★

**Food Deals 3** $1.99–$4.99 Bar food yes, but crazy-cheap and good! Pork or chicken tacos, "Shany fries" (a don't miss), steak bites, chicken quesadilla, tacos, pork sliders, mac & cheese, hummus plate, salad.

**Drink Specials 1** $2.50 domestics; $3.00 wells

**Atmosphere 2** It's a super-casual, neighborhood, Irish pub with a mysterious, magnetic charm. Something about the place makes you love it, simple as it may be. Resembles most bars in Wisconsin.

## The Rock www.therockwfp.com

**Vancouver (off Map)** 2420 Columbia House Blvd.; (360) 695-7625

**Happy Hours** 3:00-6:00pm / 9:00pm-mid Mon–Fri
★All day Sunday

**Food Deals 2** $3.99–$7.99 Half-price appetizers plus personal pizzas, mini burgers and wings.

**Drink Specials 3** $3.00 drafts, wine and wells! Plus "bucket" and "rocktail" specials

**Atmosphere 2** Mini chain of Washington wood-fired pizza joints with very fun, casual, collegiate feel.

## Tiger's Garden/Xokdee Lounge

**Downtown Map** 312 W. 8th St.; (360) 693-9585

**Happy Hours**
4:00–6:00pm Mon–Sat; 4:00–9:00pm Sun★
9:00–11:00pm Mon–Thurs; 9:00pm–mid Fri–Sat

**Food Deals 2** $3.00 Appetizers like egg rolls, salad rolls, fried tofu, wontons, satay, wings, California rolls.

**Drink Specials 2** $3.00 drafts; $3.50 wells

**Atmosphere 3** Tiger's Garden Restaurant lounge. Former wine bar, so lots of comfy, cushy, couch seating. Swanky! Artistic glass lamps, big bar, large windows.

## Top Shelf

**Downtown Map** 600 Main; (360) 699-7106

**Happy Hours** 3:00–7:00pm Mon–Fri; 6:00pm-mid Sun

**Food Deals 2** $2.50–$4.50 Bar menu with basics like Caesar salad, pork shanks, wings mini gyros, burgers, sliders, hummus, quesadillas, chips & salsa.

**Drink Specials 2** $.50 off drafts; $1.00 off wells; $4.00 martinis

**Atmosphere 2** Big U-shaped, central copper-top bar and 18-foot brick walls; comfortable, Irish bar effect; not fancy like the Top Shelf name might imply.

## Woody's Tacos www.woodystacos.com

**Downtown Map** 210 W Evergreen; (360) 718-8193

**Happy Hours** 4:00–7:00pm Mon-Sat

**Food Deals 3** $2.00–$4.00 Surprisingly delicious Mexican food for cheap! Chips & salsa, garnachas, mushroom and goat cheese chalupas, skewers, empanadas, taquitos and potato croquettes.

**Drink Specials 3** $2.50-$3.50 beers; $4.50 wells $5.50 margaritas and specials on giant microbrews

**Atmosphere 2** Order at Woody's counter, then sit out in the indoor piazza area where you'll be surrounded by quaint shops, galleries and artwork. Quite unique – quiet and sweet, especially at night.

Remember to check our website every once in a while for changes and closures.

**www.happyhourguidebook.com**

And please let us know if you see information that needs changing.

# Notes

# Notes

# Notes

# Notes

# Notes

# Notes

*Your support of this Happy Hour Guidebook will help Breast Friends continue the programs that are so needed during a cancer diagnosis, treatment, and beyond.*

Breast Friends®

## Helping Women Survive the Trauma of Cancer, One Friend at a Time

Breast Friends is a nonprofit organization dedicated to improving the quality of life for female cancer patients. Co-founders and cancer survivors, Becky Olson and Sharon Henifin understand the need for support during a cancer crisis. It is their belief that has brought hope and inspiration to thousands since the inception of the organization in 2000.

- Providing a continuum of support through programs and resources sustaining you in your journey.
- Teaching friends and family specific ways to offer support, helping them understand what their loved one is going through, and suggesting resources for the woman and for those who care about her.
- One in eight women will be diagnosed, and the other seven will know her. Our goal is to reach the seven in order to help the one.

Visit www.breastfriends.org for more information on specific programs and find out how you can become more involved.

www.breastfriends.or